GRAFTERS

GRAFTERS

The Inside Story of the Wide Awake Firm
Europe's Most Prolific Sneak Thieves

Colin Blaney

MILO BOOKS LTD

First published in October 2004 by Milo Books

ISBN 1 903854 28 8

Typeset in Sabon by Avon DataSet Ltd,
Bidford on Avon, Warwickshire, B50 4JH

Printed and bound in Great Britain by
Cox & Wyman Ltd, Reading, Berkshire

MILO BOOKS LTD
info@milobooks.com

Acknowledgements

Special thanks to Saint Syl, Sister Edwina and the dinner ladies at St Malachy's School, Brian Hughes, M.B.E., the Citizens Advice Bureau, Terry and Amanda at the Social Security office in Rhyl, Phil Starkie and Linda Moore at Rhyl Library, Scott, Sue and Lynne at Hafen Wen, Paul Atkinson for his editing, and Jana for keeping me going.

Contents

Foreword

IN THE LATE 1970s, a small crew of Manchester 'grafters' – sneak thieves, jewel snatchers, shoplifters and pickpockets – woke up to the easy pickings abroad.

They were probably the first crime crew from England to suss out that towns and villages across Continental Europe were just waiting to be pillaged. Shopkeepers were more trusting and less security conscious, while wealth seemed abundant in the ski resorts of Switzerland, the grand cities of Scandinavia, the sleepy villages of Belgium and the Dutch Flatlands, the commercial centres of Germany.

The core of this crew was a bunch of rag-arse lads from the rough Collyhurst area of north Manchester. They called themselves Collyhurst Cowboys and had grown up together in a world now gone. Many worked on the huge Smithfield Market, which sold fish, fruit, flowers, vegetables and poultry. As young skinheads they fought the greaser gangs, broke into warehouses, went through juvenile court and borstal.

Colin 'Beaner' Blaney was the livewire of the gang, its most active and influential member. He fizzed with energy and schemes, and was cool and fearless on a job. His travels began with Manchester United's Red Army in the early Seventies, and soon he and his fellow Cowboys were learning lessons from the Scouse dippers and zappers, the masters of the pickpocketing game. But their forte was stealing from cash tills – 'banging the jack' – and jewel theft.

In the late Seventies they discovered Amsterdam, which became their base as they set out to plunder every town and village for hundreds of miles, across Switzerland, France, Belgium, Holland, Scandinavia and Germany. Then they'd head to the Spanish coast to cool off, kick back and spend their loot. They devised their own slang, words which have since passed into the Manchester lexicon: geranies, jist, on one, belter, kiting, twirlers. They became known as the Wide Awake Firm, a name that summed up their opportunistic, wired attitude to life.

Arrest, of course, was a constant threat. Beaner would spend more than a fifth of his life in prisons, from Strangeways, Walton and Wormwood Scrubs to jails in Sweden, Holland, Germany and Switzerland. But it never deterred him.

By the time acid house and Ecstasy arrived in the late Eighties, they were at their peak – and the only way was down. Manchester became a more dangerous place to operate as more vicious gangs fought over drugs and territory, while the Dutch police teamed up with their English counterparts to launch a concerted campaign against the Wide Awake lads. Their crazy lifestyle was also catching up with them. Many fell prey to heroin. Beaner also succumbed to hard drugs but his worst addiction was drink.

Today he is no longer a thief. Indeed, the days of the grafters described here are all but over. CCTV, vastly improved in-store security and greater public awareness have made such opportunistic crime much more difficult. The drug trade and its associated violence now dominate the underworld.

Colin Blaney's crazy, rollercoaster story makes compelling, if at times uncomfortable reading. While he shows little remorse, he is at least painfully honest, even about his own failings. *Grafters* tells it like it was.

Peter Walsh
Author of *Gang War: The Inside Story of the Manchester Gangs*

Chapter One

The Flats

BANG AT IT. That's what we were, for more than twenty years. We hit every town and village in Northern Europe, and plenty of others beyond. We did tills, sneaks, jewellery, watches, hi-fis and stereos, furs and Capo di Monti china and designer clothes. I once read a book about the Italian who pulled off the Knightsbridge safe deposit job, the biggest of its kind. When he got home with the swag he filled his bath with wads of £50 notes, bags of pure coke and all the gold and diamonds, the jackpot. Well, the amount we had in those twenty years I'd never be able to fit into any bath I've ever seen; it would have to be a twin jacuzzi. I swear if you went into Watches of Switzerland and bought every Rolex it would not match the amount we had off.

And it all started in a rundown Manchester slum called Collyhurst.

If Collyhurst is famous for anything, it's probably as the birthplace of Manchester United stars Nobby Stiles and Brian Kidd. Being a Collyhurst Cowboy means you started with nothing and went into the world with only your wits and your nerve to get by. My mates and I all started life with no prospects and no expectations, and had to find our own way. We chose crime. I don't think any of what follows would have happened if we hadn't grown up where we did. We started at the bottom of the ladder and couldn't go any lower. 'You're in for a rough ride kid,' older people would tell us, so the sooner you accepted it, the better.

I grew up an Irish Catholic in the last slums to be demolished in the heart of the city. My dad's parents were from Ireland but settled in Bronze Street, one of a grid of terraces named after metals: Brass Street, Copper Street, Tin Street and Zinc Street. They arrived just in time for the Blitz. Dad was the fifth of nine children who all went to St Patrick's, a school which had 2,000 pupils well into the 1960s. Imagine the noise coming off the cobbles from all those clogs in the morning. They made the school football pitch by all collecting bags of ash from their parents' hearths and spreading it out over some waste ground, which immediately became known as 'the tip'. Football was like religion – even the head teacher, Lawrence Cassidy, was a part-time pro at Manchester United and became a leading scout for the team.

Dad's main interest was fighting. A schoolteacher gave him a book on the basics of boxing by the great Len Harvey and when he joined the army cadets he boxed his way to the area final of the Northern Command light-weight championship. He lost to Darkie Hughes at Ardwick Stadium. Copies of *Ring* magazine were always lying around the house and the boxing newsreels were a must at the cinema. Dad got into a bit of teenage trouble and ended up in borstal. He joined the RAF when he came out, forging his date of birth on the sign-up papers so he could join a year early. He was never a man to let the grass grow under his feet. A welterweight with a heavy punch and a strong jaw, he was picked for the RAF boxing team in 1948, fought all over Asia and became the Bomber Command champion.

Mum's family moved from Wythenshawe, a massive council estate which in the 1930s was a showpiece garden city – every house had a garden – to Collyhurst to run the Locomotive Tavern, known as the Loco. My mum, Sylvia Kitson, or Syl as we later called her, left school to join a travelling pantomime but my nana told her this was not a respectable career and regretfully she packed it in. The Loco was on the corner of Zinc Street, next to the Manchester-Leeds railway line, and was busy every evening with the kind of characters Collyhurst became famous for. One of the regulars was Tiny, who stood seven feet tall. My nana would give him a dust cloth to clean the lights and lamps for a free pint. When he wanted his next few pints he always reached over, opened the till and paid himself. The Whit Week Walks in particular were occasions for drinking, singing and dancing in the streets and takings would be colossal. The older generation took Whitsun much more seriously than Christmas or New Year; it was the only time of year you would be certain to get new clothes.

In 1952, Dad was on home leave from the RAF when he called into the Loco for a drink. Mum was working behind the bar and my dad announced at the end of the evening that he would marry her. Dad was based in Hong Kong so after a short courtship and a tearful family farewell, Mum found herself setting sail from Southampton. For a young woman of twenty from one of the roughest inner-city areas in Europe, that journey to marry my father in Hong Kong was paradise. Once they passed through the Bay of Biscay the next five weeks seemed like being on a luxury liner: the delight of sailing down the Suez Canal, watching schools of dolphins glide by, the luxury of not having to work and parties every night, the thrill of stopping at different ports and going ashore to shop after days of seeing nothing but ocean.

She loved Hong Kong just as much, though their wedding night was a farce typical for that time. My mother, being a virgin, refused to undress in front of my father, and wouldn't get in bed until the light was off. Seeing what she thought was a lazy daisy switch above the bed, she pulled it but the light refused to go out. Instead she heard a knock at the door and a Chinese boy asking what 'Missy' wanted.

'Nothing,' she retorted and pulled again on the supposed light switch.

This went on for five minutes until my mother finally snapped and dragged the bewildered servant into the room, demanding to know where the light switch was. She had been ringing the service bell.

Married life in Hong Kong was an unforgettable experience for her. All Europeans had an armah (servant) and there was a swimming pool at their shared quarters, so after shopping in the morning my mother spent afternoons at the poolside or playing mah jong, a kind of Chinese dominoes. There were ferry rides to the tiny beaches scattered around the island, and on the odd occasion they travelled by tramcar up to the peaks; the higher the people lived, the richer they were. The Catholic Club was set in the mountains and they would sit on the balcony, sipping gimlets or enjoying their famous tomato soup with croutons. If money got short at the end of the month you could go down to the Buff Club, where any member could drink all night; when you left you signed a chit which was settled by the paymaster. At 2 A.M. the rickshaw boys were waiting outside, and for an extra Hong Kong dollar a crazy race took place through the hectic side streets back to their quarters.

My father never lost a boxing match for his squadron – known as the 'Brill Cream Boys' – in Hong Kong. The newspapers referred to him as 'Black Heart' Blaney, because before fights he would make the sign of the cross with his thumb over his heart. In 1955 he won the Colony

Championships. He was decked early on in the first round and a Cantonese family behind my dad's mate Tim were shouting, 'Black Heart's down!' Their father told them to calm down: 'He'll get up' – and he did. In the next round Black Heart went to war on his foe and the ref had to stop the contest and proclaim my old man Colony Champion. Tim could still hear the father behind telling his sons he had told them so.

All good things come to an end and after two-and-a-half years they sailed back to England. On the ship the servicemen had separate quarters from their wives, so a rota was devised for husbands to visit their spouses (unknown to their superiors). I was conceived somewhere between the Red Sea and the Dead Sea. I've always been a Red and a few times I've nearly been dead, so I guess it was fitting.

* * *

I was born at Crumpsall Hospital in May 1956, the month the Busby Babes won the League. Not to be outdone, Manchester City were bringing the FA Cup back to Albert Square as my mum wheeled me out of the maternity unit. Football and music brought the city back alive after the rationing and privations of the war years.

My parents put down a small deposit on a redbrick house in Wimbourne Street, Miles Platting. It was close to a tripe factory owned by Mother's uncle and the rows of terraced houses beside it where many of the workers lived were known as the Tripe Colony. Dad worked for three years at the Bradford Coal Pit but lost his job at the back end of 1959 and this put a lot of strain on the family. We had been struggling to pay the mortgage anyway and Mum had to sell most of the hand-crafted furniture they'd brought back from Hong Kong, just so we could eat.

To get the family out of its downward tumble, they found a couple willing to do a house exchange, and shortly before Christmas we loaded our belongings onto a coal wagon and moved to 89 Burgin Drive, Collington House, in the Collyhurst Flats. Our new home was on the fourth floor. As we dragged our stuff up the concrete stairs we could see the place was falling down. Mining in the nearby pits had weakened the foundations and many of the balconies had big wooden beams wedged against them to stop them from collapsing. Inside many of the flats were gaping holes and cracks in the walls where the subsidence had really got a grip. Council workers came round with a kind of super glue to fill in the gaps. Compared to some families we were lucky, as the wall cracks were only bad in Mum and Dad's room. Green fungus oozed out during the winter months, but when the weather got warmer it wasn't too bad.

The centrepiece of our flat was a huge fireplace that only took a few seconds to get going. Dad would cover the fireplace with a sheet of newspaper and the wind would come howling down the chimney and get the wood burning like a good 'un. I'd then build up the coal over the burning wood and sit in front of it for hours looking at comic books, drawing aeroplanes and gluing together Lancaster bombers and tanks from model kits. The flat was big and had the same dark and drab wooden wardrobes, dressers and shelves as all the others. Lino was fitted in the living room and in the bedrooms, where it went round the beds and furniture so everything stayed in the same position. Mum had managed to hang onto one piece of furniture from Hong Kong, a glass-fronted corner unit with hand-carved Buddhas all round it; inside were my dad's boxing trophies and medals, with a framed photo of the great Sugar Ray Robinson in the centre.

The view from our balcony was of Burgin Drive,

Kingsley Crescent and the Gay Street Mission, which was packed to the rafters every Sunday when the protestant bands practised. Next to this was the Collyhurst Lads' Youth Club and on the left was the police station and children's nursery opposite the public hall. The nursery had a sand pit – a 'sandy' – looked after by the park keeper, who always had a coke fire blazing in his cabin. He would sometimes throw a couple of spuds on the fire to share with us in the winter and was often needed as the referee for big games of football on a Sunday or in the summer holidays to present small trophies.

From our kitchen window you looked out onto Rochdale Road, with the Essoldo picture house and Saint Oswald's church and school in the foreground. Then came a labyrinth of back alleys and narrow cobbled streets, with two-up, two-down terraced houses, surrounding the mills and factories that led up to Cheetham Hill. In the middle of this Lowry landscape were the Red Hills, huge mounds of shale and slag, and a school made out of tin. There was also Saint Malachy's Catholic School, with its domed roof and a church in the basement. At the back of St Malachy's was the railway line and the foul, evil-smelling, rat-infested River Irk. Casting a long shadow in the distance was the black tower in the middle of Strangeways Prison. We all thought this was where people got hanged, but it was just a ventilation tower.

Rochdale Road was a maze of shops, a bustling little city within a city with pubs on every corner, chippies, bakers and tripe shops. Alan's grocers was the nearest to us; he always had a basket of fresh eggs outside, which we local kids helped ourselves to. Alan was the first man in Collyhurst to wear a wig. Obvious to even the most unobservant, it never sat properly on his head and looked like it had been made for somebody else. We used to point at him and give him a load of stick, but it never seemed to bother him. On the corner of Collyhurst Street was Harry the barber: whatever you asked for at Harry's, you always got a short back and sides. Next door was the bookie and further along was May's Pawn Shop, which is still going today. These days it has televisions, hi-fis and gold, but then it was stuffed with racks of clothes that became tainted by a horrible smell if left there for more than a few days.

The men all dressed alike in white vests, heavy dark pants and black, horrible-looking boots. They all wore thick leather belts, used often on the kids. Boxing was all the talk and Jack Bates ran a gym from the back of Harry the barber's. Jack had a big name locally as a hard man: a man's man.

Mum sorted me out with a place at St Malachy's school. I didn't know any other kids from the area, but the wonderful Sister Veronica made me feel welcome. I sat next to Malachy Murphy on one side and one of the O'Rourke sisters on the other. The O'Rourkes lived on Eggington Street and the family kept a donkey in the backyard. They would turn up at school smelling of donkey piss, an overpowering acidic smell that clogged up your throat all day if you copped for a proper lung-ful. I couldn't wait for the first term to end so I would be sat next to someone else, even though they were decent kids. There were thirty-odd in my class and most were on green tickets for free school meals, which were cooked in town and delivered by van. Occasionally we were given salads, which were frowned on by all. No wonder we were always over at the school clinic getting our boils lanced. At break we got a bottle of free milk and many of the kids brought a few pieces of toast wrapped in greaseproof paper to keep them going. Although it was cold, the toast always seemed to taste better this way.

I soon got to know lots of kids, including two from the

Flats who would become my best friends for life: Eric Hostey and Anthony Gallagher, know as Gagzy. A few times a year the Catholic kids from my school would run to the Red Hills and meet up with the Protestant kids from St James's and the Tin School for a mass fight. We would hear them running down Rochdale Road, screaming religious insults and baying for blood. No one ever got badly hurt, just a few cuts and bruises and the odd broken bone, but the result was always the same: all those from St Malachy's were given the strap for bringing the good name of the school into disrepute. The teachers could see what was going on from the top floor of the school and sometimes it would take an entire afternoon to administer the strap to all those present on the hill. It didn't stop us.

Our next-door neighbours on Burgin Drive were the Kakancuses. Their dad was Polish and his voice boomed; I shook with fear when I knocked on their door to see if any of the children were coming out to play. Above us were the Dudsons, the first in the Flats to get a television set. They had to put a shilling in the back to receive programmes and switched it off when the adverts came on to save money. This was 1963 and I remember their house being jammed full of people to watch United win the FA Cup final, when Denis Law scored a brilliant goal and ran round tirelessly, snapping away at any loose balls. Law was our King: short-tempered and fiery with a cheeky brilliance adored by everyone in the Flats. The Dudsons always invited me to watch the Beatles or the Rolling Stones play live. The first time I saw *Top Of The Pops* there were twenty kids screaming and cheering at the tops of their voices as Mr Dudson stood quietly at the back grinning. He had been a prisoner of war in Japan during the Second World War and had no stomach. He was a top man, always pleasant and accommodating.

Above the Dudsons was a family who got evicted

shortly after we moved in; their stuff was just thrown out onto Burgin Drive. Their flat was taken over by a lady called Mavis, the Liz Taylor of the flats. She had three daughters whose dads were either Pakistani or Indian, all very exotic looking, and some of the kids when they first arrived would call them names like 'Pakistani Annie', but we soon put a stop to that.

Despite every family scraping to survive, this was Collyhurst – people looked out for each other. When we got our own television, one of the older boys came in and showed me how to fiddle the meter, so you could put the money in, then retrieve it and the TV would still work for a few hours. There were loads of comings and goings between Flats as so-and-so knocked on the door with a bowl asking for sugar, while someone else would be after some milk or a few pieces of bread. My mum bought Blue Band margarine for us and cheapo Stork for giving away. Often we'd have some kid at our door asking if his family could toast a few slices of bread, as their electricity had been cut off – that was when the Stork came out. In winter it was common for families to have their electric cut off. The feller from the Electricity Board and a copper as witness would turn up out of the blue and if there was no answer they would barge the door off its hinges and disconnect the supply.

For the first couple of years in the Flats I stayed very close to Burgin Drive and the surrounding streets, and wouldn't even venture to the shops alone. The reason was that there were loads of older kids in charge of gangs and as soon as they spotted a fresh face they demanded you fight one of their up-and-coming urchins. There was no such thing as refusing – you had to learn how to use your fists. I was lucky that my dad was around sometimes, not that I needed him but he always kept an eye out and made sure fights were fair. I was terrified of losing in front of him, which I realise now was probably a good thing. Near the war memorial on Rochdale Road were four metal poles stuck in the ground to form a ring and this was used for fair fistfights, with only the fighters allowed inside. The first fight my dad put me in was against a kid from the Buildings down Collyhurst Road, which were flats like ours but smaller and much older. After a few minutes of flailing we both caught each other full on the nose and, as the blood flowed, all hands declared it a draw.

Our gang, Burgin Drive, was one of the top three locally and a few weeks before Bonfire Night we launched a raid on the rival Weswells gang. We used dustbin lids as shields and hurled broken bricks or stones with our free hands, followed by nuts and bolts. We called this 'cucking duckers'. Once we had run them off we made for their prized wooden doors, carrying them back to Burgin on our backs like worker ants. We then nailed them together to make a square hut with tall planks of wood stacked over it like a wigwam. Older lads used the den inside for drinking cider and smoking while us younger ones stayed outside keeping guard. When it neared November the fog and smog came; the railways put detonators on the lines to give off a boom and let the drivers know where they were. We'd go on the lines collecting them and we would drop slabs on them to give out warnings to all Burgin if another gang was coming to have a go.

One time I heard a commotion under our kitchen window and saw Steve McGarry, who we called Maca, being tied down to the bonfire.

'What the fuck's going on,' I shouted to Alan Stuartson.

It seems Maca had been knocking around with another gang. Being a 'traitor' was heavy shit and after ten minutes of slapping him about and burning him with candles, they put Maca in the ring to fight a kid who had just joined our gang. Maca would have licked him normally but the kid was given a wooden pole, A passing bus stopped and the driver and a few older chaps made their way over to stop the fight; they soon were back on board wishing they'd kept out of it. I was gutted for Maca as I had the utmost respect for him. Only days before, a few coppers had called at his house and dragged his old man over to Willert Street police station. Maca ran after them and got stuck right into the coppers, who had a hard time coping, as all the crowd were behind the McGarrys.

Maca wasn't seen so much in Burgin Drive after the lynching. About a year later I was in the sand park with my very first girlfriend, Anne Saunders. We'd got round to our first snogging and I was desperate for more. I was busy writing on the walls 'CB loves AS' when I heard, 'Now then Blaney.' It was Maca's new gang, with the leader, 'Spamhead' Danny, over the moon at catching me in such a way.

This was much worse than having to perform in front of my dad. A quick word in Maca's ear saw him take off his top, ready for fisticuffs. I knew Maca was deadly with his nut so I kept my distance, throwing windmills and backing off, until he became frustrated and charged in blind. I caught him with my knee and we fell on the deck. Maca soon recovered but I had the better position and was able to get the odd short jab in. Suddenly Danny wrenched me up by my hair, but this actually turned the fight my way, because it ripped out at the roots and I slammed back down into Maca, my elbow catching him full on the chin. Danny really wanted to kick the shit out of me but as he was the leader and at least three years older it was a big no-no. Plus he knew I then could have involved any of Burgin's older heads, such as Dablo Dale, who would have evened up any liberty taken. A few years on, Maca and I became the best mates any person could wish for – but I still never got any snogs from Anne Saunders.

* * *

Dad still wasn't working but Mum was now a machinist at Raffles, in Ancoats, who made black gabardine raincoats. No sooner was she familiar with the job than she found out she was pregnant. Mum continued working until near the time the baby was due and then had a sewing machine installed in the bedroom so she could keep earning right up to the birth. On a freezing December evening, Mum went into labour and, with the help of the midwife and my dad, who was up and down the stairs with endless buckets of hot water, my brother Mark was born. Shortly after the birth, Mum returned to work at the Land-o-Cakes Pub on Great Ancoats Street.

One night Mum came home and told us that Dad was going back in the RAF. I watched him pack a case and walk up towards Kingsley Crescent, where my Uncle Peter lived. I had a lump in my throat and knew something was wrong. The truth was that he was up at Crown Court the next day charged with robbery. He got two years.

We eventually travelled all the way up to Haverigg Prison in Cumbria to see him. I still believed he was back in the RAF; through a child's eyes, the jail looked like a military base, plus he had bars of chocolate for me.

Dad never returned home. After serving his time, he lived in Whalley Range and Chorlton in bedsits and met a Geordie woman, with whom he had a daughter. She then left both him and the child. He did his best to bring her up on his own and would still call round occasionally to take me to see Bond films, up to Heaton Park on the boats, or for a week's holiday at Pontins. Hardly anyone in the flats had a stable family, which made things okay.

At St Malachy's there were always activities, including my first trip to Blackpool on the coach. Some of the kids were so excited that they were sick and the coach driver kept swinging the bus to the side of the road to let them off. At the seaside we headed straight for the donkeys and then sat on the beach eating fish and chips. When the weather turned nasty we hit the arcades en masse. An older boy showed us how to fiddle the one-arm bandits and we watched as he gave the arm a few light pulls and a cherry or two slotted into place. Instead of letting the cherries spin he picked a small one or two cherries win, pushed the lever and gave it a jiggle and the coins started flowing. It wasn't long before we were all winning but the workers sussed us out, mainly because of the constant noise of machines paying out. It wasn't a drama; we just moved on to the next arcade.

We must have looked a sight as we were all loaded up with Blackpool rock, pockets packed with coins, girls with Kiss Me Quick hats and boys with Dirty Dick hats, all tilted to the side, singing:

We are the Collyhurst kids, oi, oi.
We are the Collyhurst kids, oi, oi.
We learn all our manners by knocking off tanners.
We are the Collyhurst kids.

At seven years old I was ready for my First Holy Communion. This was an almighty occasion and all the mums in the flats, by hook or by crook, would acquire new clothes for their kids so they looked presentable at the altar. I wore my white shirt with a red dicky bow, charcoal grey short trousers and black slip-on shoes with elastic at the side, topped by a short back and sides from Harry the barber. Whatever style you asked for at Harry's, you always ended up with a short back and sides. First

Communion was an extra special occasion for me, as my mum had finally got her wish to be converted into the Catholic church. Her choosing to share my big day was known by all the folks in Collyhurst and I felt proud as all the kids joined with the brass band and the choir to march round the Flats and nearby streets in celebration.

It wasn't just the big occasions that made us all excited. My old lady came home one night shaking: she'd won £50 on the bingo. For nearly a week she spread the money out on the table every night, staring at it with a lovely smile, wondering what to buy. We got a carpet for the living room that went straight over the lino and our first fridge, which was gas. The joy of having ice cubes in drinks, even in winter, was indescribable.

A buzz used to go up round the Flats when Raffo's ice cream horse and cart came into Burgin Drive. The mums saved up their carrot and spud peelings to feed to his horse, and in return Raffo would fill up the bowls we waved in his direction on tick. All of the kids loved jumping on the small ledge at the back of his cart as he pulled away, getting a free ride along the cobble street. Raffo knew the kids were safe for a little while, then out came his horsewhip, which he would swing behind him. This was the signal for the kids to jump off the back before he cracked the horse's behind and trotted off up one of the other drives. Everyone at the flats appreciated Raffo. Mr Whippy made his first appearance in the mid-sixties, turning up before Raffo was due one hot summer's day. I swear not a single person went out to buy anything. Then we heard Raffo's tune as he turned the corner into Burgin Drive and a massive cheer went up. Whippy knew the score and was forced to move on.

Everyone loved a new salesman knocking on the door, whatever the product they'd be selling. The word flew round when they started their rounds. I remember the bedding salesman knocking on our door: double sheets, single sheets, you name it, he had it all for two shillings a week. But as soon as he left the Flats, every family could be seen trotting off to May's Pawnbrokers round the corner, and a good night followed for all. Over the next few weeks the salesman would call round for the payments and I would open the door and say, 'My mum says she's not in!' His face looked like last year's rhubarb, as he'd had the same treatment from all the other families. It wasn't long before he put up the white flag and moved on to another area.

Not all salesmen got the same treatment. One from a firm in Ardwick sold us a three-piece suite for ten shillings a week, reduced to half a crown after a few months. Once we'd paid back half, my mum stopped paying for it. The salesman had told us when Mum signed the papers that if we paid half of what it was worth, then by law no-one could take it away from us. He said he was sick of climbing up and down the steps of the Flats trying to get money and had had enough of the abuse he received whilst doing his rounds. Telling people the score made his life much easier.

The Flats were full of characters. Wally was a little feller in his sixties, very smart with a small pork pie hat that barely managed to stay on his swaying head as he stepped out from the pub at closing time to make his way home. He was constantly drunk and sang 'Underneath the Arches' as he took one step forward and two steps back. He had a purple conk and looked like Mister Magoo and I remember that the smell of booze from him was always sweeter than from the other drunks. Sometimes it would take him the best part of an hour to traverse Burgin Drive, with some of the kids singing along and joining in the 'Wally Walk'.

One Boxing Day, 1964, a crowd of us went up to a funfair on Hulme Hall Lane. I didn't know all the kids with us but one was a young girl called Lesley Anne Downey. Evil was also in the area: Ian Brady and Myra Hindley were also lurking there, Hindley wearing a dark wig to hide her blonde hair. Hindley carried boxes wrapped in Christmas paper and dropped one as she passed Lesley. The little girl picked it up and then helped her to carry it to the car, where Brady was waiting. She was dragged in and knocked out with ethyl chloride, then taken away and was never seen alive again. When we all got back to the Flats there was panic that Lesley was missing, and the parents had us all down at Willert Street police station trying to get information out of us. No-one knew at that time that she had become the fourth victim of the Moors Murderers.

Chapter Two

Collyhurst Cowboys

BY THE TIME I was ten I was mixing with lads from all the other drives in my area. Gagzy had all but moved into our house as his mum had done one, leaving him to fend for himself, so my mum became his mum, and his dad, a former pro boxer called Pat 'Kid' Gallagher, became mine. Four of us in particular hung around together: me, Gagzy, from Southern Drive, Eric from Central Drive and Carl from Kingsley Crescent. We played football on the flat roofs with a deflated ball (so it didn't bounce too much) and spent loads of time smashing things up around the small cobbled streets and in the derelict flats that were being pulled down. There was something about destroying things that appealed and the noise we made was something else.

A few of us were in full destructive swing at a pub that had closed down when this huge feller came in and lost his temper. We bailed out into the backyard and jumped over the wall, but broken glass was slotted into the cement to stop people from climbing over. We all got cut up pretty bad while the feller who chased us just laughed and didn't give a fuck. Every one of us had to go to ossy and I probably came off worst: once I had realised my hands were being cut to shreds I had fallen from the wall and broke my arms, a wrist and a thumb.

We were regulars at Ancoats Hospital, known locally

as 'the Butchers'. I stood on many a rusty nail, fell off many a roof. I once hit the deck and a metal spike sticking out of the ground got me between the eyes, where the forehead meets the nose, and opened my nose up like a tin of beans. I broke a leg and an ankle and lost count of the stitches they put into me.

The recuperation that followed never stopped me or any of the others from going into places we shouldn't once we were back to full strength. Factories, cotton mills: they were all too enticing. Danger was part of the excitement. One factory had hundreds of the tube lights, perfect for sword fighting. We loved the noise when they broke up and were fascinated by the white powder that shot out – until one of the younger boys began screaming when he looked down and saw two of his fingers hanging on by a bit of skin.

Another day out for us all was down on the River Irk with an airgun or catapult, trying to kill rats. On Sundays we went to the paint works, which had a square in the middle filled with toxic waste and water. This was our Tom Sawyer day out, as we always built a raft for messing around on, knowing it was a no-no to fall in. It all added to the excitement – until one day Willy Dale fell in. He surfaced, covered in leeches, before the weeds pulled him under again. We managed to drag him out and that was the last time we ever built a raft. There was also an old air raid shelter by the River Irk that we used to take time out for cigs and cider – which we nicknamed bareback rider.

Some of us began venturing further afield. I helped one of the older Colly lads, Pete Kank, to sell papers outside Old Trafford football ground. We'd get in the ground with our papers and leave them with the staff selling food and drink so we could watch some of the game. Near the end we would collect them and wait outside the gates for the first people to start leaving. As soon as we had sold out, we would get into one of the *Manchester Evening News* vans and go back into town to collect the *Football Pink,* which sold very well. In the late sixties it would become too much trouble selling the *Pink* because the skinheads and hooligans would kick you and your papers all over the place.

I also started to earn a few bob looking after people's cycles and motorbikes. My nana and grandad lived in the houses over the bridge from the Stretford End, off Railway Road, and the back entry to their house was one of the widest and longest in the area. Loads of people wanted to park their bikes there on match days, so it was a steady earner minding them while they watched the game. Afterwards I often stayed with my grandad while the crowds died down and nana used to make Mark and me beans on toast with Daddies Sauce, cutting the toast into the shape of a castle with the beans in the middle. When he'd finished, grandad always said the same thing.

'Nelly, that was lovely, love. Just one thing wrong.'

Nana always gave him the cue: 'What's that love?'

'There wasn't enough!'

Nana worked sometimes at the United chippie on Chester Road, so after a game I could pop my head in and no matter how busy it was I used to have my fish, chips and mushy peas straight away. Nana also worked at the White City dog track during the week and I'd nip over to see her whenever I could. She'd give me a top parcel of food to take home for my mum and Mark. Grub like that was a luxury. In those days even jam butties were a treat because of the cost; if you went to a mate's you'd most likely get brown or red sauce between two slices while girls would dip theirs in condensed milk. Sugar butties were also popular, while old folk would have theirs with

Oxo or dripping. I loved only one type, vinegar, even better when all soaked into a crust. Later in life I suffered terribly with heartburn and when I finally got to see a private doctor he shoved a camera down to suss it out and said, in his German accent, 'Vot voss you eating as a child? Many bacterias I see from your youth.'

We spent Christmases with Nana and Grandad and their German sausage dog Fritz – Grandad was a Dunkirk veteran. The streets where they lived were so quiet and peaceful and I used to love going to the Dog and Partridge to tell Grandad dinner would be ready in half an hour. He would give me half a shandy to drink and it allowed me to tune into all the older men's talk, mainly about the War and the docks. I used to love the way my grandad smoked his Capstan Full Strength cigs; every now and then he'd pick a speck of tobacco from his lips and expertly flick it into the ashtray.

Grandad took me to my first Manchester derby at Old Trafford. It was 1966 and everyone was talking about United's new goalkeeper, Alexander Cyril Stepney. They'd paid a record £55,000 for him the previous day. In the pub, grandad and all the other dockers would discuss their number one United player, Duncan Edwards, describing how he stuck out like a Colossus, an England regular at eighteen and a born leader and winner, who of course died at Munich after fighting for life for two weeks with injuries that would have killed any other man instantly.

As we crossed the railway bridge on the walk to the ground, Grandad told me the history of United: how the club had been called Newton Heath, how it was stuck for cash at the start of the century and how four backers came forward to finance it. They decided to change the name, rejecting Manchester Central and Manchester Celtic in favour of United. Once over the bridge he took me into the Stretford End seats, which were right up in the heavens. Only 2,000 could fit up there but what a view, plus you could soak up all the crowd's chanting.

Sixty thousand watched a close game with United edging it 1–0, Denis Law scoring the winner. We went on to win the League without losing another home game. Going back over the bridge, Grandad started on again, telling me about the first-ever derby at North Road in 1891; about the infamous old ground at Bank Street in Clayton, next to the smoke-belching chemical works, and how the pitch was ankle deep in slime and mud; about how we were the first club ever to be relegated after losing to Liverpool in the last game of the season.

'Mind you,' said Grandad, winking as we came down onto Railway Road, 'them bloody Scousers got relegated themselves next year.'

As we arrived at the house he gave me his last fact for that big day: in 1910 we moved to Old Trafford and lost 4–3 to Liverpool. He ruffled up my hair and gave me a few pretend boxing digs, then came out with the punchline.

'Yet, laddie, we went on and won the League the next year.'

I would go to games often with my grandad, and hear those same stories many times. As a kid it became a bit boring but when I think back now I get tingles.

*   *   *

The boys I grew up with were footie mad and some could really play. In fact we first became known as Collyhurst Cowboys – a nickname that would stick to us when we later became grafters – because when we played football against the posher schools and colleges, they viewed us as a bunch of cowboys, wild and untameable. Gagzy was one of the best and when he and I were picked for

Manchester Boys it was a buzz for everyone. I was fanatical about the sport – my only ambition was to turn pro. I would spend hours on my own reading in the library whatever I could find about the sport and became a complete football brain, able to answer questions about crowd attendances, nicknames, past histories, the lot.

When the 1966 World Cup kicked off, Grandad got me tickets for all I asked. The new cantilever stand at Old Trafford was unveiled and I was soon smitten by Eusebio, the great Black Panther from Portugal. We even made the trip to Goodison Park to watch Portugal play Brazil. My everlasting memory is of the sheer power and speed of Eusebio and how he tried to get his teammates to play like him. The chip shops were giving out free chips to all the Scouse scallies, which I soon put myself in for, like you do.

After England had won the Cup, Pete Kank and I got summer jobs at the Willert Street Hall, where they served free dinners to the Colly kids when they were not at school. My mum worked there and sorted us out with a bit of cash in hand work. We had to set up the long tables and benches and help with carrying in the food that was cooked in town and brought in a van. With the few bob we earned, we went to the arcades on Tib Street or the Golden Goose in Piccadilly, or saved up for a couple of weeks for the zoo and fair at Belle Vue. It was like having Blackpool on your doorstep. We would sneak in over a huge spiked fence at the back of the bowling alley. Once we were all over the fence, a row of bushes gave us perfect cover until the coast was clear. There was only one ride at the fair we could jib for nothing, called the Selnick Railway. Every now and then the guys who worked on it would throw a load of used tickets into a large metal bin. With a bit of cover, one of us could lean over and get a handful. Then we'd go offside and mooch through them to find ones that hadn't been ripped. Our best ever haul was twenty unused tickets, a proper result.

Sometimes we'd also head up to Heaton Park, where the route home was sometimes the dreaded walk on the train lines, dreaded because of one long tunnel and the possibility of an oncoming train. This walk took around two hours and I shit myself bad the first time a train did come through. We all did the same: shagged the wall screaming, 'Aaarrggh,' or 'Maaam!'

A school up on Grey Mare Lane was open all day for sports and music during the summer holidays, so Gags, Eric, Carl Bailey and I went up to see what was what. All seemed fine until the one-hour break, when we made our way to the yard. As soon as we got to a corner to light a fag, we were surrounded by a mean crew of locals a year or two older than us, which at that age means a lot. Before any kind of script had been put before us, Carl slipped off his jumper, rolled up his sleeves and stated he'd take on the Daddy. None of us knew that Carl had just started boxing training over at the Tin School, which catered for eleven years and under.

What we saw of Carl that day was the best performance in a street fight ever. He boxed and busted the main three kids into submission, so it was no big surprise that we all joined the boxing at the Tin school two nights a week. Later we were all old enough to join Colly Lads' Club, which was even better. Within a few months Carl was a well-known boxer, beating kids his own age with ease, and within a year he held all kinds of titles. Micky Duplex started boxing on the same bills and every other week we'd all go to support them. Mick was harder than Carl but lost his head in the ring now and then, head-butting and fouling, while Carl's speed and skill looked like taking him all the way. He turned pro in 1976 and I went to see him in a big boxing event at Rotters on Oxford

Road, with John Conteh and Alex Higgins at ringside. It was good to see Carl in action and even better to have a good old chit-chat in the bar after. We had a laugh about my debut in the ring, which was three rounds with Carl. He busted me up bad but the trainer kept telling me I'd get a full bottle of ice-cold Coke if I lasted and somehow I did without getting knocked down. That Coke was the best drink I've ever tasted.

Another memory of Carl was one lazy afternoon up at the Grey Mare Lane school, when two female student teachers took him and me to a bench in a nearby park and taught us how to French kiss. We still hadn't got round to any kind of sex but this experience boosted my confidence when it was needed – in the very near future.

* * *

My final school trip at St Malachy's was to Blankenburg in Belgium, not far from Ostende. This was really big stuff for us and before we got on the train to Euston my mum took me to a twenty-four-hour café near Piccadilly called Snack Time. It was full of loonies and drunks and had clocks on the wall showing times from places all over the world. This was really exciting for me, knowing I'd soon be in a different time zone, even if it was only an hour difference. When we arrived at Euston we all went mad and tried to slide down the middle of the barrier leading to the Tube trains. The Tube was just as exciting as a ride at the fairground. After a rancid bag of chips at Victoria we were on our way to Dover, singing Collyhurst Kid songs nonstop until we saw the White Cliffs. On the ferry I got over-excited and started snapping away at the Cliffs and the other ferries with the camera my mum had borrowed for me. By the time we got onto a coach at the other end I had used all the film in the camera and the spare one she'd given me. She was speechless when she got them developed.

We had a short road journey before arriving quite late at the hotel in the main square. After omelette and chips we were off to bed. The next morning we were up early and down for breakfasts, which were these amazing bread rolls, the best I'd ever tasted, and as much jam as we could load on. We decided to get off before the teachers crawled down for their breakfast and headed for the sea. The beach was deserted and as I looked along the coastline I could see a red flag flying in every section all the way into the distance. None of us had a clue what this meant, so we all peeled off, leaving our undies on as trunks, and made a dash for the sea. Just as we were about to leap into the foaming tide there was a load of shouting, from some people who looked official and were running in our direction. We all doubled back to grab our togs, thinking this part of the coast must belong to someone, and ran further along the sand to the next part of the beach. Then another two official types came running over, so we stood our ground to find out what was going on. They told us it was dangerous to swim in the water and said they wanted to escort us back to the teachers.

Without thinking, we all made a dash for it and split into two groups, soon losing them. My group ended up in the shopping precinct just as the shops were beginning to open. A woman was pulling up shutters at the first one we came to, so we strolled past her into the shop for a mooch around. There was a cabinet full of these mega cig cases with a lighter built into the corner. We all grabbed a couple each and moved back to the forecourt, where the woman was still busy arranging things. There were all new kinds of trunks, goggles and flippers for swimming in the sea. I picked up one of the flippers and shoved it down the back of my trousers. As I was manoeuvring the next one down the front of my trousers the woman clocked me and started screaming, grabbing hold of my ear lobe at the same time. Everyone else was off as a couple of the other shopkeepers came out and got a firm grip of me. The police arrived and took me back to the hotel, where the woman pointed out a few of the others. I felt terrible, as I thought I had brought it on top for the other boys. The teachers were fuming and I ended up losing all my spends.

My first trip abroad and I'd been nicked. If ever there was an omen in my life, this was it. Still, it was my first proper brush with the law and I was so relieved when we got back to Manchester that no one mentioned it to my mum, who was waiting for me at Piccadilly Station.

I moved to Saint John Southworth School in September 1966. Boys who had been cocks at their previous schools lined up to fight each other, so the pecking order could be sorted out quickly. Our own Vinny Healey – whose old man ran a scrapyard on Collyhurst Road and was once involved in a brawl that left one man dead from shotgun wounds and made the *News of the World* – was pushed around like a pussycat by another cock, much to our astonishment, until finally Vinny snapped and bounced this kid's head to and fro off the wall for a clean kayo, firmly establishing himself as cock of our year.

Our form teacher, Mr Archdeacon, who loved to swish his cane around, also came a cropper one day when Eric had one of his fits. We didn't understand that these were a build-up of temper – we all believed they were real fits and got out of his way if one came on, thinking he'd kill anyone in his way. He went berserk on Archdeacon and we all had to do something or he would have dropped a desk on the poor old feller's napper and could have been in serious trouble. Archy was in a bad way after.

But the school was a dream. All the dinners were cooked on the premises. Cornflake flan with treacle was my favourite dessert and I loved the bread and butter pudding with raisins in it. We also got a free bottle of milk every morning and the fish and chips on a Friday were as good as Frank's chippie in the Flats. The new gymnasium had ropes that pulled out, a trampoline and 'horse' boxes, and we were shown new games like volleyball and basketball. There were even nets inside for playing cricket. We didn't have a football pitch but a quick bus ride to Smedley Lane, next to Queen Mary Flats, took us to our grass pitch, which had hot showers and changing rooms. The hot showers were the best thing of all, while the icing on the cake was the weekly ride to the baths in Ancoats, where I ended up with a swimming medal and countless verrucas along the way.

Despite somehow finding myself in the 'A' stream, I wasn't interested in lessons, particularly maths, which I could never understand. The teachers were a mix of good and bad but all had different ways of inflicting pain for those who misbehaved – a wooden cane across the knuckles or the inside of the wrists, a strap across the backside or across an open palm or fingertips.

Mum bought a secondhand music box that she paid off monthly and was mad for Matt Munro, Gene Pitney and Shirley Bassey. I loved the Beatles, Amen Corner and the Hollies, while Gagzy was into Tamla and soul stuff and Eric was 100 per cent Elvis. I also noticed that when friends called round a lot of them were ogling my mum and talking about how good she looked, and at first I was embarrassed. But she really was the best-looking woman in the flats and I was proud of her and how she had looked out for Mark and I. So for her next birthday I saved up and bought her a huge bunch of flowers from the florist on Queens Road. I dreaded the walk back through the Flats, as the sight of a bunch of flowers carried by a kid like me just didn't fit in. Yet once in I didn't give a fuck and to try to explain the joy it brought her is impossible. And she still looks fantastic today.

One Saturday afternoon Nana took us to New Brown Street, which was Manchester's Carnaby Street, where I pleaded with her for a pair of Wranglers or Levis. All she could afford was a pair of cream Wrangler cords two sizes too big. Although I spent six months looking well dodgy, after countless washes and a bit of growing by me these cords were my big intro into fashion – even though Mum maintained they were a waste of money. Fashion was becoming important to us – and so were girls.

* * *

One Saturday night, Jimmy Ford brought over to our house two friends and a big ginger-haired girl who let us play around with her tits. A short while later we started going to Belle Vue to see the speedway on Saturday nights, and afterwards in the fairground Kank pulled Mary, who was a spit of Dusty Springfield with all the makeup on her face, bleached blonde hair and massive false eyelashes. Mary lived at the back of the abattoir. She and Kank started off a necking session, then we all got a turn.

From then on, Mary turned up at Hulme Hall Lane Fair with a new mate every other night and we all got a bit of a snog. On the last night she said she'd bring an older friend, a greaser girl, to the Playhouse flicks on Oldham Road the next week. She also hinted she might give out one handjob.

So there's me, Kank, Eric and Gags, sharing one of my mam's Woodbines and waiting in unbearable expectation. We heard them coming and the nerves jangled even worse when we saw her mate was older than expected and weird looking. Anyway, we sneaked them into the cinema as fast as we could, and once settled down we started sharing bits of necking, and sure enough Mary was giving out a very sly rub up. I got a bit of tit on the outside of the bra from Mary's mystery mate before she pulled my hand away – I'm sure I was doing fuck all for her in that department.

I moved over and let Gags try his luck but he struggled even to neck as he was the smallest of all our lot. He moved back over so before Kank came in I went straight for her knickers, only to find she had tights and a girdle on as well. But she pulled me in close so I could get a firm grip of the top part, then work my way down to heaven. Gagzy nearly had a fight with the others as he pleaded with me to show him her beaver while trying to keep the others at bay.

The flicks finished and Kank was now cert for a wank as he led Mary over the road to the corner of Miles Platting train station. Over we all go into the coal yard. I grabbed Mary's mate again and made my way to the top of a pile of loose coal. She leaned back onto the filthy wall and parted her legs a touch. I worked as best I could to get the three sets of trolleys off – it seemed to take ages and the noise from the trains passing above didn't help. But then with perfect ease she had my hotdog out and slid me in.

I'd forgotten about the others until they began almost cheering me on, Mary the loudest. I realised that my bare arse was on show, pumping away. I doubt if I lasted more than a minute but I clung on tight, moving for as long as I could to impress the Cowboys. The coal was getting loose and I needed her help to get my pants back on. We shared another couple of Woodbines, then the mystery girl spoke.

'We'd better fuck off if we're going to make the chippie.'

That was the last we saw of her, but Mary started coming over to my house on Saturday nights. For the next few years it became known as the 89 Club, as my mum had a weekend bar job and so was out of the house. I was the only one to have access to two single and one double beds, plus the three-piece suite, almost every weekend. Many a time they were all in action.

My old lady was working Friday, Saturday and Sunday nights at the Osbourne Irish Club on Oldham Road and I got a job there too, clearing up the bottles and mess and cleaning cars. It had two long bars, a regular showband and a room at the back was where you handed in your ticket for a boiled burger and chips. They sold Irish poteen, so no wonder it was the worst gaff for fighting in all north Manchester. My first ever watch came from my old lady, who slotted it during a fight.

Next door was the Ram pub, which had a big room with Irish bands, a vault and a snug. It was run by Cassy, a frail woman but a real whisky head who when she came down in the mornings would grab a shorts glass and in one movement hit herself a wee dram, only one day it backfired as when she swigged the whisky back the glass was full of drawing pins. The priest from St Pat's would nip in now and then and was given the green light to slip behind the bar and help himself to the top shelf.

The Ram was where Syl, my mum, met my new dad, Jimmy Smythe. He came up to Manchester from London to open a sand-blasting firm, which became the biggest in the country. Jimmy was from Lurgan, near Belfast, and looked like Rab C. Nesbitt, even down to his string vests. He was a pure whisky monster with a fine rebel singing voice. Trouble was, no-one in his sober times ever knew if he was Welsh, Scottish, Eire or Northern Ireland. His conversation was short and often repeated: 'Hey boy, hey boy,' like you'd want to salute him or he was shouting for his dog.

Only about twenty per cent of the kids who came into the 89 Club got round to shagging. It was more of a learning process for girls who wanted their tits rubbing so as to 'get them bigger', while others came over for the necking or until they got their mate to ask the chosen boy, 'Will you go out with my friend?' The first one I said yes to was Lynn Ward, who was top funny and a good looker. I never got much off Lynn and the next girl I went out with would be a couple of years later – and she bore me a son. But I did learn a lesson from Lynn: I realised I wanted to get the most out of life while the going was good.

The first couple to kick off the shagging big-time was Holly and Dot, on the night we all tried to drink a bottle of whisky and ended up chucking it on the fire for the effect. That night Dot left her bra in Syl's bed and there was murder when she found it. We had to start paying off my brother Mark to keep quiet, as Mam was paying him to grass, so Mark had it both ways.

Mr Coglan was now in charge of a female borstal and started bringing a minibus load of them every Saturday to our youth club disco. The first blowjob I ever got was from a Glasgow arsonist upstairs in the kit room. We also started going to a hall in Cheetham Hill for the roller skating. Maggie McEwan and Lynn Beaumont, who were older started to come with us, and soon asked me, Wodger and Cooky to go to Gorton for a bit of necking at a house where they baby-sat. All seemed to be going well when the door went and two older lads – they looked like grown fellers to us – burst in. It seems they were involved with the girls and, as I looked the oldest in our group, I copped for a black eye. They wanted me to come outside for more but Maggie saved my bacon.

That same week, just as my eye was getting better, I was wagging school at Gagzy's when the door got a hammering and who was out there but Andy McEwan, armed to the teeth with Mick Jones, who was known not only as a right hard cunt but a blade merchant. They wanted me to go round the back of the shops to have it out with Andy. I was having none of it but it was out of control, so Gags said, 'Let them go for it in the living room.'

Having to clear the chairs and tables while knowing you're going to get a hiding was a nightmare. Anyway, off we jolly well go. What a fight – it was like two puppies. I had Andy down in two seconds but had to let him back up when he shouted over to Mick. This went on for fifteen minutes with Andy not able even to catch me. In the end I let him land punches to my sides and let out stupid cries of pain while Andy demanded would I give in. That was no problem as I was shitting myself that Mick was on to this farce and would lose it. Andy later worked as a barrow boy at the market and whenever I passed he always let on like we were the best of friends, which I let ride.

It was also around this time that I was introduced to proper thieving. The two leaders of Burgin at that time, Billy Beaumont and Roy Clarke, took us into Manchester to show us what he called the 'five-finger discount', where you grabbed a handful of whatever you could just for the sake of being in a thieving gang. We lined up at the two main entrances to a big department store and walked through the counters lifting anything we could get our hands on. I came home with a few locks for my bike. We also started blocking up the change compartments of the photo machines dotted across Manchester with thin pieces of metal. We would put the metal at the top of the compartment out of sight so it prevented the change from falling down. Then on our way home we would visit the booths again with a piece of wire to liberate any change that had collected during the day. It didn't add up to much when it was divvied up – but it set me on the grafting road.

Chapter Three

Skinheads

I WAS A FULLY-FLEDGED Stretford Ender by the age of twelve and was lucky enough to witness much of United's triumphant European Cup campaign in 1968. My favourite game of the tournament was the quarter-final against Gornik Zabrze, the Polish champs. We lost the first leg and my God did their goalie play well in the second but we came through 2–1 on aggregate. Packed inside were 64,000 and it was the first time I knew what a big Euro game was like. The Stretford End were all getting their voices tuned in with school bells, horns and rattles mixed in, and I was fascinated by the floodlights on full and the fine rain floating down. Clouds of steam rose from under our duffel coats into the night air. All the older workers wore donkey jackets and the Mods had parkas or Army coats on.

We went into the semi against Real Madrid, with United the underdogs. Gags and I had both been picked for a game up for Oldham Athletic's youth team but I was finding the trip up there and back on the bus a bit of a norse, so I made some excuse, as I just had to be at Old Trafford for this one. I couldn't get Stretford End tickets so went down the Scoreboard End and saw Georgie Boy give us a 1–0 win to take to Madrid two weeks later. Next day the *Manchester Evening News* had a big photo of Best's goal and among the clearest faces on it were

Eric and I to the right of the goal. Thank fuck we didn't go in the Strettie. As for the final, I was in hospital having an operation on my big toe and watched it with all the staff. The shock of the night was the great performance by Johnny Aston, who became an instant favourite of mine.

Weekends were dominated by football but during the week, youth clubs were all the rage. Soon we were old enough to join Collyhurst Youth Club, the best in the area. All of Ancoats and Miles Platting came as it had a top weekly disco. The senior football team was run by Brian Hughes, who was also in charge of the boxing and would go on to train many top fighters. Jimmy Kidd was number two under Brian with the boxing while his younger brother Brian Kidd, the Manchester United star, coached us all at table tennis. Round the corner in Willert Street was a hall where Brian's number one boxer, Kenny Webber, ruled the roost. At his Saturday night fights we would peek at the most fearsome feller we had ever seen as kids, Jock McAvoy, the old Rochdale Thunderbolt, sat right at the front. He had a face like granite and huge, gnarled fists.

Violence had always been part of Collyhurst life but it was slowly taking a turn for the worse. I saw my first skinhead in late 1968. I was terrified: I thought he was going to pull a knife or chain out on the lot of us. I'd seen the lad around previously and thought nothing of him, but his newly cropped hair, his clothes and his attitude suddenly made him a somebody. Soon more skins appeared in the Flats, aping the behaviour of others they'd heard or read about in the newspapers. One Friday night I was in the chippie when I heard them all walking past singing, 'Hey ho the lights are flashing, we're all going Paki bashing.' And that's what they did. Another of their favourite antics was to steal a copper's helmet, which would be wedged on top of a lamppost in the small hours outside one of the pubs on Rochdale Road. We would wait around the next day for the poor copper to bumble along and try to retrieve it, while we all took the piss.

I started hanging around on the fringes of the skins, listening to Desmond Dekker and Judge Dread and reading a book Ashy gave me called *Skinhead*, about a violent young character called Joe Hawkins. Then I got an introduction through Eric from Central Drive to his cousin Richard Tschikowski – Chike for short – a top rag-arse tearaway. Chike had just come out of his second lot of borstal. He'd done approved school and been to detention centre twice and was a great storyteller, a real spinner. He loved to add spice to his tales, like how in borstal he'd wasted a greaser and then put him in the washing machine! Chike was a big Beatles fan and got us all into 'Yellow Submarine'; the girls outside Frank's chippie used to join in with him when he sang.

I was soon knocking around with Chike and my life and schooling began to slip. First I wagged classes to hang around the arcades, then I went into the big stores to nick whatever we could get our hands on. We went for boxes of goods, not single items; the boxes were always in the cupboards under the goods themselves. Chike's favourite things to nick were Marks and Sparks cardigans to sell on to the skinheads in the Baked Potato café on Brown Street. They gave us good money, as they were right into fashion. Any we had left we'd knock out to the older window cleaners or the fellers at Smithfield Market. I treated myself to a striped Ben Sherman shirt and a secondhand pair of black, steel-toed bovver boots. When I tried it all on with my newly acquired red braces I looked a proper idiot, as there was no way I'd shave my head and go full skinhead. I took the boots back, got a nice pair of black brogues and kept the braces in the draw for the time being.

The violence around the skins was always bad. One night we arrived at the youth club and in the disco saw two Gorton skinheads who were older and even harder-looking than Ashy and Co. They were carving their names on the wooden rail by the DJ box for all to see their cut-throat blades. I swear they glittered, the size of them. I froze and waited out of the way in the corner, hoping they'd fuck off out. But as they left they got slashed up wicked, the first time I'd ever seen razors used.

A few weeks later, old Tom, our table tennis manager, took me as captain and several other B team players to Gorton for a match. Besides skinheads there were real greasers in their club and I was so scared I wanted to lose but it would have looked so obvious that we would have been killed. The two cut-up skinheads came over and showed us their scars. Even old Tommy sussed it was bad and got us out of a side exit when he saw a bus coming.

The very next week the Gorton Greasers stormed into the Flats on their motorbikes and wasted a good few lads outside Frank's chippie. Ashy got a hiding with bike chains.

For the 1969 Whit Walks, my mam took me to Burtons to buy my first ever suit on tick. I went for a navy blue, single-breasted, three-button pin-stripe with a twelve-inch back vent, one ticket pocket on the right side, and three buttons on each of the cuffs, and straight trousers with turn-ups. That Whit Friday I bowled down to town and all the lads in their own new suits were giving me the thumbs-up, reason being we were all cert to get served in a pub. I don't know why but I said I'd meet them later on and walked over to Swan Street, hearing the bagpipes from the procession in the distance and feeling pleased with myself, and went straight into the George and Dragon (later the Band On The Wall) to try to get served alone for the first time in my youth.

The pub was one very large room, so I was on show as I walked up to the bar.

'A pint of mild, luv.'

It worked. Away she went to work the pump while I sparked up a Woodbine. What a feeling. I went over to the jukebox, then played the pinball. After three pints I was bladdered, singing to myself as I staggered out the door.

My ruinous love affair with the demon drink had begun.

* * *

Around Easter, Chike and his mates invited me over to an area full of warehouses, near the Express Newspapers building in Ancoats. Everyone seemed to know the plan, which was simple. The new kid on the block – me – would scale the drainpipe to the seventh floor and use a crowbar I had been given by Chike to break in. I would come down two flights of stairs and use the bar to burst the main door. This would set off the alarm. I then had to run down the stairs to the ground floor and let the lads in. From there it was every man for himself, though Chike said I could stick with him.

Together we carted out two massive binliners full of sexy women's underwear. Most of the lads made their way over the Rochdale Canal to hide or creep up bit by bit till it felt safe, as the coppers were soon all over the place. Chike bailed over to Stevenson Square, to where the black cab rank was, and the fellers there seemed to know he was coming.

'Now then Chike, what's what?'

He told me he'd used them for years. The same night

we dropped the gear off at the Sparrow pub with Jimmy Fox – who was a fox with his prices – and Chike had to really haggle to get £20 for the lot. I couldn't believe it when he went right down the middle with it and gave me a tenner for my night's work. I bought myself a black blazer and a Lancashire Rose to sew on the breast pocket. Soon I had a pair of Prince of Wales pants to go with it.

Kank and I started to go to our first club, the Ritz, though we were only in our early teens. Sundays and Mondays was Soul and Northern Soul, fast stuff with the dance floor bouncing. Just as we started to get into the scene, we got jumped on Oxford Road by a right old firm. I got slashed twice by a steel comb on the back of my neck as I was giving it legs, while Kank was knocked cold and ended up in ossy (hospital). A few months later I started to go back and it was an even better buzz, as it was free on Friday afternoons – and live on BBC radio.

I pulled a bird who asked me to meet her on the Saturday night in the Red Lion in Blackley, one of the liveliest pubs in north Manchester. Afterwards I had to walk her home – to a farm. I went for a snog and a bit of a squeeze until her old feller appeared and gave us loads. I jumped on a bus back to the Flats and spotted Kank in the opening with two birds I'd seen at the Ritz but never talked to. Both were Ancoats girls: Legsy and Smiler (Sylvia Bollard). I made a massive bid for Smiler and got to walk her home. I knew without doubt after our first necking session and bits of grinding hips that we'd be seeing a lot more of each other.

Smiler was working as a machinist and loved a drink and footie. In fact she was the leader of a big girl gang of real hard City fans who went right in where the action was. She'd come home with police charge sheets, busted ribs, cuts and bruises. Once she got into the Shed at

Chelsea with all City's top boys and it was in the Sunday papers how they'd taken over, with seven or eight stabbings. She wore a long black coat with 'Smiler Man City' across the back. I loved her accent, real inner Manchester.

The landmark event of that summer was the World Cup in Mexico. On my fourteenth birthday I went with Chike to the Hat and Feathers pub to watch the opening game live. Everyone was singing 'Back Home' and I reckoned the England team was as good as 1966. Well, as we all know, England were doing the Krauts 2–0 until Alf Ramsey pulled off Bobby Charlton to save his legs for the semi, then England crumbled with the Cat from Chelsea flapping in the nets. We were all in despair. Still, we got to see the best team ever, Brazil, when they turned it on in the final – on the colour TV at the Heywood pub on Oldham Road.

Ashy was now telling me about all the up and coming skinhead versus greaser fights on certain fairgrounds and I got to know other older skins and bootboys. The one I most admired was Steve Wilson, known as Snake Hips. He was the first I'd seen in a Crombie overcoat and he looked cool and hard, plus I'd seen him go and he could fight. I saw him and Jack Horner chase off a pack of greasers one night and was well impressed.

I felt I'd earned a stripe myself now so was okay to go on the Paki-bashing or trips up to Cheetham Hill to rob a Crombie coat, be it light brown or navy blue, from the Jewish area (I once came back with a trilby hat which Smiler wore for the City games). 'Paki-bashing' was a youth phase that lasted for a few months but we were definitely not racist; in fact you would not find a less racist crew. Everyone was equal round our way, regardless of colour or creed. Burgin Drive, where we hung out, had two massive black families, one of which was the Clerkins, who could really fight. Because we knocked about with them from such an early age, racist thoughts never entered our heads.

The skinheads' biggest enemies were the greasers or bikers, most of whom were a lot older. One night I went up to Hulme Hall Lane fair on the Red Rec, and was stood around the speedway with the lads, skanking slightly to a massive ska tune – 'Al Capone's guns don't argue' – when a massive firm of greasers from either the Ten-Ten gang or the Skyways from near Manchester Airport, the two biggest biker mobs at the time, sprang on us. I was happy to come away with a busted lip. One kid who was up on a ride when it kicked off strolled right into them just after they'd finished us all off; he spent the night in Ancoats Hospital.

The next night skins and bootboys from all over north Manchester were on the fair wanting to have a real good go at any greasers but not one turned up. So Brian Gaftney took charge and led the mob on a mini riot, with police soon on our trail and plenty getting nicked. Around the same time, a skin was killed with a blade by a group of greasers in south Manchester and the next night there were over 1,000 bootboys hunting for revenge. The truth was that eighty per cent of greasers were much older and wiser than the bootboys so they were pissing in the wind thinking they'd get revenge.

*   *   *

I wagged school more and more. One sunny summer day I was getting pissed with Chike in the Spanking Roger pub in Miles Platting. I was fourteen years old. We decided to go to the school on Holland Street for a sneak around and ended up in the staffroom with a fistful of purses, though unbeknown to me I'd been clocked on the mooch through. Like an idiot, when I got home I gave my mum one of the purses as it looked brand new, so when Officer Dibble arrived at the door I was bang to rights. I had to go over to Mill Street Police Station for a caution.

It didn't make any difference. A few weeks later we screwed a factory on Collyhurst Road that made nice handbags and when I came back from a rare visit to school, there was a police van outside our flat loading up all the stuff from my secret hiding places. They charged me with burgling £480-worth of handbags, though I doubt if I'd had £100-worth. The funny thing was, almost every woman in the Flats had a new handbag swinging from her shoulder as soon as the Dibble were off the estate. I got three years' probation. My mum was frantic with worry; a week before the cops had come knocking she had found a television hidden under my bed. She made me promise I'd sack Chike and all the screwing that went with him and even sent for my dad to come and have a word. He caught up with me outside the Colly Lads' Club with some of the skinheads and pulled me to one side. It must have been difficult for him and whatever he said went in one ear and out the other.

In the summer holidays I did a bit of cash-in-hand work at the fruit market, then a couple of the lads who had finished school said they were going to Blackpool for a break before they started full-time employment. We put together a homemade tent from a few bed sheets and two snide poles and headed for the station. We walked all day before we found a campsite that would take us, deposited the tent and finally headed for the bar – and got served no problem, despite our youth. But when we got back to the tent and tried to fit things together, it was clear that it wasn't happening. So we had a mooch and found an empty caravan in a nearby field, popped the lock and were in like Flynn. We used the homemade tent for storing our dirty clothes in. During the day we'd shoplift all the latest stuff: V-neck sleeveless jumpers, Stone Whites that were like Chinos, and Jaytex shirts, which I thought held their shape on the collar better than Ben Shermans.

After half a dozen days of successful shoplifting, we decided to call the thieving a day. As we were walking back to the campsite I remembered that the batteries had gone in the torch we'd been using to navigate through the fields, so I decided to catch up with the others later and headed into town. Call it over-confidence or whatever, but I slipped a few batteries into my pocket and strolled out of Woolworths. Straight away, two fellers outside the main entrance pulled me, but before they could say anything, whoff, I was over the road and away. A tram nearly hit me on the Golden Mile and every time I looked back the fuckers were still chasing me, all the way up to the open-air swimming pool. I then doubled back along the sand but a copper had joined in the chase. We went through the fairground but just as I thought I had half a chance of getting away, one of the fair ground workers nearly took my head off and before I knew what had happened I was on my way to Blackpool police station.

The problem was my mum, Mark, Grandad and Nana were also in Blackpool on holiday and were staying in a hotel. There was no way I could send the Dibble round to their hotel as it would have killed my nana and ruined their holiday. So I decided to say nothing to the Old Bill, no name, nothing, and they were really pissed off with me. They put me in a cell where the only thing I could see was the Tower and every day they'd throw whatever runaway kids they'd caught in with me, knowing I'd see them being sent home that same night. Most of the kids were messed up and some had been forced to work as rent boys. All of them smelt bad and after a few days my head started to spin.

Once I knew the family were back in Manchester, I told the coppers who I was. They went round to tell Mum and she came up on the train to pick me up. We went to court and I got a fine, then Mum took me for lovely fish and chips before we hit the train home. She told me how worried she was about me and I tried to convince her that I'd get my act together. But as soon as I got home, one of the lads came round with my share of all the stuff we'd nicked in Blackpool. I sold it on the next day and on my way home I bumped into Ashy, one of the skinheads I'd met through Chike. He was wearing a new pair of Doc Marten boots from the Army and Navy store next to Victoria Station. He told me that many of the skinheads were properly getting involved with aggro at United and that there'd been big kick-offs at Hull and Reading. The following Saturday, plans were afoot for the Watney Cup final at Derby in August 1970. The Watney Cup was a short-lived pre-season competition between the two top scorers in each of the four divisions of the Football League.

I felt like I was being asked to join the other lads, but in truth I had no idea what football thuggery was all about. I'd seen all the skins in the Stretford End but no away fans had caused any aggro since Everton years ago, when some of their lot got into our end. I'd been to a couple of away games but that was on cheap Ribble buses to Burnley and Blackburn, with only a faraway view of the mob trouble at the opposite end of the ground. I decided there and then I wanted to be part of it and thought about it on my way to the Army and Navy store to get sorted with some dark brown Docs with the yellow stitching all the way round the rims. A lot of the lads ended up getting the cherry red ones, bought for ten bob cheaper up at the abattoir as they were worn by the slaughtermen there.

Saturday couldn't come soon enough.

* * *

It was boiling hot so I left my jacket at home and pulled out my red braces from the drawer, twanging them over my shoulders. I'd had a medium crop earlier in the week, so it looked like a skinhead that had started to grow out. When I arrived at Piccadilly train station, the platform was awash with shaved heads and Doc Marten boots: 500 bootboys and thugs – and this was the third football special of the day, as two were already on their way to Derby. The Collyhurst lot were soon all stood together: the Flecks, the Simpsons, the Gaftneys, the Critchleys, Nutty Norman, Mick Farrell, Steve Wilson, Dave Willis, Tommy Beard and many more, including Maca McGarry, who was to be my oppo at United's games for the whole of the Seventies – we always watched each other's backs.

When the train arrived we piled on and were soon singing 'Manchester la la la, Manchester la la la' to the tune from *The Banana Splits*. Ashy pointed out some of the Salford lads: Mick Grogan, Little Des, Marnie, Yowdy and Ged the Red. Then the lads from Wythenshawe: the Terrible Twins, who were like Tasmanian devils, the Gillams, Big Gibbo, Jeff Lewis, Pearsy, Pubby and so on. As we neared Derby the volume rose with each judder of the train. All hands dismantled the light fittings and anything else that could be ripped off to throw; light bulbs were a favourite. As the train edged its way into the station, every door and window was opened in preparation to bombard the waiting police. Any coppers with dogs were a particular target. Even before the train had stopped, everyone was piling off and with almost no effort we broke through the thin police cordon and were marching through the back streets on our way to the Baseball Ground, chanting, 'A . . . G . . . A.G.R . . . A.G.R.O . . . Aggro!'

The plan was to make our way to their end, but lads from the earlier trains had beaten us to it. Normally in the early Seventies it wasn't difficult to breach the home team's end, but because this was a final at the end of the pre-season, the Old Bill were more together than usual. We were blocked in a section with just a few turnstiles to get us all in. There was lots of pushing and shoving and a bit of cursing, particularly from a guy behind me. When I turned round I couldn't believe my eyes: it was a priest with a dog collar on who was swearing and trying his best to cause havoc with the police. The turnstiles were a token gesture for a lot of the lads, as they just jumped over them without paying. It was a very common thing in the Seventies, like not paying on the train, and we called it 'jibbing'. Everyone waited until we were all through the turnstiles before entering the stadium itself en masse. I looked round the ground and couldn't believe United's following – not just that there were seven or eight thousand for a pre-season game but that every one was a thug.

We made our way to the fence that separated us from Derby, the same layout as the Kippax at Maine Road, and plenty of missiles were flying. I could see the St John Ambulance in action on the touchline, scrubbing people's heads, and I soon realised why: some of the missiles were condoms full of a kind of acid and they were raining down on plenty of heads. A few United were trying to get onto the pitch to help a group of Reds who had been sussed in the Derby end. They were getting a good beating with lots of boots going in, so we all got our loose change and began to pelt the Derby. This seemed to help the lads and they were able to get onto the edge of the pitch and back amongst the Devils with a little help from Plod. The game itself was not going United's way and we were getting a real good hiding, but despite this I couldn't believe it at half-time when all the lads were buzzing, saying what a brilliant knobble it was.

The second half on the pitch was worse than the first as United let another couple in and on the terraces Derby were really letting us have it as they pelted us with heavy stones and coins. When the full-time whistle went, we all made our way outside and I couldn't believe it when I saw a massive group of Derby waiting for us. I didn't think this could be possible but there they were – and they looked evil. Seeing as it was my first street brawl, I held back and watched as the lads steamed in. The fighting intoxicated me. As soon as United looked to be getting the better of it, I went in to christen my Doc Martens and booted the nearest Derby fan, who already looked like he'd had enough. I doubt I really hurt him anymore than what he'd just copped for. All of a sudden we were running and singing back to the train station, tipping over hotdog carts and smashing up cars and windows, as police sirens blared away nearby. The carnage looked like Northern Ireland on the telly. We were buzzing all the way back, and wrecked the train again every time we passed through a tunnel. As we piled off at Piccadilly, we felt as though we'd been to Dunkirk and got our revenge. I was hooked, and could hardly wait for the season to begin.

Chapter Four

Doc's Barmy Army

STARTING OUT IN the hooligan game you quickly learn how to keep with the pack, listen to the old hands and make sure you know where the meet is. The older ones make the places for meeting before and after the games. In London it was Mr Fogs and the Cockney Pride, in Birmingham it was the Yates's and in Newcastle it was the Victoria Comet, which we called the 'Spit and Vomit'. The Comet was near the train station and had an old wooden floor covered in sawdust, with a revolving door. It was funny to see well-to-do people struggling to get through the revolving door with their cases, only to take one look at us and leap back out sharpish. As for Liverpool, we didn't have a favoured watering hole, as you would never catch a Mancunian supping Higsons' Scouse beer. The truth was if we'd have pitched up at a boozer it wouldn't have lasted more than an hour before we'd have had some serious shit on our plates.

Going to the Smoke with the Red Army was the biggest buzz of all – like going to a rave twenty years later. We would pile into a Salford Van Hire Transit around midnight, slinging in some dirty old mattresses, and think of songs to sing on the terraces the next afternoon to tunes Snake Hips played on the guitar. We'd reach Euston around six in the morning; some of the lads would sleep off the booze in the van, while the rest hit the Superloo, which was upstairs near the comfy chairs and black and white TV. We'd see other United starting to mill around. Some came down in stolen cars, while others jibbed the overnight train or hitchhiked if they were really desperado. Around eleven o'clock, people started to have a proper mooch about. Most lads who had not been to London before would do the tourist thing for a couple of hours, while others would have a huge game of football on the grass outside the station. We'd often nip to Carnaby Street or Sloane Square, then along Kings Road, where there were always one-off things to nick that you never saw at home. Some were even worth breaking your bank for, like the black leather Chelsea stacks that Gagzy and I bought.

The first time I went to Arsenal was a mega day of drinking and singing, with a load of United steaming into the North Bank and staying there during the match. After the game, Gagzy and I and a load of United were making our way to the North Bank to join the rest when I heard this enormous rumble. I looked up and saw countless Gunners charging down the stairs leading from the side entrance to the Bank. Everyone got on their toes and Gagzy and I got cut off from the rest, along with a small group of others numbering no more than 100. And those fucking Gunners hunted us high and low. Fellow Reds were getting a good kicking nearby and it was panic, with us having to tug the coats of unknown Reds in front of us as we felt the heat of the Gunners pack breathing down our necks. By the time we'd made it back to Euston we'd missed the special home and the station was filling up with incoming Cockneys. Nightmare. We had to keep our heads down and hang around waiting for a service train to jib home, both of us sticking out like true northerners.

Jibbing the train was a way of life for us – we never

considered paying. I went to one game with Gags and we hid under a table when the inspector came round. Unfortunately, he brought two coppers with him who decided to sit at the table opposite, so we had two hours of bad cramp by the time we got into Piccadilly. Gags, who wasn't into the bootboy thing anyway, never bothered with any more away games.

For Bobby Charlton's last ever game, at Chelsea, I took Eric and we sneaked onto a coach outside the Midland Hotel on the Friday night, both pissed up. We woke at Watford Gap with everyone off for a tea and a piss. As soon as we hit the forecourt, we saw trouble on the other side of the car park between Mancs and Scousers. Eric pulled out a blade that I had no idea he was carrying and ran over to get involved – inadvertently chasing four Mancs into the fists of these now very happy Scousers. We then had murders with the rest of the Mancs and ended up running off, then sneaking back just in time to jib the coach to London. The game was a real bore with Peter Osgood getting the only goal in the dying minute; it was used for years to end the credits to *Match Of The Day*, with Osgood's face saying it all.

Another time in London, Maca and I got down to White Hart Lane a bit late after a small kick-off on the tube. We jibbed into their part of the ground, then slyly edged our way round to the United section, which was marked by a line of coppers. Just as we were about to make our little break to join the United fans, there was a massive surge behind us, which we tried to ride all the way to safety with our own – but at the same time the United backed off, leaving a big gap with just me and Maca in it and all these TV cameras pointed at us. We thought nothing of it until a few weeks later, when a *World In Action* about armed police in the Smoke had the pair of us on full show – the Met were apparently planning to bring armed police into football to calm it down, one bad idea that fortunately never caught on.

We rarely carried weapons ourselves bar the odd steel comb; we could always find weapons in most situations if the need arose. Car aerials could be extended and used like a steel lash; very good for keeping a person at bay even if they had a knife. Milk bottles, fences or the small square garden doors, we'd all give the same spot a good kick and break off a lump of wood that could be used like a bat or pole. Shops were always good for finding things to use as missiles, but you'd only really do this if there were a handful of you who'd been cut off from the pack. DIY shops were the best because of the nuts and bolts; I'm not a bad darts player so hitting a Geordie or Scouse head wasn't that difficult. But the best weapon of all is your legs; I always thought it was a load of bollocks when I heard lads say, 'We never run'. I gave it my fair share of toes and I was not alone.

The real bonus for any hooligan is the derby rumble. A lot of fighting at United between rival mobs took place at the roundabout near White City. My first United–City match as a thug was at Old Trafford for Bill Foulkes's testimonial. The game passed off without incident and at the final whistle some of the other lads and I made our way to the roundabout. When we got there, battle lines had already been drawn. Two proper firms were massed and ready to get stuck into each other. I took one look around, realised I was out of my depth and almost without thinking jumped on to the first passing bus. The next day at school I bumped into Chris Tiner, a mad City fan. He kept winking at me and ribbing me about the night before, as he'd been in the thick of it and I'm sure he had seen me disappearing.

There have been many things said about United versus the Scouse and in the early Seventies it was dirty tactics by both sides. When the football specials pulled into Lime Street they would get pelted with bricks, but to be fair we did exactly the same to the Leeds trains when they were close to Victoria – as Gagzy knew only too well, as he got nicked for doing it. The Scouse loved robbing of any kind from us, be it a star jumper or a Harrington jacket as they were sticking the boot in. They also loved using razor blades, even sticking two together so when they slashed it was a real messy job at the hospital trying to stitch the wound back up. They had a certain song for us: while jumping up and down with one arm extended in the air, holding a pretend knife jabbing away, they would chant, 'Stab a Manc, stab a Manc, stab a Manc!' to the tune of 'Here We Go'. I've seen many bad things but nothing so bad as a Red from Northampton or Norway – meaning a total Mr Average – who was not aware of the Scouse dirty stuff and was walking around with his brand new MUFC hat on. All of a sudden this Scouser lurches forward and slashes him across the face. Half his face just peeled off and ended up dangling down his neck. It was really snide with no warning of trouble.

You had to feel sorry for the United dreads like Banana Bob, Buttie, Pele Roy and Black Sam, who were all prime targets in Scouseville. When the pack was almost on you, especially round the Scotty Road area where the flats were just like Collyhurst's, their cry was always, 'Get the nigger.' Mind you, the Scousers were easy to spot as they all used a tailors on Walton Road that made these massive, horrible jeans, called Flemings or something similar. Joe Bloggs got his jeans into the *Guinness Book of Records* during the Madchester era as the widest ever but these were even baggier – and cost more than a Levi jacket. Several thousand Mickeys marching down the road in them was quite a sight.

The first time Liverpool arrived as a mob they came

into the Scoreboard Paddock. They grouped at the bottom
but were charged from behind, forcing a few onto the
pitch. Then we steamed on from the Scoreboard. I got
nicked with thirty others. Buses took us straight to a
gymnasium in Stretford where another thirty were all
awaiting bail. I helped a young Scouser to Oxford Road
Station as we got bailed at the same time and he hadn't a
clue, this being his first away game. He would have been
caught out in the town for sure, and in life I've learnt it's
not a bad thing to do a good deed.

I was nicked again at Leeds, when we went right up to
their main pub and parked our Salford Van Hire Transit
but forgot to take off the Salford stickers. It came right on
top (think of fifteen Leeds guys driving a Leeds-hired van
straight to the Dog and Partridge – pure suicide, but we
liked it!) and we soon had no choice but to bail out and
all get stuck in, as we were surrounded. I was nicked just
as things were looking good, as other Reds were helping
the Cowboys out. The police gave me bail around seven
o'clock with a lad called Alan Haslem, better known as
the 'Ghost' – he turned stone white when stoned or angry.
We got a couple of cans, jibbed the train and had a good
chat on the way home. When I saw the Watneys Brewery
I knew we'd be stopping any minute at Miles Platting, so
I got up.

'See you at the next big game.'

I saw the platform, finished my can, opened the door
in no rush and after a few seconds hopped out. Only
thing was, the train didn't stop – in fact it picked up
speed. I missed the platform by a long way and I landed in
the middle of the intersection, where other trains were
passing every few minutes.

I was lucky to survive. I cannot remember a thing after
opening the door, but Graham Cook was cutting across a
part of the lines as a shortcut to Oldham Road and found

me walking in circles with blood pumping from my head. He took me from the lines straight over to the Salvage pub, where Gagzy said there was no way he could help as he was just getting the taste, so Graham took me to his house and phoned the ambulance. I came round on Monday with a whopper of a headache and stitches in my head. They told me how lucky I was not to be sucked under the train. The next time I saw the Ghost was on the way to Millwall on the football special. He'd thought I was a dead body for sure.

For an FA Cup third round tie, Alex Ross and I hitched down to Wolves, but got there way too early, around four in the morning. We were freezing in the train station when we met this Glasgow Rangers loony who was mad for any violence. He'd been with the Red Army all season and had been nicked a few times in the bargain. We decided we'd mooch round the town and find a warm café. Now Chike had taught me to always look above new shops, as most have three or four glass panes that are opened in the day and that they sometimes forget to shut at night. Some, like dry cleaners, were always open and it was a doddle to take the panes out of the frames and in you go.

We found one that was a suede and leather centre. We let loony tunes do all the fetching and carrying and he even came out with the till instead of just ringing it and clearing the 'Jack' (Jack and Jill = till). We split up and met back at the station around pub opening time. I'd hidden my coats in an old shed by the station while Alex had put his in the lockers, but the Rangers loony was wearing a spanking new sheepskin, pissed as a newt, and had sold two others for next to nothing to the landlord of the pub we met in.

More than 15,000 Reds were there that day, with lots of trouble before and after. Even though we lost, United

fans were the loudest I'd ever heard sing and I still get
tingles up and down my arms and back thinking how
deafening it was. I swear it was Maca who started every
song. Us Collyhurst lot had heavy Manc accents, perfect
for the match, but none of us could bellow like Maca. In
the pubs Reds from all over the UK would latch on to him
to learn all the new chants which normally Snake Hips
and Mick Farrell had written that week, so Maca hardly
ever had to buy booze as it was always flowing his way.

Back at the train station we saw loony again. His new
sheepie was now in bits: the collar had been ripped off
and it had boot marks and mud where he'd been kicked
around like a football. His face was a mess yet he was still
pissed and in merry mood and when he saw us he wanted
to jib the train and come back to Manchester. We needed
to stay low key to get our stolen clobber on the train, so
we had to pack him off back up to Glasgow. Shame, as he
was a real Cowboy. We sold our coats in the Sale Hotel
for £30 each that night.

Every away game was a similar adventure. When
Sunderland met Leeds in the FA Cup final, Maca and I
decided to go down to support the Mackems against the
Sheepshaggers. We caught the late bus to Altrincham,
where there was a twenty-four-hour transport cafe called
the Bear's Head. This was where you'd get your first lift
to one of the motorway service stations, where battles
with the Scousers would often commence – it was open
warfare. At the cafe that night was a City fan called
Dicko; he had just sorted a lift but we took it instead. As
we got near Brum we saw a van with a few heads piling
in. Maca was straight over and put us right in it – this
firm were all Scouse dippers (pickpockets). After a few
heated remarks, we realised we had a lot in common so
soon broke the ice. Later they sorted us out, meaning all
over the weekend they boxed us off with a booze and

scran. They were all from Kirkby, the massive council estate on the edge of Liverpool, very similar to Wythenshawe. They hated Mancs but in the future we would bump into each other in all sorts of funny places and got on okay.

It seemed like Sunderland had everyone in the UK behind them. After their win it was pure carnival time around Leicester Square and Trafalgar Square. Everyone was buying us beer as we were Mancs with Sunderland caps and rosettes on, singing their songs plus throwing in our own: 'We all hate Leeds and Leeds . . .' We got back to Manny on the Sunday night feeling like United had won the cup.

The biggest mob I ever saw appeared as we were cutting through Oldham Street over to Piccadilly one afternoon for a bus to Old Trafford to watch the Reds play Norwich City. Three football specials from Wolves had arrived together, stretching from the top of the Piccadilly ramp to near Woolworth's, with a shitty police escort at the side. They were playing Leeds at Maine Road in an FA Cup semi and they were right up for it.

This really was my proudest day as a thug. The first thing I noticed was a few bootgirls right at the front of this huge mob dressed in white boiler suits, those stupid monkey boots that came and went in fashion for about five minutes in Manchester, and silly black bowler hats. They really wanted to have a go; I wished Smiler was with us, as she'd be first into this crew. We were only around thirty-strong but this was our town and no twat was going to walk through us. I'm sure this same feeling ran through all the Cowboys, as without any of the usual 'Let's go' we ran straight into them. I went for the three girls, wanting to break a nose or crack a rib; Smiler and her crew had suffered in their frontline fights and so could these fuckers.

Just as I was on them, a tall skin wearing specs came forward and Simo caught him a lovely crack, dropping him to the deck with his specs in bits. That set in the panic and we had them scrambling over barriers, cars, the lot. Within seconds other United came out from hiding places. They must have thought the whole of Oldham Street was on them as I have never seen anything like the panic that gripped this mob. I didn't get the chance to smack one of the boilers but still had the pleasure of slapping around kids near them with painted *Clockwork Orange* faces, now minus their bowler hats.

That day was ours but it wasn't always like that. Glasgow Rangers invaded our city for a friendly match arranged at short notice by Tommy Doc because both sides had been knocked out of the Cup and there was a spare Saturday in the calendar to be filled. I passed near Newton Street on my way into town on the morning of the match and saw this crew walking out of a pub carrying a ciggie machine and the one-armed bandit. They smashed them both up, filled their pockets with money and went back inside for more beers. I passed another pub and heard all these unfamiliar songs being sung. Thinking it must be a rugby team passing through, I walked down to the Ram and hit the vault. A few United there were frothing at the mouth with anger: Rangers were all over town. Several pints were sunk for Dutch courage before we made our way to Oldham Street to look for their mob, but there were just Mr Averages everywhere. Then the word came through that they were all over Piccadilly Gardens near the big statue of Queen Victoria. I arrived there to see a Union Jack draped over the statue.

We all started to run towards them but with each stride forward it was clear we were outnumbered three or four to one, so we bailed onto the nearest bus heading for Old Trafford – though not before we had pulled that flag down from the statue. As we drove up Chester Road towards the ground, all the pubs we passed were full of the Hun – Rangers. None of us could believe what we were seeing. No-one in the Stretford End could get their heads round the turnout and to this day I have not seen a firm as up for it as Rangers were that day. We ended up toe to toe on the halfway line and it took fifteen minutes or more for Plod to restore some kind of order after Sir Matt and the Doc had called for calm. We tried to give it to them by the scoreboard in the second half but were beaten back by very stiff resistance.

The game itself was a thriller, with the Hun winning 4–3. We kept our heads down afterwards, having arranged to meet outside Chelsea Girl off Piccadilly. Everyone had a weapon of some kind. One kid had warpaint on his face and his mate had a cricket bat. But as we started to make a move we were again outnumbered big style and ended up offside at a pub on the edge of town. We sank a few more beers and all came back into Manchester around nine o'clock for one final push, but the police had closed the place down. Every pub had its doors locked except for the Shakespeare at the side of Lewis's, which Rangers had wrecked – one of them was nicked for swinging his axe at a copper.

Rangers were the first to come and party in our town. Most Saturdays offered up something different. Another memorable afternoon came when we played Sheffield United. Three of us hitched a lift near Oldham from a Yorkie fella who said he would drop us off near Sheffield. About ten miles into the trip, we had the Old Bill right behind us and Yorkie puts his foot down and does a Steve McQueen over the Snake Pass. I was frozen in the back and couldn't believe it, as he looked such a straight member. He tried to do a fancy manoeuvre cutting through a little village but got it terribly wrong and we ended up crashing head-on into a wall. We gave it toes as the front of the car burst into flames and I ended up buried in a hedge for two hours until the coppers got bored. At the game we properly got stuck into the Sheffield mob and there were a few arrests. One lad from Northern Drive got nicked. He was a Mod with all the chrome on his scooter but when he returned to court in Sheffield he went in a Reliant Robin over the Snake Pass and was killed in a crash.

* * *

By now school was a waste of time for me. I'd lost interest and I was spending more and more time with Chike. We would scout the Thompson Street train yard but all the best stuff to nick was out of bounds, as it was too close to where the railwaymen worked. The kids from the Flats had robbed it silly in the past, kamikaze style, breaking into the nearest carriage and heaving anything they could grab over the wall. Chike reckoned it was still worth scouting out the movements of the nightwatchmen and the coming and goings in the train yard at the back of the shops nearest the Flats, where all the goods trains were parked up for the weekend. So we hit the roof at about one o'clock in the morning one Saturday. We soon realised that hardly any of the trains in this section got touched, as a lot of the guys who worked in the yard spent most of their time in the Sparrow pub or the large signal box. Chike swore blind a lot of these men carried coshes or metal chains; I knew they didn't but he still managed to get me at it.

We sneaked into the yard and opened a few containers, but they were full of wood and other building materials, no good to us. We moved further along and over the bridge at Queens Road, hiding until we saw one of the guys pass on his rounds. Then we carefully opened a container. Bingo! It was full of strong, brown-paper sacks containing catalogue orders: cashmere jumpers, leather boots and shoes, even three-piece suites – all top of the range stuff. We could carry only three bags at first but on each subsequent visit we managed to lug four. Chike had a thing going with an older woman in one of the Flats who would store any bent tackle we brought to her door, no questions asked. We used an old pram with a blanket tossed over to transport the stuff from the bottom of the embankment, where we'd stashed it, to Kingsley Crescent. We would push it along the railway all the way to Frank's chippie and then cut across through the estate.

It didn't take long for a few other firms to make themselves busy in the railway yard we'd hit upon – they saw us blowing money in the arcade at Tib Street and buying all hands booze in the Pineapple opposite Ardwick Youth Club and soon got into our ribs. A firm from Miles Platting opened a counter full of coins and managed to get away with a fair few grand. This really brought it on top and there were a load of house raids, with a couple of people getting nicked. The yard stepped up security with dogs so we turned our attentions back to town.

Eric, Gags and I went looking for casual work in the area around Strangeways to sort ourselves for Christmas 1970. Our dreams of being pro footballers had gone. Duddy got picked with me and Gags for Oldham Athletic's youth team, so every Wednesday night the three of us trained on 'Little Wembley', the first-team pitch up at Oldham. We also had to be back on most Sundays for a game, as we were expected to make the grade. Now I was also playing for school, Colly Lads, Manchester Federation and Manchester Boys, so having to travel on those old slow buses all the way up to Oldham as well became a nightmare. I got sick of it, and when they found out I was also getting involved with the police and courts, then I was out. Gags wouldn't go without me for company so he never signed.

We found work with a Jewish feller called Victor who bought burnt stuff from factory fires then salvaged what he could to re-sell. We got cash in hand every day until December 23, when he came back early and found us playing conkers with his electric sockets. Truth was we were pissed from a few jars in some pub nearby.

Smiler and I were really getting into each other and were in turtle dove. At New Year we hit the CIS hall near Victoria Station. One of the upper floors was a massive, first-class disco but the problem was getting into the bar, as you had to look eighteen. Smiler and I looked okay but were not confident we could blag past the two bouncers on the door, so our jib was to wait at the side until Micky Duplex or Fat Neck's brother, Rob Powell, had started a fight, then slip in while the bouncers were occupied. After half an hour we'd nip to the toilet, asking the bouncers what went down, then we'd have it sweet as a nut in and out of the bar for the night.

Eric from Central Drive, Chike's cousin, had been mixing it down in Moss Side at the shebeens and then came back into the Colly Lads' disco and danced to the music with such rhythm that all hands were well impressed. He also had a full set of sideburns and was the first to know about weed and whizz and downers. He started wagging school with Chike and me. We were looking at the factories and stuff around the back of Edwards's meat market up near Newton Heath. All the small, old terraced houses were being knocked down in the area, though a few people still remained in them.

As we walked down one of these sad, scummy streets, Chike just booted the front door of one of the houses and was in. We followed as he went straight for the meter, busting it off the wall and grabbing coins as they cascaded from the bottom. Before we had a chance to help ourselves we heard footsteps and shouting, so we legged it into the back yard and away, not stopping until we reached the White Hart pub on the corner of Collyhurst Street. We were bent over gasping for air when brakes screeched and a firm of Paddies jumped from a car. It was the workers from the house – so again we were off. I made the mistake of not heading for the roofs which were a maze for the outsider and where we knew which panels were loose so you could drop down into the flats. Instead I got trapped by the Rochdale Canal. They grabbed me and gave me a few sly digs in the ribs, cursing as they dragged me to their van. I couldn't understand why they were so upset, but it turned out they had the job of stripping the houses before they got knocked down and were being blamed when things got nicked.

Chike was picked up the next day and Eric ended up on an ID parade. There was no passing go for Chike and he got nine months that very week. Eric and I went to juvenile court and I got a short, sharp shock in detention centre for three months while Eric got thirty days at Rose Hill Youth Centre, near Wythenshawe. As the judge sent me down, Mum burst out crying, which made my head spin, but as soon as they'd put me in a cell they allowed her in to see me. I gave her a big hug and asked her for a sandwich, which seemed to cheer her up and she went off and came back with a massive chip butty. We felt much better after this, but when we were parted for real I felt sick and a big lump lodged in my throat.

I was driven to Foston Hall, near Derby. It must have been around teatime when I got there. The other couple of kids who'd been sent down had already been processed through the reception area, so the main screw was having a break. I ended up sitting with another lad whose job was to help the screws out in reception. He was about sixteen years old but he seemed to me like he was in his twenties. His hands were covered in home-made tattoos. He was from Derby and was on my case as soon as he heard I was from Manchester, saying Derby had taken out United in the Watney Cup Final. Like a top divvy I rose to the bait and started to defend United.

When the main screw came back he took my clothes from me and gave me new stuff before pointing to the shower and telling me to go and have a good scrub down and a shave. I'd never shaved before. The shower was very welcome, but as I was running the razor across my face I realised there was no point, as I was just shaving fresh air. I bent down to rinse the remaining soap from my face. Someone cracked me from behind, causing me to lurch forward and hit my chin on the steel taps. It was the lad from Derby and although I wasn't cut, a huge lump started to form, the remnants of which are still there today. I lost my head and caught up with him, belting him from the side when I knew he wasn't looking. We both managed to get a couple of real body winders in before it got broken up. Derby lost his job over it and I ended up in a cell by myself for four days. Normally you only spend the first night in a cell before going over to the dorm with the rest of the lads.

After the four days I was marched over to see the housemaster, Paddy Moore. Everything was done military style: standing to attention, thumbs in line with the seams on my trousers, shoulders back and chest puffed out. I had to shout out my name and number and then the charge was read out. I pleaded guilty. Paddy asked if I had anything to say and so I enquired when I'd be in the dorm with everyone else. Paddy got up from his desk and walked over. Without saying another word, he pinched both my nipples and twisted them, lifting me off my feet. I tried not to scream but couldn't help myself and with that he started to shake me. Paddy then went back to his chair and added five days to my sentence, saying I would lose my first week's wages. I was thrown back in the cell, and about an hour later a screw opened the door and escorted me to the dorm, saying I would be getting a haircut the next day. There was no choice – everyone had a crop, which was worst for the greasers, as it was done in the middle of the dining hall with all the others watching and loving it.

The cock of my dorm was a giant of a kid from Moss Side who was in for dealing weed (ready-made joints for five bob each!). There were two Scousers, a kid from Stafford who was training to be a wrestler, and a lad with ugly spots from Bolton, who never spoke to a soul. After a couple of weeks, he got done in by a load of Scousers in the casting shop and was put on a cushy job cleaning the paths and roads on the small housing estate next to the centre, where the screws and their families lived. He couldn't handle doing time and bolted back to Bolton but was caught an hour down the road and got another six-month lump added to his sentence. You should have seen the look on his kipper when he walked back through the door. Tomo was from Warrington and Jeff was a United fan from Nottingham who was the first greaser I'd ever met. He was full of stories about lads throwing up on their jeans, then rubbing it in and never washing them – really hanging stuff. Jeff had proper biker tattoos, but his pride and joy was a Man United crest.

Every new kid in the dorm had to go through a 'reception course' and there was a choice: either run a gauntlet of kicks and digs, with the lads lined up in two rows and you legging through the middle, or try to go under then over all the beds while everyone again got stuck in. The beds could save you a fair few digs if you were fast enough, otherwise you could get trapped and receive a proper leathering. There was a third option: stand naked on the table in front of everyone and sing 'God Save the Queen' while wanking. I chose to run the gauntlet and came out of it okay, I suppose, before learning that if you picked the song, straight after you got a real good beating from the lads anyway.

The next morning I awoke to a loud thud from the dorm next door and then this cockney screw bursts into our dorm, shouted, 'Hands off cocks and onto socks,' then grabbed the side of my bed and tipped it over so my face squashed into the lino with the weight of the bed on my back. He then disappeared and I could hear him doing the same thing in the next dorm and so on down through every dorm. Another screw then marched in screaming for us all to have our bed packs made and to change into our PE kit. We were marched downstairs and everyone was made to run on the spot in a long wide corridor. Yet another screw arrived and started checking us all out, then barked at us to start shuffling past an open hatch cut into the side of the kitchen. Each of us, about 130 in total, had to grab a mug of horrible black tea that was only half full to stop it from spilling, as we were all still running on the spot.

Then the routine began. I looked around at all these bobbing heads trying to take gulps of tea, it looked really comical and I wanted to burst out laughing. But at that moment I clocked this particularly unpleasant-looking screw in a tracksuit unbolting two big metal doors. A blast of ice cold wind came whistling through the corridor and right up my spine. I thought I'd pass out if they sent me out into the cold and it was still only 6.30 A.M. Then the shout came up to drink the rest of the tea – *now!* Suddenly it didn't seem to taste so bad. Then we were on the move, tossing the mugs into a bin in the corner by the exit doors.

The yard had spotlights in each corner to light the area. We had to run on the spot for ten minutes to warm up, before lining up to face the tracksuit. He would do a certain exercise that we would all have to copy, then he'd move on to the press-ups, which we'd do even if it was snowing. All the time he was looking and checking to see if he could spot the jibbers. Anyone he didn't like the look of would have to stay on in the freezing yard for an extra ten minutes, sometimes longer. The lads who were fit and doing all the moves correctly would get picked out, but they were the first ones allowed back into the lovely warm dorm.

Once back in the dorm it was time to get down on your hands and knees and get on with the cleaning. We all had a certain section of the dorm, corridor and stairs to get into good order. Then it was wash and shave time, before getting ready for work or in my case school; there were seven or eight schoolboys like me. Most of the older lads wore denims and denim jackets, the kitchen staff wore white, and the trusted lads wore grey trousers with a short navy blue jacket like my dad wore in the RAF. Breakfast was served in the dining hall, where you were only allowed to talk for fifteen minutes while you were eating. I ate fried bread for the first time and loved it, and thought the porridge they served up was sound as well, even though most of the boys thought the food was shit. Then a bell rang out and if you spoke after that you were guaranteed to either lose wages or lose some time, so it was very rare for anyone to speak. Pure silence. On Saturdays and Sundays we'd be in the dining room for two or three hours and the big treat was the radio. There was a quick run down on all the sports results and I remember hearing that Joe Frazier beat Ali. 'Ride A White Swan' and 'I Never Promised You A Rose Garden' were the two big hits of the time.

After breakfast we all went into the boot room and the older boys changed into their garters and boots. Us schoolboys wore plain black shoes. Then we went out into the yard for a count up and a small inspection. We marched around for a few minutes, before the main gate opened and everyone trooped down the path leading to the workshops and gardens. The younger boys were at the back and were the first to break off to a small classroom stood on its own. Schooling was a nightmare; we were all as thick as fuck and all on different levels. I felt the odd kid out as none of the others had been to a match or a pub or talked any kind of sense about girls.

We were in the gym every day and undertook a gruelling weekly circuit that was almost impossible to cheat on; if you were caught skipping a push-up or pull-up, the whole gym had to start again, so you can picture the proper hiding the offender would get in the showers later. We could also browse in the library for ten minutes once a week; each table in the dining hall would be called up in turn to choose a handful of books during the afternoon silent period. I always came out with stories about Edge, a Cowboy whose wife had been raped and murdered. He was a real bad dude, with a cutthroat blade in a tricky pouch at the back of his neck.

A certain screw crept around the dorms late at night slipping his hand over a kid's mouth to give him a pure fright, and keeping it there until he'd done what he was going to do. It was mostly the same two kids but there were other things going on, I'm sure. It seemed like kids who came from broken homes were the main targets, the kids who had been passed round local authority homes from when they were little. Many of these had not been through the courts or had a good grounding in the crime world. I came from a broken home but compared to some of these kids my background was super solid. I had a few visits whilst I was there, from Smiler and from Jimmy and my mum. They brought me three packets of Jaffa Cakes that they passed to me one by one under the table. Smiler told me the Colly Lads football team had just won the cup but it was marred when Pete Kank's dad died from a heart attack at half-time. The odd things was, Gagzy's dad Bill died over a decade later after shouting to Gags that Scotland had just scored against Brazil.

The weeks and months disappeared in Foston Hall. Before I knew it, I was lying in my cell next to reception for my last night of DC. I couldn't wait to get back to Collyhurst. The next morning Pickles, a screw who made life as difficult as possible, walked me to the main gate and told me I was a certainty to come back, or even worse, end up in borstal. I didn't even look at him, just headed for the bus stop. I felt like everyone on the bus knew I'd done a bit of bird, not really a surprise given the state of my hair and the fact I called the bus conductor 'sir'. I got myself a packet of five Park Drive cigs and a *Daily Mirror* and boarded the Manchester train.

Chapter Five

On The Road

SMILER WAS WAITING at the station. She took me into town and bought me a Jatex shirt, then it was Don the barber on Oldham Street to do his best and Collyhurst-bound as fast as my legs would carry me. I walked past the Ram as it was opening and Syl (my mam) was all smiles and big hugs and gave me a pint of mild to drink, which tasted so sweet and never touched the sides. Then it was off to 89 Burgin Drive with a chippie. When I first walked into the Flats off Collyhurst Street, I got down on my knees and kissed the ground. I felt like the Pope. A couple of old dears were leaning over the balconies nattering, as usual, and both said how fit and well I looked. All those gym sessions and daily workouts meant I was in tiptop condition.

Eric was first to call round telling me all about the derby game against City that I'd missed. He was wearing a black Ben Sherman shirt and gave me the rundown on the latest fashions hitting the terraces. We headed for school, where Gagzy was in bulk laughing at the state of my hair; thank God he hadn't seen it before Don worked his magic. All the lads were glad to see me. After school I went to see my old fella in Tib Street Café and he gave me a joint coming-out present and a birthday present, which was a cracker of a racing bike, with gears and one of those things to carry water. Soon as I got home, I took our Mark and my old bike to a shop on Conran Street and got an okay price for it. Then I took Mark to New Brown Street, where I bought him a pair of kids Levis with the studs instead of the buttons. I'd missed him and wanted to start looking after him more, as I'd been a bit of a bastard to him in the past, as older brothers often are – eating a full bowl of cornflakes with a full bottle of milk while giving him an egg cup with five or six flakes and a teaspoon of milk, sending him to the shop to buy a bucket of steam or a tin of striped paint, that kind of thing.

At school they were letting us have the odd afternoon off so we could look for a job, which wasn't that difficult as there were so many about. Apprentices were paid terrible wages for anything from three to five years, but after that they rocketed. Gagzy and I chose apprenticeships as cabinetmakers at a place where Kank was working on Collyhurst Road, next to the Irk. We didn't tell the teachers we'd been fixed up but instead asked them almost every afternoon if we could carry on looking for work. They had given up on us by now and so they let us go. We'd often end up in the Cheshire Cheese, a famous pub on Oldham Road run by the old Collyhurst boxing champion Johnny King.

Gagzy and I started work at the Italian cabinetmakers. They made units for Kitchen Queen and paid a fiver a week so long as we worked Saturday mornings. It didn't take us long to suss out that there was no real apprenticeship, we were there as cheap labour to do all the shit jobs. I had to load and unload sheets of hardboard and other materials, then cart them upstairs and cut them up on the most dangerous machine I'd ever seen, before tossing them over to the lads who knocked things together. But what a top feeling getting my first pay packet. I couldn't stop grinning. I treated myself to a sole-and-heel job at the cobblers on Oldham Street and had enough to get steel tips put in. This helped with the wear and it was mega trendy to click your heels with a swagger as you walked.

This was the start of the smoothie boys. We were all still boot or bovver boys at the football, and there were still plenty of skinheads for a good few years, but the Royals, Oxfords, brogues and Comos were now seen and heard clicking away everywhere, nowhere more so than in the two big cafes in town, the Blackbird and upstairs in Lewis's. Smiler and I would sit there for hours checking out Salford, Wythenshawe and the rest, with all the new fashions and faces. Comos were the latest shoes, ox-blood or black with a plain soft top and extra wide rim along the soles. They looked better worn in, especially when topped off with a Fred Perry and the latest Slazenger jumper – the cardigans were even better but out of our price range. All of us carried umbrellas for the smoothie look plus for the Manchester weather and for fighting.

One day we were in the Blackbird when Tommy Ack and Mant strolled over for a chat. Behind appeared two real greasers who were after them for jumping a mate of theirs. We shit bricks and bolted – pure chaos. Fortunately Smiler had gone to the ladies' and never saw a thing.

After a few months on the Irk job, I told the boss I wasn't up for the apprenticeship and said I was looking for other work. That same Saturday night at the Colly Lads' disco I saw Nogger, a lad from the Flats, who'd just started work at Smithfield Market for Frank Coleman on the fish. I asked Nogger to call him and Frank said I could start first thing Monday morning. If it worked out I'd be getting more like £15 a week but it was an early start: I had to be up at five o'clock and walk on to Rochdale Road to stand with a few other workers from the Flats waiting for the first wagon to come rolling down the hill.

When I jumped on the wagon on the first day I immediately saw familiar faces, including Bomber, who was completely covered in tattoos with 'Fuck United' across his back. He was much older than our lot and worked as a fruit porter and barrow boy. He had massive strands of thick black curly hair, Rasta style, with a pair of cheap black-rimmed glasses with those milk bottle lenses. He once saved my bacon during the annual punch-up under the Albert Square clock at midnight on New Year's Eve, when it was traditional for United and City or us and Salford to steam into each other.

Smithfield Market was its own world, selling wholesale and retail fruit, vegetables and fresh fish under huge canopies. It was chaotic, noisy, vibrant and buzzed with life. The barrow boys had their own language, which more or less followed the alphabet backwards: one was eno, seven was neves, ten was net. The fruit market in particular was enormous and it could take up to an hour to get from one side to another with a fully loaded barrow. Smithfield was also a bit of a closed shop: Collyhurst, Miles Platting and Ancoats ran it, just as Salford Docks was a guaranteed employer if you knew the right Salford people.

As we arrived at the market, a lot of the guys were putting on their wet bib and braces; these were the men who filleted the fish, rabbits and chickens. Our three were Jimmy Sword from Moston, a well-built stocky fella who was the coolest Ted in town, with slicked-back hair and long sideburns with a thin bit at the end that joined his lips, and the two Tommies. Irish Tommy was a slim feller with carrot-coloured hair and a smooth Cork accent; he took his break every day by downing a few pints in the Lower Turks Head on Shude Hill. Only the chosen few could gain entry before nine o'clock in the morning. German Tommy was always grumpy for the first few hours, and would only perk up when the women office workers cut through on their way to the CIS building and the market erupted in wolf whistles and shouts.

Nogger and I wore brown porters' coats over our thick jumpers and standard working jeans and everyone wore clogs, which were vital to avoid the cold setting in – it was so bad it could make you ill. The clogs were good for your feet and so efficient at insulating that we never had to wear socks. My first job was to empty the piss bucket from the office into the toilet that all but faced the stall. I could never quite work out why it was there. I had to throw a bit of Daz detergent in after rinsing it with hot water, which I got from Alan's café next door to the toilet. It was the smallest café imaginable yet did a roaring trade and was noted for the best chip butties in town, serving from five o'clock in the morning until one o'clock in the afternoon.

I had still not met Frank Coleman and Irish Tommy was keen to fill me in, saying he had a short temper but not to take it to heart, as he was just a flapper. The workers on the adjacent stalls to ours knew all about Frank, and Irish Tommy said they would wind him up when they saw that his head was going west with all the simultaneous deals he was trying to conduct. He said Frank wore all the top jolly clothes, those Scottish-looking hunting waistcoats, tops, caps and ties and had a very posh accent.

All of a sudden the huge fish wagons from Aberdeen started pulling up and everyone jostled for a good position so they could make a quick, clean move back to their stalls. Our stall was at the end of the main fish market so we were told to get back sharpest, as the punters who spent the most money were there as early as the workers to get the best deals. I started to unload the boxes onto my barrow. It might sound easy, but far from it. Looking around, I realised there was an art to loading the boxes, but my time had passed and I had to get the stock back to the stall. I pulled the two handles of the barrow and was taken aback by the weight as I struggled to get the small metal wheels to turn. Nogger was on the move and I managed to get going and follow him through the hustle and bustle, but as we moved through the main market area I realised he was picking up speed – and so was I. I could feel my load begin to sway all ways, more so when I hit a patch of cobbles and the metal wheels sent shockwaves through the load, which I now realised I'd loaded upside down. I tried to slow the pace but events gathered their own momentum. A few of the workers clocked my swaying and the noise level rose, along with my blood pressure. I was only a yard or two from our stall when all hands gave it, 'She's going to go!'

I glanced over at our stall and saw a tall man stood there, looking like he was ready to go out on a hunt. It was Frank and his mouth gaped like a goldfish. The barrow was out of control and heading for the road when the inside wheel sank into a gap where a cobble had been removed. As I tried to swing her round to the right, 'Wahay, there she blows!' The whole lot ended up on the floor, right in the path of the fish and fruit porters, who slipped and slid as they fought to keep their own barrows balanced. It was best Scottish haddock, Frank's prime catch, and worth a small fortune. Frank turned purple and went into orbit as Nogger and the two Tommies helped me rescue some of the fillets before the local tramps arrived on the scene. We were able to save about fifty per cent of the load, which we washed and repacked with a touch of fresh ice from Fred the Iceman (that's all he sold). I think this made the difference between me keeping and losing my job.

Sometimes we'd have to pick up things from a fruit

stall and this was always a challenge, as they would take the piss mercilessly. Once I got stuck in the hectic market traffic and finally arrived sweating at a punter's van only to find they fruit lads had replaced my box of chickens with a sack of turnips. But at weekends we traded with each other and I'd often go home with a 'swinger', which was all the best fruit and veg with some best fish and a capon. Our Jimmy liked goose, for the fat's really nice and good for you, or sometimes I'd bring him a duck home.

I got a sideline 'on the offal' with a feller called Albert from Harpurhey; we collected all the slimy fish waste and poultry skin and bones and loaded it at lunchtime into massive boxes on a wagon to go to the pig farms. Albert was the horniest feller I knew, always shagging in his car and giving out the details. He took me a few times to see the pornos which were shown on certain stalls, always with a few good mags to buy after the show. The market coppers ran this sideline. On Fridays Albert would sometimes take me to the Royal George for a pint; this was where I first met Barney Hamilton, Georgie Derbyshire and all the Quality Street Gang, many of them Scottish fellers and all massive boozers. You never wanted to get in a round with them – they'd drink double Camparis with chasers all day long. Many years later I'd have a few this-and-that deals with them.

Eric and Gagzy started working on the fish after about six weeks. We had our breaks at the same time and would go to Mother Mac's for breakfast around nine o'clock. What a huge feast: bacon, beans, toms, sausage and chips with bread, fried bread and toast, and she would always shout over to see if we wanted any more, always. We finished work around twelve o'clock and a lot of the lads went to play the five-in-a-line machine at the Tib Street café, a kind of cross between pinball and bingo with thirty holes for five balls to enter and if you got five in a line you won the jackpot. I saw many a fella lose their full wages and the odd one win a small fortune. After the New Year, I started running round Chinatown a lot on the bike, dropping off fish here and there. Frank had bought himself a new Triumph Herald and I also went with him on business trips to Sale and posh places in Cheshire; that car could really go.

Driving fast gave me a buzz and soon I joined the car thieves from the Flats, who spent their time joyriding. Sometimes we would change cars two or three times a night as most of the ones we nicked ended up crashed. We never made any money out of them, it was pure pleasure. One Sunday afternoon we pinched a big wagon with metal shutters on the side and drove it straight through the wire fence and across the rubbish dump. It was the best ride of our lives as we bounced along the uneven ground, our heads hitting the roof. We drove it round Collyhurst like something out of *Wacky Races* until a couple of the lads started fighting in the back and it came on top. The Old Bill dragged us down the station and we ended up getting slapped wrists at court.

My mum had had enough of my trouble and was in bits because our Mark was also running round with his gang and had started screwing warehouses. She was on to housing every day trying to get an exchange, but no one was interested in taking up her offer. Then they said she could move into a new house on the Racecourse Estate near Partington, on the edge of Sale, an overspill estate for families moving out from the inner-city slum clearances in Moss Side, Hulme and elsewhere. The place was like a building site, with no proper roads or paths. If you wanted to get a bus, it was a hefty walk onto Washway Road or into Sale. Mum didn't really care, she just wanted to get us to a place where we might calm down, so she took the chance of a cottage flat with all mod cons. My 'uncle' Jimmy hit all the shops, putting down deposits for goods the day before we left, loaded the lot into a wagon and then we did the bunk. One shop caught up with us years later but still didn't get a carrot. Sale was a big shock for our Mark, as it took him ages to find new friends, and for the first six months he travelled back to Collyhurst to see his mates and to rob. I had to get up for work an hour and a half earlier than when we lived in the Flats, and spent a good few nights staying in Ancoats with Smiler and her folks when it got too much.

Smiler and I were thinking of a future together. I bought her an engagement ring, which cost the earth, and we planned to have our bash in the Salvage, which had changed its name to the swankier-sounding Manhattan. Once they had changed the back room into a disco it was full to the brim with people from all over the north side. I got to know Gilly (the Mike Baldwin of Manchester) well and his fighting partner Vinny Ross, the best one-on-one fighter I'd seen; he'd take off his jacket, roll up his sleeves and slug it out with anyone on that cark park. There were always fights after the disco, often involving women.

That Easter, the talk on Smithfield was that the council wanted to build a new market on another site, which would mean over seventy per cent of the lads losing their jobs, including me. They wanted to flatten the old market and build a car park, wiping out over 150 years of history. I looked for another job and had a word with our Jimmy, who was running a company called Clean Walls. They sandblasted the outside of buildings and had just started on Manchester University. He said there was a job if I wanted it, but I found it hard to leave the market, as the crack was so good. Eventually I decided to move on and took everybody to a real old pub called the Glue Pot, where I blew my last wages. I swear I had an apple in my throat to leave the market.

I soon got into my new job as a pot man, working directly with one of the blasters. The 'pot' was the name for the container where the sharp sand was kept, and it was up to me to make sure the blaster always had what he needed. I had to sheet up part of the scaffolding where we were blasting and feed the pipes to him, sometimes up to thirteen levels high. You knew within a few days whether you had a head for heights. All the pipes had to be connected together from the top to the pot and another pipe went from the pot to the compressor, which made the whole thing work. The blaster needed a firm grip on the pipe when the sand started to shoot out, and as soon as the sand hit the wall it buffered away all the caked-on grime and pollution. We communicated on the job by signals because of the noise. I had to learn when to bring the pressure up or take it down and when I needed to cut the pot. When he needed you to cut the pot, the blaster would signal by bending the pipe, which blocked everything up for a few seconds and caused the compressor to slow right down. Once I heard the dip in the compressor I knew to turn off the pot. We all used the university canteen and I was amazed at the taste of yoghurt and the cheapness of the breakfasts. At dinnertime we'd hit the pub for a few gargles and a pie, then it was back to work.

Early in the summer of 1972, I had scraped together enough money for a week's holiday and decided to go to the Sunny Vale holiday camp in Rhyl with Smiler and a few of her mates. Kank and Gagzy came along. When we arrived it was straight into the QC sherry, then on to the camp bar and disco. The main tune all weekend was Hawkind's 'Silver Machine' and we stood in lines doing the Hell's Angel dance with your thumbs in the waist of your semi-flares, shoulder swaying in and out. We hammered the drink and Smiler and I slipped back to the chalet early for a bit of privacy. We were just moving up a gear when we heard a thunderous knocking on the door.

'Lively Beaner!'

'Beaner, it's on top!'

I opened the door and Gagzy and Kank steamed in and dove straight under the bed. Before I had a chance to register events, a size-twelve foot prevented me from closing the door, followed by a rather large Scouser whose chest was pumping with anger. The veins were sticking out from the side of his torpedo-shaped head and as he stood in the doorway he tried to grab me by the throat, saying there were two shitheads in the room who had done his car in. Smiler jumped between us and that seemed to put him off a bit. He stepped back, then blasted the door with his iron fist, cracking the wood.

'You must have the wrong room, mate,' I said.

With a bit more persuasion he called it a night, grumbling away that he was going to get the coppers. Smiler and I were finally able to continue where we had left off, and later that night our son Lee was conceived. It was a mad holiday.

* * *

I now worked on the blasting with a Scouser called Page, who lived near the River Irwell in Salford in a big old house with his wife and two kids. We had left the university and were working in Little Hulton, near Bolton, which was a pain to get to. Page asked if I wanted to move in with them while the job was on, so we could get a bus together from Salford depot round the corner. The room cost me almost nothing but my bed was a mattress resting on top of a dilapidated wardrobe laid flat. I had to get used to the rats, which scuttled around in the night; I put a tray in the corner with a few chips on it, loaded with rat poison, to keep things manageable. In the morning I'd sling the dead ones in the bin on my way out to work. Smiler came round a couple of times and wasn't impressed. On one visit she told me she was pregnant and we both put it down to the night the angry Scouser burst into the room. If only he'd knocked on the door earlier! That said, we were both made up with the news. Coming up to Christmas 1972, we booked our wedding day for the following Easter at a small church in Ancoats. I bought a ring and put down a deposit on a suit (purple!) for the big day, though my family didn't yet know anything about it – or about Smiler being up the tub. I knew it was going to blow up, as I was still just approaching sixteen and would need parental permission to marry, but I wanted to leave it until after Christmas before I told them.

The Clean Walls bosses paid a top Christmas bonus in recognition for all the graft we'd put in over the year and laid on a full day on the ale for everyone at the Holy Name Club. Uncle Jimmy and a few of the other top workers, including the Plank (Jimmy's best mate from Salford, George McNally, known as the Plank because he's as thick as), got a turkey and a bottle of whisky. Gagzy and I hit the free booze as we watched Blackpool's Big Pat necking pints in one gulp before moving on to the top shelf. Hours later, we stumbled onto Oxford Road and were walking into town singing away, when I bumped into what I thought was a student carrying a briefcase. In my stupor I went to kick him up the arse, but missed in a spectacular way and stumbled. As I was regaining my balance, the 'student' pulled out a hammer and started cracking away at me with it. Everything went black and I ended up in the hospital.

Shortly after this, I let it slip to my mum about the

wedding and she flipped, particularly as she'd just given birth herself to my new brother James. Even Jimmy and the Plank were on my case and I started to think they were right, that it was too early to go all the way and get married. Yet when I went to Smiler's house and spoke to her mum and dad they thought the opposite, so my head was in pieces about it all.

I was working on the pot on Salford Cathedral when I got asked to do a job on an old shopping centre in Bradford with a Yorkie feller who would pay me double time. We worked away on it until twelve o'clock, then the Yorkie disappeared, leaving me sat there for one, two, three hours without a carrot for a scran or a pint. From my seat on the scaffolding I clocked an Army and Navy store that was covered by the Clean Walls sheets and had the old slat windows at the top that Chike had shown me how to remove. So I dropped down the scaffolding, carefully slid out the panes and, with barely an effort, was in like Flynn. I grabbed a bin-liner and filled it up with Levis, then went over to the Jack and was about to take the fifteen or twenty quid float when the owner and his son walked in. I bolted through the window and offside up the scaffolding to hide. The problem was, I still had my Clean Walls overalls on, so within a few minutes the site was surrounded by coppers shouting for me to come down. All I could think about was whether I'd be in time for scran at the nick. I got two jam butties and a charge sheet and a message came through that I'd blown my job.

I was bailed and headed for my mum's, but when I got there I just stood outside for a couple of hours, thinking how everything in my life had come on top. I finally went inside and crumbled; I tried to stop myself but it just kept coming. My old dear was a diamond and I really listened to what she wanted for me. She said our Jimmy would be able to take me under his wing and get me my job back, once the boss had had time to cool down. She didn't want me to tie myself down and I knew deep inside that my life was going to move forward without Smiler, though it really broke me up for weeks when I cancelled the wedding and the suit and gave the ring to my mum. I think Smiler knew things had come too far and we were at an end, but neither of us ever had the conversation, we just let it drift.

I got my job back at the Walls and ended up working with our Jimmy and the Plank. They had moved off the blasting and were now working on the inside, paint washing. Jimmy loved knocking out a seven day week and no-one earned as much as him and the Plank. The first things to learn on the washing were all the tricks about 'bumping', which means making it look like you've washed the ceilings, radiators, windows and frames, doors, pipes that run down the walls, light fittings, the whole Monty, but really you've washed hardly any. It was an art form and Jimmy was the best, as well known for his bumping as he was for his boozing. He also had the knack with the clerks of works, local fellers whose job was to keep us in check. They had the power to sling you off a job if they caught you at the bump. Jimmy had the eye for sussing out which ones liked a drink and from there they were putty in his hands; he'd have them out on all-dayers with a wee bung at the end of the week.

The Plank was one of the funniest guys I'd come across and he showed me how to do tricks with money. One was where Jimmy went into the vault of a pub and got a pint with a tenner that had a telephone number written on the corner. Then Plank and I would go into the best room and the Plank would order a couple of drinks for us whilst waving a tenner about. He'd switch the tenner with a fiver in his other hand and pay for the drinks with the fiver. When the change came back, the scream would go up that the Plank had paid with a tenner, not a fiver. There would always be a bit of barter and banter and then the Plank would declare the £10 note he'd handed over had a telephone number written on it. It worked every time.

Another one the Plank put me onto was the ten-bob trick, which Gagzy and I did for years after. You'd buy a pint or a packet of five Park Drives and hand over a pound, but have a two-bob coin in one hand so as soon as you got your change you'd switched their ten-bob coin with your two-bob coin and say, 'Excuse me, is this right?' They'd check it and think they picked out a two-bob coin from the ten-bob section of the till, so everyone was a winner and ten-bob could buy four or five pints!

I worked all over the north of England with our Jimmy and the Plank. They used to get mullered every night on beer and whisky. Walking home from the pubs, Jimmy would throw his change on the paths and demand it be left there for the kids to find in the morning, shouting out his pissed mantra: 'Get it spent and be content.' Sometimes I would nip out early in the morning for a paper and pick up the change he had tossed away the previous night. He would even burn money in the ashtray when he was really out there. Sometimes when our Jimmy stayed at home, mum and our Mark joined me in dipping his pockets while he was in his whisky coma. I'd been telling them for ages it made sense, as he'd only end up blowing it or burning it.

The drinking on that job was merciless. If we were working around Manchester, come Friday around noon we'd nip down to the yard in Irk Town, have a chat with Stan and there'd always be a few of the painters or blasters gagging for an all-dayer. I had to go through the pain barrier to cope – even though at my age I could already keep up with older fellers, these all-day binges were a different ball game. I was up for it but it took a year before I was at their level. Many a time I'd have to be carried out and slung into the nearest doorway or, if I was lucky, I'd just about make a bus in Piccadilly, often getting on the wrong one or waking up in Partington or Altrincham, or even back in the Dilly hours later with the driver saying how he'd tried to wake me up.

The Friday session would start in the Ducie Bridge Inn opposite the CIS insurance building at the back of Victoria train station. The best thing about the CIS was that every Friday there'd be a girl leaving or a birthday, so it was packed with women on a binge. Many a kop or a date was set up. Around 3.30 P.M. we'd hit the shady back-street drinking dens which were all over the town. Jimmy's number one gaff was in Spring Gardens and had a coded bell ring with the wee peephole where Manchester's top bouncer, a half-caste called Ronnie Scott, worked; he also worked at Papa's in Newton Street, better known as 'Snappers', the roughest club in town. I tried every one and I thought they all were dives, probably because I was never in the company of any lads my own age. I never saw a woman under twenty in these gaffs and almost all the women were ex-pro's or still on the game. Many a time I'd see one get a hiding while everyone else carried on drinking and singing away. At one place near Victoria Station a few Paddies put money together and a woman did a streak right through the station, then came back in and bought everyone a beer. I was that gone that I had to tip half of it away under the table. My all-time favourite drink was Chesters Mild. It was black and smooth and I really miss beer like that.

We always made a bit of extra money fiddling the petrol costs and when Jimmy and the Plank were desperate for booze money we'd send a load of snide receipts for buckets and stepladders to the office. We worked on government buildings, hospitals in Leeds and Bath, a loony bin near Darlington – where I cleared £100 a week after my digs and expenses – and banks and offices in Newcastle. One of our biggest jobs was doing thousands of offices for the shipbuilding company Swan Hunter. The problem was getting digs, as we were in Wallsend, a rundown, depressed gaff around five miles from the Toon with the view of a massive working docks, all grey and black. It was real *Get Carter* land, yet I had a ball there. There was a massive dosshouse called Simpson's Hotel which looked brill from the outside but inside housed around 100 hobos, stinking to high heaven. We tried it for a few nights but it was mental, with fights, singing and bawling all night.

Then the Plank copped off for a gem of a local lass who let him move right in lock, stock and barrel. I was pleased for him, as he needed it and is still with her today. I got digs with a load of Paddy road workers who slept in their work clothes after fifteen pints every night. You had to watch yourself not to upset the landlady as she threw many a Paddy out every other day.

Lunchtime was a classic. The main gate would open right on twelve with the hooter blasting away and hundreds of men in black work clothes and hobnail boots waiting for this race to dinner. The sensible fellers would open up their snap tins or 'bait boxes' and get ready for the afternoon graft, watching this mad charge as all the rest bolted up this steep hill to the workingmen's club, where the staff had already pulled a few hundred pints for this lot to neck real fast, as they had only half an hour then back to graft.

We'd first nip further up the road to the pub, then have a couple of Newcastle Xs or Browns. Brown is known as a Bottle of Dog; it comes from the feller's blag to the

missus every night: 'Just taking wor dog for a walk pet.'
Then straight into the local battle cruiser. We'd have
another couple in the workingmen's club, as you now
could move and breathe in there. Half the time we'd stay
on the piss all day.

The Geordie workingmen's clubs were the best in all
Britain, with strippers on every other hour. Disco nights
were funny at first as you made the same mistake as all
new-comers to Geordieland, dancing and chatting and
buying any spare women drinks until at the end of the
night all these same women had their boyfriends waiting
at the bar and the wrong look would get you in serious
shit. I used to love the pie-eating competitions, as they
were home-made, plus I could get myself in the top three
so I'd always get an invite.

For six or seven weeks I stayed every weekend, but it
was shady in the pubs and clubs in town on Friday and
Saturday nights. I was in big danger with the local thugs,
who would all suss me out as being Scouse, for some
reason. It was worst waiting in the main bus depot after
the clubs shut, a nightmare when I'd spent my taxi fare.
After witnessing several brutal fights I'd be ready to jump
on a bus to anywhere just to get away.

So what I started to do was go back Friday afternoons
to Manny when there was a big United game on. If the
Reds were away I'd get to Maca's in Burgin Drive around
tea-time, have a scran, hit Manhattans then take the trip
to wherever for the game, sleep at Maca's Sunday nights
and get back Monday.

For New Year I went over to Sale and ended up in the
Cock Robin with Syl and Jimmy for a real local sing-song
in the vault, then as usual everyone back to ours, with
loads of Southern Irish and Glaswegians all singing rebel
songs. My favourite was the one where they all ducked
down in the dance to the words, 'Duck boy, the bullets

are coming.' Everyone had to sing a solo tune at a certain
point of the night. I always went for a United one:

> We went down to Wembley one fine day in May
> With a load of supporters so happy and gay.
> And when it was over and when it was done
> We defeated Benfica by four goals to one.

> The first was by Bobby, he outjumped the rest.
> The second was scored by wee Georgie Best . . . etc.

It always went down well with everyone joining in at
the death. Our Jimmy was a famous singer and boozer on
the Manchester scene; he spent money like a madman,
buying everyone shorts and pints, even more so in the
dives, and boozed with the likes of actor Peter Adamson,
George Best, Thin Lizzy singer Phil Lynott and the rest of
the in crowd in the Brown Cow in Salford, which was run
by Jimmy the Weed and was the best pub in town. Jimmy
was the only boy from a big family of sisters and my old
lady loved her times out on the piss with them when she
went over to Ireland. The very first morning the women
went off to the corner shop straight after breakfast, carted
a large crate of Guinness into the pub and hid it under a
table to start off the session.

I could outdrink everyone my age and many older
fellers. People years later would ask how I could drink
so much and the truth is it was through our Jimmy and
the Plank. I thank them in a crazy way not for the booze
itself but for looking after me as much as they could, as
they were both killing themselves through beer and
whisky. Both sorted themselves out some years later. I
hope I can.

* * *

We started using the Piccadilly Club, which had soul downstairs and Bowie, Mott the Hoople, Rod Stewart and Gary Glitter upstairs. Gagzy and I were the only ones in the Flats to get the real glitter boots, which cost £40 a pair, a fortune then for shoes. People would choke when we told them how much they cost. Eric went into one fulltime over Dave Bowie; he even had the Aladdin Sane flash coloured into his hair and the bits of make-up put on in the club's khazi. The dance floor was the classic chequered one like in *Saturday Night Fever*. The sight of female Bowie freaks trying to kop for him on the dance floor for a shag was untrue; it cracked us all up. Even when Eric came up to Syl's for a Sunday dinner, all the birds would be round, running up to the windows screaming he could take them, some even believing he really was Bowie. Eric lapped it up.

Another club we frequented was the Silver Moon on Shude Hill. They gave out a ticket for boiled burger and chips when you went in. One night one of the lads pointed out a feller in there called Brian Dunne, 'The Bear', who was a legend on the north side of Manchester for his fighting prowess. In the Teddy Boy days, Harpurhey Baths was the main dance hall at weekends and the Bear ruled the roost there. He was famous for steaming into the Top Derby pub with an axe to attack a firm of Jocks who were on their way to Wembley for the yearly game against England.

Anyway, when this lad pointed him out it was one of those 'there's so-and-so but don't look over' moments. You can't help yourself, and he clocked us looking at him. He stood up, raised his fists and blasted his chest King Kong-style, then pointed straight at us, his unflinching glare making my stomach turn over. We were in deep water but as we were about to bolt for the exit, the Bear burst out laughing at our panic. He'd got us properly at it and kept it up all night, as we had to pass him to go to the toilet.

The Moon could get a bit rowdy. George, Maca and I got stuck into a group of Scousers one night and when the police swooped all the Colly lads got nicked while the Scousers got off with it. We spent a night in the Central Detention Centre above the courts in Manchester and got fined the next day.

Another popular dive was Deno's, which is name-checked in the Thin Lizzy tune 'The Boys Are Back In Town'. It had a jukebox and a little dance floor in the corner and was full of snappers, brasses, nightshift grafters from the newspapers still in overalls and gangs of workers from out of town on the piss all day then getting the last train home. Around the corner from the Silver Moon was the Picador, where Geordie, the main bouncer, was gay as Paree. It was a tranny and dyke gaff on the lower level and had cabaret and a first-class mix of girls from the north side, Salford and Cheetham Hill upstairs. The DJ used to play the full album of John Holt's *1,000 Volts of Holt*, which got us all into reggae. There was lots of speed and acid on offer, though most of us stuck to the odd joint.

The Picador was a top place for pulling, as it was so close to Collyhurst Road. We'd take girls into the railway carriages near the Flats; it was Chike who first put us on to them, as he'd been sleeping in them for years with the runaways and tramps. The best carriages to shag in were the ones with separate compartments for privacy, but you were not always up to looking for one, as the task of getting up there was a nobble in itself. Four or five couples, all pissed, would cross over the River Irk, then climb this steep grass embankment, with a few always losing their grip on the tall grass and rolling back down; you were fucked if you rolled into the Irk (they used to say that if you went in the Irk you were a cert to catch something bad as it was so toxic, and I swear it haunted you thinking about it). The noise was too much for the gypsies who had a camp at the bottom so after a bit they'd come out and turn on their torches to guide us all up.

Once up it was every couple to themselves, looking for the best train and compartment. I always made my way to first class, shut the door, pulled down the blinds and took off the mega cushions to place on the floor. I swear it was as good as any hotel. It was common to feel the train pulling out around seven in the morning and hilarious trying to get dressed and jump off with most your clothes in your hands.

* * *

Gagzy and I were now working together at Clean Walls and spent a bit of time with the Plank in Whitley Bay, where he had taken to wearing a Newcastle United shirt and was sorting out starting his own business. We got a massive job at Benton Park in Newcastle, where everyone's national insurance documents are stored. There we met the funniest washers ever seen on scaffolding, a pair who dressed better than the pop stars of the time and often came to work still in their gear: silver jackets with lightning flashes, penny-round collared shirts in freaky colours, special Dan Dares or Lionel Blairs covering huge plat-formed boots. How they grafted on scaffolding in that gear I'll never know.

Andy Chips and Steve Rouff were both from Old Trafford. Andy was a Greek whose family lost their business in Cyprus when the Turks invaded. His icon was Rolling Stone Keith Richards: he looked the spit of him, with his hair cut the same way, and I swear he took just as many drugs. Steve, known as Roufy, was the spit of Phil Lynott with the same colouring: his mother Elsie was from Old Trafford and his dad came from Bombay to Liverpool on a boat, then worked his way up to owning Indian restaurants.

What top characters they were, always telling us about piss-ups and shags and being collared by landladies going through half the bed and brekkies in Newcastle. After they'd done their work they asked me to call in on them the next time I was in Manchester, and we went to a superb curry house in Chorlton that blew my mind and helped get me into all other types of food, as before that I was a pure fry-up and chippie man. Then they took me just round the corner to an after hours bar in the Whalley Range hotel run by Phil Lynott's old lady Phyliss, which was frequented by the likes of George Best and top Granada celebs. I ended up in stitches at the bar all night hearing their stories.

A few years later I bumped into Chips and Roufy in Amsterdam and we have worked, lived and played the field with each other all over the world ever since. To this day they're both my brothers.

* * *

On a break from the blasting, Gagzy and I went to Blackpool for a weekend. Walking from the Pleasure Beach to the Pontins holiday camp, we talked about getting a job there, or possibly at the bigger Butlins. Our idea came from the film *That'll Be The Day* with David Essex and Ringo Starr, and all the pussy they got working on a fairground. Maca, one of the Colly lads, had also been talking about getting off to work the holiday camps in the season but had been nicked for assault and sent to borstal.

We applied to Butlins and within a few weeks received a letter offering us summer work at the camp at Minehead in Somerset. We went to see Maca in the nick and he was gutted, but we said he could always do it with us next year, though his head was too bashed to think that far ahead. The offer was from the beginning of May; they needed us to help clean up the camp ready for the start of the season. Because United looked a certainty to go down into the Second Division and were playing City on the last game of the season, I thought it was best not to be in Manchester when the inevitable relegation happened.

That was when our very own King, Denis Law, backheeled the winner for City. For the only time in my life I didn't even listen on the radio.

Gags and I bailed down the Oasis, the new top shopping place, and spent all day buying everything we needed. Birmingham bags were massive at the time, with large pockets on the side halfway down your legs. We took the piss out of them, saying you could fit wardrobes in them, and chose the same style of kecks without the wardrobes, with massive three- or five-button waistbands, no back pockets, tight as possible on your arse and fly area. Then, whooff, massive Tony Blairs which covered our platformed boots. My boots had black and white stripes on the sole and a black heel with stars on and were full-size, which meant they came right up to the knee. Funky-style clogs were also in, and the thing to do if you got into a fight was take them off and use them as a cosh. We wore our cheesecloth shirts as tight as possible and the style was real Medallion Man, so the top three or four buttons were open, showing the best part of your chest. You'd even see the odd massive coin on a chain; I'd just got my last tattoo from the legendary Manchester tattoo artist Cash Cooper – 'M.U.F.C.' on my chest – so I never bothered with the coin.

Our jackets were very much blazer style without those gold buttons and box-like pockets, very smart and really the only sensible part of our wardrobe. The shirt collars were called Concordes because of the size, ending in penny rounds or sharp points, and when worn with a knotted kipper tie the collar tips would almost be touching your belly button. Without a tie the Concorde collars would be worn outside, as though they'd been ironed flat over the lapels of your jacket. We'd also hang a silk hankie out of the breast pocket. Hairstyle was crucial. You used a hair dryer to cope with the massive curls that had to be tucked in neatly with a sorted curling brush, as very long hair and sideboards were well in – think of George Best and Pat Jennings and that's how it was. Skinheads would only be seen at matches now. The Brut splash-on was big but I stuck with Old Spice.

They sent us tickets for the train down to Minehead, which was just as well, as jibbing with two huge suitcases would have been a problem. We were on our way.

Chapter Six

Dippers and Zappers

MINEHEAD WAS SET on a picturesque coastline with a beautiful harbour. It had one of the biggest Butlins camps in the country: accommodation for over 10,000 guests, with over 1,000 staff to look after their needs. It had a huge Pig and Whistle in the middle, which was the main bar and disco, a Select Bar where the likes of Bernard Manning and Bob Monkhouse entertained the adults, other bars dotted about and a kids' disco.

The staff chalets were tucked into a corner away from the holidaymakers, in lines like an army camp, with the washhouses at the bottom with baths and showers. For Gagzy and me it was luxury. Being among the first staff to arrive, we had our pick of the chalets. We went for one in the middle of the block nearest the staff club, which sold the cheapest booze; on staff disco night a lot of the campers would try to sneak in because it was the best night of the week. They sold Brain Damage, the local cider that did exactly what it said on the bottle and had bits of apple floating in it. It had the mother of all kicks and the unfortunate side effect of making me piss the bed. I wasn't alone: every morning there'd be mattresses on the roof or drying out on the grass. The rooms were smaller than most prison cells, so we covered the walls with tinfoil and threw up loads of freaky Bruce

Lee and Pink Floyd posters, topped off with a fishing net on the ceiling. It was a top pad.

The work was easy at first, cleaning all the kitchens and stores, but then the first campers arrived. We had to work split shifts serving up the food to the waiters to dish out in the main dining rooms to the OAPs and the handicapped, who were the first lot to arrive. The *Hi-De-Hi* mob would not start arriving for another two weeks and then the work really picked up. We had to do all sorts: take the eyes out of spuds before they went into the peeler, scrub pots and pans, clean the floors. Sometimes we wandered round selling seafood; at other times we could fill in and do some waitering, which was where we could do a bit of a fiddle. We got to know one of the girls working the bar, so every time I got an order to write down on my sheet I'd get another one as well and keep it in my head. The friendly face behind the bar would put one round through the till and bin the other for us to split at the end of the night.

We enjoyed serving up the scran to new staff so we could flirt with the girls. The first-timers were often nervous about facing new people at work and for many it was their first time ever away from home, so Gagzy and I were both super-helpful, telling them useful things like the best time to use the bath. Most nights we ended up going out with a firm of Chalet Monsters, the girls who cleaned the staff chalets and were the horrors of the camp. They'd buy us a couple of glasses of Brain Damage and get a grip of us at the end of the night, when fourteen stone does not look too bad. One night one of the Monsters called me over to tell me what she would like to do, then said we'd have to wait because she had a dose to sort out. We ended up doing it anyway. A bus went once a week from the camp to the hospital so people could get themselves sorted out, so I hopped on a few days later for a check-up. I got a mega shock when they said I was all right on the VD but had a dose of the Sandy McNabs (crabs). This wasn't the only time I got on the bus, as the girls just kept on coming.

What a buzz it was telling all the stories of what went down at United games, pitch invasions and giving it to City from all sides. This was the start of the Red Army years, when United's travelling mob took it to everyone. The best storyteller was George Lyons from Burgin Drive, who had just arrived for the season. He was a very handy United lad who filled us in about all the going on, including coppers getting done in. Even though United did indeed go down to the Second Division, we knew they'd bounce straight back. We got to know a load of good lads like Cockney Bob, a Gunners fan who used to drive a three-litre Ford Capri with a top stereo and his clothes smelt of money. The best thing was, he never drank a drop, he'd buzz off us lot losing it on cider and say he was well happy just driving us around. We never gave him a carrot for petrol. Then there was Alan, a Birmingham City fan. People say Brummies are boring and have the worst accent but that's pure bollocks; Alan and all the other Brums we met were right on our wavelength. Two lads from Bristol moved onto our line and their accent *was* something else: they sounded like Wurzel and had both done borstal down on Portland, where all the snappers from down south ended up. They loved their weed but found it hard to keep up with us on the cider. They'd end up slumped over the bar asleep at the end of the night. Geordie Rogers was from Ashington, the north-east mining village where the Charlton family came from. I was the only one who could understand him and had to translate to the rest of the chaps. Our line also included Scousers, Paddies and Jocks, a real mixed bunch.

Often we'd finish for the night around eight o'clock

and crash out round the swimming pool. We'd smoke a joint and drift away from the pace of the job, listening to Pink Floyd's *Dark Side of the Moon* album. We met a couple of chic Brummy girls who were bang in with the in crowd (they'd once copped for Bryan Ferry and Brian Eno) and knew all the right people who worked the Oasis shopping centre in Birmingham (not the Manchester one). They nodded a few parcels through to us with all the latest stuff. We'd clear out my chalet and bang out the clobber on payday; the place looked like a boutique. Everyone was delighted with the clothes and we'd slip a few things to the side for ourselves, as expected.

I still used the ten-bob trick the Plank had shown me on all the new bar staff and shop assistants. It would take only half an hour to get the starter for the day and you met all kinds of different people whilst on the mooch. I got talking to a couple of Scouse lads who were dippers or zappers – pickpockets – and they invited me to Newton Abbot Racecourse, offering to show me some of the basics. Apparently Scouse zappers are the best pickpockets in Britain, then it's the Dublin dips and Manchester and Glasgow are close behind. There are some top Cockneys doing it but many of them work in Europe and Australia; the best dippers in the world are trained at special schools in South America and the best in Europe are French Algerians.

The first thing to learn is the pattern of teamwork without any talking and to stay cool, alert and ready to do your graft when the time is right. My first move was the simple one, receiving the wallet, known by the Scousers as the zap. You can receive two or three at the same time from different directions and then you have to go offside and empty them out. When you've got all the cash and cards together, you hand it over to whoever is the Guv, the top man, then get back in close to collect some more. They all told me it wasn't worth trying to shark a few bob out of the pot down your undies, as everyone got virtually strip-searched on the way back and you could get cut up bad if you were at it.

The next stage to learn was 'the block' for the main dipper to do his thing. There were loads of different techniques, but the one they showed me first was for crowded streets, where you would just breeze into the intended victim and knock into his right shoulder. In that split second, he would turn his head to the right, leaving his inside breast pocket exposed, which was an easy lift for any decent dipper ghosting in and out from nowhere. The Scousers said football matches and other sporting events were ideal for dipping because of the normal crush and jostling from the crowd. You could get into some terrible trouble though, especially if you were in the other team's end, so the chaps liked to have an extra one or two on the firm for protection.

Shamefully I must admit that I also found supermarkets a doddle; you'd always find a woman or two who'd walk away from their trolleys and turn their backs. The Scousers said that escalators were good for dipping too and that it was best to have a coat or jumper draped over your arm as cover. Clothes store changing rooms could provide rich pickings if you got dressed up well and looked like you were up for spending a few quid. The shop assistants would not give you a second look and as people wandered away from their cubicle to change the size or speak to their partners, you could be in like Flynn. I'm ashamed of this graft now and in mitigation I did try to target upmarket shops to avoid stealing from working class people, but I'm sure that many times I must have robbed my own kind.

Towards the end of our season at Minehead, the

management employed a new head of security. We called him Action Man because he lifted weights outside his chalet on sunny days and his missus had whips and chains hung up in their room. He built a nasty little firm who started to knock around a few of the lads, real bully boy tactics, bursting into people's rooms at four o'clock in the morning. So we decided to deal with them. One of the lads went into the Pig and Whistle at last orders and made a few snide remarks to them all. The rest of us hid on our chalet line waiting for Action Man and his cronies to take the bait. There were Brummies, Taffs and Scousers, many of whom I hadn't met before, all with coshes and other weapons waiting for the fight to happen.

We saw the kid who'd made the snide remarks and sure enough he'd brought a gathering with him. He was a banker to get a good hiding, and just as they were about to get stuck into him we jumped in and gave them a proper beating. The only one that got away was Action Man, who was straight on his toes, but he and the rest of the nasty security fellas packed their bags and left Minehead that night. The Old Bill turned up the next morning and were at the camp for a good few days, but ended up charging only George Lyons. George got sacked, so all the waiters, including me and Gagzy – who had recently been promoted – went on strike. It was a panic job because they had to bring in Redcoats to serve up the campers' food and Billy Butlin himself turned up to try to calm things down. Eventually they put George back to work, so we all went back, but by then it was near the end of the summer season. The football season was about to begin, with United playing Second Division football for the first time in their history. We wanted to support them all the way so we worked a week's notice, which meant we were okay for getting jobs the next year, though clearly not at Minehead, and headed back to Manchester.

* * *

I got my job back at Clean Walls straight away; the boss liked all the young grafters from Collyhurst, because we would work whenever and wherever he asked, even at short notice. I was put back with our Jimmy and went up to Newcastle to finish some government building with the Plank, then on the following Monday it was over to Glasgow to do a hospital. As we came into Glasgow, the Plank tried to get me going, pointing at all the fellas waiting on corners for the bars to open. In every group there was one or two busted-up faces from kick-offs at the weekend, and he kept telling me how much they hated the English. The truth was they did hate the English, but not really Cowboys like us.

The only place I knew was the Gorbals, which was like Collyhurst Flats with its massive tenement blocks, and we booked ourselves into a bed and brekkie on a shady street nearby. We headed straight over to the Gorbals to see our Jimmy's Irish friends, all pure Celtic, and we were off on a mind-bending drinking session. We even forgot to meet the clerk of the works to go through the job with him. We went to the local Celtic bar and Jimmy hit the whisky; the measures were much bigger than in England and that was pretty much it for him. We hardly saw him until the following Friday dinnertime, when we were getting a lift to Newcastle so we could catch the train back to Manchester. The job ended up a complete disaster. We got kicked off it by the inspector, who couldn't make sense of what our Jimmy was trying to blag him with.

United were playing Hull the next day – we'd just bought Stuart Pearson from them and this game was part of the deal – and I got a lift in a van with some Colly lads. We had a good day, stopping in a few pubs on the way and singing. For a while we followed Sir Matt Busby in his Rolls-Royce with its number plate LAW 1, and we all cheered and hung out of the windows as he speeded up to get away from us. The next week I blagged a lift to London with Maca from the Flats, who'd just come out of borstal, to see the Reds play Leyton Orient. We got to Euston at ten and nicked a few sandwiches while we waited for the pub to open. By one o'clock we'd sunk a fair few pints, but as usual in those days the cockney beer missed the mark. So we got a load of bareback (cider) from a shop and jibbed the Tube to Orient's ground. It was boiling hot, with all Tommy Doc's Barmy Army up for a good sing-song: 'Six foot two, eyes of blue, big Jim Holton's after you.' Then a mob of us steamed into an off licence shouting, 'Hello, hello, United aggro, United aggro,' and carted out as much booze and cigs as we could carry. The shopkeeper went mad but could do nothing.

We were amazed at how many Reds were wandering round looking for a pub, or crashed out kipping in doorways with United flags wrapped round them, having found the pub. And what a sight the ground was. The Red Army had taken it over: hundreds were scaling the walls and a load had climbed the floodlights. The Old Bill tried to get them down, but every time they came close all the boys from above pissed on them. When they wanted to get down, we all pushed the coppers a decent distance away so they could drop and mingle in without getting their collars felt. We started shaking the scaffolding holding up the commentary box, and after a few minutes the Old Bill came running in, as it looked a certainty to topple over. If it had it would have killed a few of us for sure but we didn't care, as we had shared a kind of mob brotherhood where you'd willingly die for the Reds. We even smashed down the iron crush barriers on the terraces and threw them on to the pitch. After mobs had twice invaded the pitch, the Doc came over and asked us to keep a lid on things, winking and waving at the same time, as if to say, 'Save it for later, chaps.'

Millwall were the next vistors to Old Trafford. They were the most feared firm in the lower divisions and a heavy reception committee was planned. We met up in the Dilly and marched up the train station ramp, only to be forced back by the coppers. We turned a sharp left down London Road, then halfway down it went left again under the big arches near Sparkle Street, an area nicknamed 'the Dardanelles' because it was once so rough. The local pub was a Chesters house where all the local characters used a side vault called the Carrot Yard, which was a knocking shop; when the police got a call they used to have to strap the women to a two-wheeled stricter to get them back to the cop shop.

We sent a few lads back up the side entrance of the station to scan what was going down and they came back down screaming that it had already kicked off and Millwall were all over the place. We later found out that they had shared the train up with fifty Cockney Reds, who promptly attacked them from behind as they left Piccadilly Station and chased them out towards some waiting Mancs who happened to be on the walkway at the right time. By the time we got involved, Millwall had legged it into an old fire station, with police protection, and were refusing to come out. One copper told a Millwall fan: 'The next time you come to Manchester you'd better bring your mothers with you.' The dibble escorted them back to the station and they went straight back to the Smoke.

The next big one was Cardiff City. They had a bad reputation in the hooligan world and only the week before had run riot in Bristol, with over 100 getting nicked. I had a good few pints with Maca on the Friday night, then we got on the 263 bus to Altrincham. Straight into the Bear's Head transport café, where we soon sorted out a lift to a service station on the M6. But we had no luck finding another lift, so we ran across the motorway and I saw a top-of-the-range Jag parked in a crazy place, near the entrance to the service station itself. A feller was slumped over the wheel. With a bit of effort we managed to rouse him. He wound down the window and the smell of whisky nearly took me off my feet. He gestured to the back and we got in. It turned out his missus had left him and he'd tried to kill himself with pills and whisky. We blagged him to drop us off in Cardiff and he was on a real downer at first, driving blind and nearly killing us. We polished off his whisky and cigs, which put us right on form with the patter, so we ended up getting a few bob out of him as well. He was thinking of coming to the game until we arrived at the railway station and he saw police and thugs milling round. Every train coming in from the Valleys had hordes of rednecks on board, who were right up for it.

We had a bit of scran, then scouted round town. There was plenty of activity, with large groups of Valley skins picking off unsuspecting United fans. We just got through a shady scene ourselves near a sports complex, then headed back to the station bar, where we met up with a group of Reds from the Midlands who'd been well busted up. Maca and I were starting to get edgy. Then came a gift from above: a service train full of Cockney Reds, who piled off and gave out some digs, which restored order around the station area. Reports starting coming in from all over town of pure running battles – and it was still only 1.30. Nearly every pub by this stage had either bolted its doors or been trashed.

About a half-hour later, the Manchester football special pulled in. The noise was something else: 'Tommy Doc's

red and white army! Tommy Doc's red and white army!'
First off was Alan Twigg, a top boy who was ready to
rumble. With the Cockney lot we were over 1,000 strong,
and once we were together we burst through the police
lines and into a pack of Valley skins. It was fun and
games all the way to Ninian Park as we turned over
hotdog stands and ran into every shop and off licence to
nick booze so we could get tanked up freemans. When
we reached the ground, we all jumped the turnstiles into
their end, but realised it was a no-go as they'd spent
fortunes on fencing and barbed wire for the visit of the
Red Army. So we were caged into this stupid corner with
Cardiff a stone's throw away – and plenty of stones and
missiles did rain down on us, all through the first half.

We were separated from the bulk of the United mob,
so me and a couple of the others went to the toilets to
see if we could get through them and rejoin the rest. The
toilet was in the top corner and there was no way
through, but as we came back out of the other entrance
so we could get a drink, a very nasty-looking mob of
Cardiff were waiting with some of their main boys at the
front. They started throwing kung fu stars and darts. I
was right at the front so there was no way I could bail
out of this one. The lad in front of me looked like he
could have a fight so I took a big gulp and landed my
best shot on his chin. It was a real beaut and before his
legs had a chance to buckle, everyone else steamed in. I
was buzzing so much off it, I felt like I'd won the Pools,
more so as everyone had seen it.

At the end of the game we all knew it would kick off,
particularly as we hadn't managed to get into their end.
To get us in the mood, one of the lads cracked a copper
full on the chin as we left the ground. Then it went mad,
real mob fighting in all the side streets. By the time we
reached the station we were the usual body or two short,

and later on when I watched *News At Ten* they said Snake Hips from Collyhurst had been given six months at a special court held on Saturday teatime – and he'd gone down to the game with his dad! The next day everyone was talking about it and the Sunday papers were full of photos of Cardiff getting a kicking, with some thugs dressed up in *Clockwork Orange* gear.

The next big away game was Sheffield Wednesday. We caught an early service train and then a bus up to the ground. Wednesday bricked the bus as we neared the ground, so it was no surprise that we were straight into a bit of aggro in a park next door. Then, instead of finding a pub, we blagged our way into their social club and got involved in a yard of ale drinking competition. It went down a treat, though I got soaked by the bit in the bubble at the end. The social club was attached to Hillsborough and had an exit that led straight into the stadium, so we were through without paying before they knew what was happening. Police arrested over 100 people during the game as we kicked their mob out of their own end. Fans were being stretchered out throughout the game, which was a classic 4–4 draw, with United getting the equaliser right at the end. A copper on a white horse galloped along the touchline trying to keep order, but there were kick-offs everywhere.

Ashy, who was with me, was now a pure rocker with long curly hair down his back, into Deep Purple and Led Zeppelin. I must admit he got me into 'Killer Queen' and then Wishbone Ash and an album by Jethro Tull called *Too Old To Rock 'n' Roll, Too Young To Die*. He was always going on about Tangerine Dream. It was quite a change, from the most fearsome-looking skinhead to this heavy rock head. Meanwhile Gags and I were getting into Roxy Music: we fell in love with Bryan Ferry's dress style, which was double smart, plus the music was spot-on and still is. I remember seeing him stroll onto the stage at the Kings Hall in Belle Vue in 1975 dressed in Levi's, green Dunlop trainers and a navy blue, faded Lonsdale boxing top and singing 'The Bogus Man', and I said to myself then and still believe that he was the Godfather of Cool. We eventually slung all our platforms, flared collars and loon pants to the secondhand shop and to this day have stayed dressed in what was later labelled the 'casual' style.

A club opened at the back of Manchester Cathedral; the old Time and Place and a club round the corner called Nice and Easy joined together and re-opened as Pips. It had four or five rooms all playing different things. The best to cop in was the one always playing 'The Bump', with 100 per cent of bodies doing this crazy, really funny dance. But the main one for us was the Roxy Room. You had to be a member of Pips, carrying a card with your photo on, and this cut down all the fighting, as no-one wanted to be barred.

* * *

George Lyons, who'd been sacked for the fight with the security guards at Minehead, asked if I'd go to Exeter Magistrates Court to back him up. I got the Plank to send a letter on company-headed paper confirming I'd be losing two days' pay due to travelling to court. We jibbed the train down and decided to go to the holiday camp to see if there was anyone there we knew. We jumped over the fence and headed for the staff lines and were well pleased to see a few Chalet Monsters cleaning away in preparation for Christmas. We were both taters deep by midnight.

The next day George got nine months, so if he kept out of trouble he'd be out for the end of the football season. I went down to see him in the cells and he was gutted that the security guards had told a pack of lies to get him sent down. But he soon got over it, winking and saying we'd still have the next summer season at Butlins in Skegness. Archie, from Kingsley Crescent in the Colly Flats, had worked his way up to top chef and was trying to sort us all out with good jobs for the next summer season. I went to see George's solicitor about my loss of earnings, return fare from Newcastle to Exeter and the price of the bed and breakfast that I'd stayed in (not). I couldn't believe it when he paid me out in cash; I wasn't expecting a carrot. I went straight back over the camp fence and into the mauling arms of two Chalet Monsters. I ended up working at the camp over Christmas and it was one of my best Christmases ever, even though the work was harder than in the summer. We served wine with the food, so all ended up in some bad states ourselves, as the campers demanded we shared a glass with them.

I spent New Year in Liverpool and then travelled up to Newcastle to continue on the job with the Plank and our Jimmy. On the first weekend back in Geordieland, I decided to stay up and chance my arms with the local girls. We went to Ashington, which was in the *Guinness Book of Records* for having twenty workingmen's clubs on the main street. I got talking to a married woman who said her husband was at home but would be getting the midnight bus to his nightshift down the coal pit. At the end of the night, she went home while I waited across the road with a chippie that nearly choked me when I saw the size of this Geordie brute at least fifteen years older than me – I was still only eighteen – coming out of the door and off up the road to catch his bus. A minute later, the lights in the house flashed to say the coast was clear. Once inside, the first thing I did was bring the ironing board down the stairs and wedge it against the front door. I made sure the front window opened and that I could climb out of the back kitchen window in an emergency. She totally took control and it was a wild night as she bounded round the house in stockings and suspenders, or Stretford Enders as we called them. On the Monday I told one of the Geordie lads who worked with us and he wised me up about the dangers of getting involved with married women on the side. He said I'd soon get sussed because it was such a tight community and her husband would put me in hospital or worse if he found out. I never went back for more.

George had got out of Exeter jail and the first thing on his list was the second tie of the League Cup semi-final against Norwich. They got up to the usual mayhem, coming a cropper in a Chinese chippy on the way home, with buckets of boiling fat flying about and a mad scramble as all hands slipped and slid, screaming to get out through the door. I went to the next away game at Bolton and United were there early in force, taking over their town centre pubs. None of their lot was anywhere to be seen, but at the ground there was about 15,000 of them in the open end. So we jibbed in and steamed into them. I got a bloody nose and my white Starsky and Hutch cardigan was soon covered in claret from my conk and a bit from some Bolton who'd also suffered. It was no surprise when I got collared; the real surprise was that they only chucked me out of the ground, so within ten minutes I was back in through another exit. At full-time, the coppers had had enough and locked up about thirty lads, including me. On the Monday morning our Jimmy brought me some cigs and a book by the Glasgow gangster Jimmy Boyle called *Sense of Freedom*. We went in front of the magistrates for £100 fines. The following day the papers named and shamed us, printing our names and addresses.

A lot of clubs were now terrified of our fans. At Oxford, they put up banners saying 'Welcome United' and laid on buses to the ground. It was the most boring away game I've ever been to, but we more than made up for it when we went to Blackpool away. Maca, George and I got there the night before and, after booking into a B & B, hit the Manchester Arms, then went on to the former boxer Brian London's club. It was jammed with Reds and a lot of them didn't have any digs. Because the weather was bad, we let a right few come back to sleep on our floor. The landlady's kipper in the morning when she came into our room was a picture. She went ballistic, as some of the lads had vomited and pissed all over the gaff. Luckily we'd got up early and had a huge brekkie before she made herself busy. They reckon 17,000 made the trip and we filled their massive old kop end to bursting. The only trouble was with the coppers. Eric stood in the middle of a mob chanting, 'Kill, kill, kill the Bill, kill the Bill, kill the Bill,' and I saw a couple of bobbies getting kicked up and down like footballs. Plenty of the Red Army still sported bovver boots with massive flares over them and sheepskin coats were also in.

The away game at Millwall was changed from the Saturday to midweek to cut down the number of travelling thugs and give the police a better chance of controlling it. Although it hurt my pocket, I was going. I knew our Jimmy wouldn't mind me having a couple of days off, as he knew the score with me and United; he was the same with Celtic. We met at the Manchester Arms, a pub opposite Victoria Station that had topless barmaids and strippers on all day, then wandered up to Piccadilly, pissed and singing. Every Red on the train was in his working clothes and hardly any wore United colours. This felt good, as every head on the train was someone I'd seen at the front when it had gone off at previous matches.

As always, we chatted to other Reds on the train but one kid stuck out: he was alone and without doubt the youngest person on that train. Coco was a big, strong half-caste who lived in the bullring flats in Hulme. He told us he'd run away from an approved school in Southport so he could be on the trip to Millwall. We asked what got him into United and it seems his first game was a Manchester derby and whoever won he'd support for life!

We were met in London by a crew of Cockney Reds and walked from Euston over to Euston Square, where the police split us up before allowing us on to the Tubes. We had to change a couple of times, and by the time we reached the ground everyone was huddled into small groups. The main stand at Millwall was all seats, with the two ends and the other side for standing. The unusual thing was that you could walk round the ground and get into any of the three standing areas. It meant that as soon as United had grouped together, Millwall charged from all sides, having been joined for the night by Cockney thugs from other clubs. Steve Coppell scored a penalty but we didn't jump up or let out a peep, as we were surrounded by docker thugs in their thirties and forties. After the game we kept our heads down and were lucky to avoid a good kicking. All the way to the Tube, Reds walking with us were picked off and dragged away for a shoeing. It was without a doubt our shadiest trip to London.

All the games at Old Trafford were a good sing-song and a time to watch the Reds doing their stuff with one of their most exciting teams: Steve Coppell, Gordon Hill, Lou Macari, Sammy McIlroy and Co. United's average home crowd that season was around 56,000, with hardly ever an away supporter to be seen. This lack of away fans was true for a few years until the police got their act together with special escorts to and from the ground and tactics like keeping the away fans back for fifteen minutes until they'd had a go at dispersing the home crowd.

An away game at Notts County was to be our last that year, as we wanted to get to Skegness right at the start of the summer season, as we'd done in Minehead. The ground was so rammed that a toilet wall collapsed onto a load of people, with a few getting badly hurt. United's win meant we had taken the Second Division title with a couple of games still to go. We felt we'd done our duty to see the Devils safely back into the First Division, so that week Gagzy, Maca and I got on the train and headed up to Skegness.

We received a nasty shock. They didn't need anyone to clean the camp, as it had already been done, so we had to doss around for two weeks waiting for it to open. Things got really bad, as Skegness is a ghost town and the winds blew gale force all day. We had to hang around cafes on the lookout for people who had only half eaten their meals; we'd swoop in lively and polish them off. Maca was still on his borstal licence and had to keep reporting to a probation officer who more often than not gave us a few quid to keep us from going on the rob. He even told us about the Sally Army and born-again Christians who would give out a few sandwiches if you were prepared to put a couple of hours in. The one good thing was that we'd brought a record player with us and would try to drift away to Al Green's greatest hits during the day.

Then we met Billy, a pisshead from Glasgow who worked the scam taking people's pictures without any film in his camera. Most punters paid there and then in cash, with Billy handing them some kind of ticket to keep them happy. He ended up moving into our sweaty flat and supplied the booze until we could return the favour a few weeks later. When the camp did open, the weather was still bad and the campside beach was a health hazard, with an ugly smell and things floating in the water. It was the oldest Butlins in the country and almost the spit of the Minehead, with the same bars and dance halls, though instead of the Pig and Whistle they had a massive German Bierkeller, with wooden benches and the oompah band giving it plenty. The biggest disappointment was the staff club, because it was miles from the staff lines and they wouldn't put on a separate disco night for us. I went there only three times: for the FA Cup Final, the European Cup Final when Leeds lost to Munich, and best of all, to see England beat Scotland by a fistful of goals, with Gerry Francis scoring the winner. I got a letter from Scouse Mac, a top lad who we'd worked with at Minehead. He was now at the camp at Bognor Regis and said it was an awesome crack. He and a load of Scouse dippers from Kirkby also went over to work the Leeds Euro final.

Opposite the Skegness camp was a big caravan site, which had a mega bar with talent competitions every night. Most times we went out we'd start there and then return to the camp for the last hour or two to see the Chalet Monsters, who were all from Sheffield and Doncaster. I was working as a waiter, Gagzy got a top job as a cook and Maca and George were kitchen porters, but I couldn't settle in the place. After a few weeks, I told the lads I was going to put in for a transfer to another camp. The weather was getting to me. It was grey and bleak, the beach remained the saddest I'd ever seen and even the area around Skegness was dull. I tried the ten-bob trick in all the village pubs and it worked a treat, but there was no life in the gaff. Maybe I'd been spoilt by the beauty of Somerset but that's how I was then, I loved nice-looking places and good weather. I knew the south coast was going to be sunnier than Skeggy and I'd heard that the area around Bognor was buzzing, with tourists from all over Europe. Brighton was only thirty minutes down the road with the UK's first real nudist beach.

So Maca and I put in for a move and got transferred to Bognor – and continued our thieving education.

Chapter Seven

Learning The Sneak

THE HOLIDAY CAMP had a small pier with a nightclub, and facing towards the main area was a big pub where hordes of holidaymakers sat outside on benches at long wooden tables. We went straight to the beach and who did we see but Scouse Mac, lounging around with a load of other Scouse bandits smoking big cornettos.

These guys were pro's. The main dipper was little Ronnie Cadey, who had long, jet-black hair like a Red Indian, and the main sneak thief was Gerry, the first person to explain to me the simple facts about being a sneak. He said you have to be prepared to talk normally if you're caught somewhere you shouldn't be, and have plausible excuses at the ready. One of Gerry's favourites was to produce a bottle of tablets and say he needed the toilet and some water. He said if you were calm with your speech they'd always point the way or else escort you there, though you had to be on guard for the one who appeared to have it but then called the coppers as soon as they could. While on the sneak it's all about weighing up situations – like an apprenticeship really – and Gerry said it took a few years to polish off the rough edges, no matter how much nerve you had.

You should never wear boxer shorts on the sneak as the best place to put cash, cards, jewellery – or tom as we called it, short for tomfoolery – and other small items is down the front of your undies. With boxers on, your stash will slip down and end up coming out of the bottom of your trousers. It's always better to avoid contact and confrontation if possible. Say it's the afternoon and you're in the master bedroom, looking for the cash box, tom box or safe and you hear someone coming up the stairs. Rather than bursting out, it's better to hide, as they may be coming upstairs to change their clothes or have a nap. Under the bed is always a good option – and you'd be amazed how many times you can come out while they're asleep to find they've brought up the takings and put them on a bedside table. Some sneaks will even remove the rings and watches of people who are sleeping; the trick is to put your hands inside the bed so they get to the same temperature as the sleeping person before going to work. Some thieves even carry a small pair of metal cutters to remove difficult rings.

When working in a public building it is worth having an old hand with you, a blagger who can talk sensibly to staff if needed and distract them while the sneak slips in and out of the private areas. Most sneaks and blaggers have their own codewords or signs, often light clicks of the fingers, with certain noises meaning certain things. It's also vital for a blagger to learn how to be a sneak, as many times the main sneak has no choice but to blag, so the blagger then has to turn sneak and slide in. A sneak thief never stops learning his trade, things like the way you creep up stairs by getting as firm a grip on the rail as possible, then taking four or five steps at a time. Always making sure you stand on the edge of the step, not the middle, as they can make bad noises if you walk up the middle. Always be prepared for different kinds of dogs – often it's the small ones, like Jack Russells, that are harder to control.

You need to learn what time is best to hit certain

places. Small shops often cash up in the last hour, then leave the takings in the office until they close. Usually it would be in a drawer or cashbox, but even if it was in the safe the keys would often be in the office or around the till area, sometimes on the keyring in the till. Places like bakers are attractive in the summer, as they leave the back door and windows open because of the heat. Small, family hotel-restaurants are often very busy from around eleven o'clock to two in the afternoon, as all the family are working; this is the best time to hit the living area and bedrooms. The best thing about the sneaking game is you can work every kind of business: tom shops, garden and DIY centres, family supermarkets, anywhere that has a back office or a small house attached.

After talking to the Scousers, we sorted ourselves out with a chalet and then went straight to check out the staff club. It was just as good as Minehead, right on the corner of the staff lines. I bumped into a lad who worked the hotdog carts at Old Trafford; he said it was sound, though there weren't any Chalet Monsters, the reason being all the girls working the staff lines were top darling southerners – to me and Maca they were Cockney babes. There was so much to do in the place that after a couple of weeks we got to thinking about telling the office we were living off camp, which meant we'd get a few extra bob in our wages. I was seeing a Scottish girl called Irene who worked in the staff office and she said she could sort us out with a chalet on the sly, so we still had a chalet and got the extra dosh as well. Maca was working in the kitchen and I ended up doing just about every job on the camp – the dining hall, the bar, the kitchen, even the bins. I liked the constant change to keep things fresh.

Towards the end of the season, a Scouser called Kelly and I had a proper little scam and nice earner going on. We gave people a tenner to open an account in the Post

Office on the camp or the local ones around Bognor, then gave them another tenner to report their book lost. We then forged the entry in the book to change it from £10 to £100 and mocked up a new Post Office stamp in the book, using a silver ten pence coin, which was exactly the same size as the stamp. After making the alterations, we'd spend our days off in Brighton with a good few Post Office books, taking it in turns to draw out money from every one. We only took out fivers to begin with so as not to arouse suspicion. Once this had been done, the book had a genuine stamp in it for the last transaction and so it was sweet to draw the lot out the next time we were in town.

We drew out a good few bob one day and went on the piss all afternoon. I took Kelly for his first tattoo, a Liverpool FC crest up the top of his left arm. I got a heart and arrow across my chest and a Union Jack with my brother's name in a scroll at the bottom. I looked like I'd been at the Battle of the Boyne. Then we hit the beach with a couple of bottles of bareback and a couple of spliffs and Kelly asked me if I'd fancy doing the last book in the Post Office right next to the train station. I stupidly agreed and ended up getting chased down the street. I ran back on myself in a big loop and slipped back into the station, running straight through a crowd onto the Bognor train. Unfortunately it wasn't due to leave for ten minutes. The cops carted me off and charged me with defrauding the Queen.

The duty lawyer put me straight the next morning and said I should expect at least a six-month lie down, possibly even a year, which was the most the magistrates could impose. I arrived at court and Maca was there smiling and giving me the thumbs up. The lawyer said he'd brought me a bag of clothes and some cigs and newspapers, as he'd told Maca I was due to go down the steps. Just before the magistrates passed sentence, my solicitor called Maca to the stand to be a character witness for me! I think he got the art of talking sensible when needed from his old man, who was the best seller of dipped gold bracelets on Oldham Street. Maca took the court by storm, going on about how I'd been led astray by others and how determined I was to keep out of trouble and get back to a proper job. Even my brief loved it. He made the difference and I ended up getting a fine and six-month sentence – suspended!

We headed for Brighton and scored some weed on Orange Street, the main place for fags but great to get good weed, then hit the nearest pub and were soon stoned. Kelly carried on doing the Post Office books and a few weeks later got twelve months, doing his jail in Lewes, further down the south coast. Before he went down he started grafting with Miriam, the best Geordie bird any of us had ever seen: her accent wasn't too rough and what a darling. She loved the buzz of being around the bad lot. She and Kelly worked a scam where they went into a tom shop, both in their swimming gear so the staff thought they wouldn't have much chance of binning any tom. Once they'd got one of the staff warmed up, Kelly would palm a gold chain or two into his mouth.

When Kelly got stuck down, Miriam and I tried our luck. We were quite successful with the chains but we had more results by doing the switch. You go into a tom shop with a snide ring on your little finger and ask to look at some nice rings. When the chance comes, you put the snide one back and keep the real one on your little finger. Soon after this I started to have even better results by picking a pad of rings that had a few missing and clocking the dearest ring on the pad. When the staff ask which one you want to look at, don't choose the dear one, choose a ring near the one you want to rob.

When you put the ring back, your little finger can hook the dear ring you want. It happens in a flash and, like everything, the more you do it the better you get. Working with a good-looking girl always makes this kind of thieving much easier.

Halfway through that summer, we started to go on the rob every chance we got. Maca and I worked together only on the best shops, using my favourite method as used by Chike, where we removed three or four window panes high up that could be slid out, then in we went and cleared the lot. We only bothered with fashion shops with the latest denims tags that all the Cockneys wore. When we grafted with the Scousers, we were both learning their methods of thieving so it made sense to split up. Maca took to the zapping much better than me and was soon able to pickpocket solo, whereas I soon picked up the art of screwing tills. We all gave up our jobs – except Ged the Red, who was sacked for fighting with a few Spanish lads – but still lived on the staff lines, eating two or three times a day in the staff canteen. We even had chalet parties and invited the security – it was their job to kick us off the camp but they didn't even think about it, as a lot of them were up to all kinds of things, selling weed and whatever. There was many a snatch from the person carrying the night takings from the bars and shops over to the main office, until they brought in an outside security firm to collect the money.

The way we did tills then was a bit clumsy and my first ever one went pear-shaped. It had been a few years earlier in Manchester. On Sunday afternoons after the boozer, Eric and I would sneak into the blue movie cinema on Oxford Road, where we'd see a Swedish film and come out around ten o'clock to catch the last orders in Tommy Ducks, a top pub with hundreds of pairs of knickers pinned up on the ceiling. A lot of funky jazz bands played

there. This Sunday we left the bluey a bit early because
the film was so bad. We were on the third floor and saw
that the woman who collected the money had pulled the
shutter down and left her kiosk. We could see she'd left
the keys in the till, in a position we could reach through
the shutters. Without exchanging a word, we banged and
cleared the till, though in the excitement we made a lot of
noise and notes and coins fell all over the place. We
bolted down the staircase, past the women and all the
other staff, who were baffled by the sight of Eric and me
charging by holding pockets loaded with money. We
probably left half the cash in a trail behind us, but we
didn't care as it was such a thrill. We thought of it as the
crime of the century. On Oxford Road we both jumped
up and down, screaming with joy and in tears of laughter.
Instead of going up to Tommy Ducks we ran straight into
the Salisbury, at the bottom of the steps to Oxford Road
train station. What a booze-up we had. It was so obvious
we had just robbed the money that it was amazing the bar
staff didn't phone the dibble.

Anyway, we eventually got wind that the Bognor Old
Bill were onto our activities and were after us. So when a
couple of Colly lads visited us to escape the heat *they*
were under from the Manchester police, we all decided to
go to London armed with some sound Scouse wisdom.
We went to Marks and Sparks on Oxford Street, where
most of the tills were in fours in a square formation, so
were almost impossible to get to – we called them Fort
Knoxes. But next to the side exits were single tills which
could be banged, and even if the staff heard and put up
the scream, you could easily get away. I had sussed out
that when the person working on a till had a break, or
went to dinner, they just unplugged the till and did not
lock it with the set of keys they all had. They also emptied
the tills only an hour or less before closing. Within six

minutes of walking through the door we'd banged two tills, or Jacks, in one Marks and Sparks, then crossed Oxford Street to the other Marks and banged another few, like you do. A good thing about Marks and Spencer's tills was that the money was stood up in the drawer, making it faster to clear out; most tills had the money lying flat and secured with heavy clips.

We sacked the train back to Skeggy, as the weather was perfect, and instead went on an all-night bender in Soho after scoring a weed in the All Saints Road area, ending up in Ronnie Scott's jazz club. Next day we got into Skeggy around dinnertime and had a mooch down to the high street to suss out a few tills. Maca and I were picking up the Scouse lingo and decided to use our own words to replace theirs, as we sounded stupid speaking their slang. We called a weed or hash a 'Denis', which stands for Denis Law, while the Scousers called a smoke a 'draw'. This was perfect in the nick when you needed to ask your partner for a smoke – you'd just twist it around a touch and say, 'I haven't seen Denis for a bit.' Or you'd say, 'Tell Denis to come and see me.' It's a real Mancunian thing, as the King played for City and United, so everyone picked it up easy. A snatch, where you grab the takings going to a bank or an office, we called a 'Tony Hatch' after a big cheese on a Seventies TV talent show. After a bit it became simply a 'Tony'. A till was a 'Jack and Jill' and eventually just a Jack. When we opened the till we called it 'banging' and scooping the money was 'clearing out the Jack'. Scousers called the police 'bizzies'; One of our favourites from being kids was the Yank cartoon show *Top Cat* (renamed *Boss Cat* in the UK), in which the copper who was always messing things up for a crew of alley cats was called Officer Dibble. So we started to call the police the dibble – Maca and I lay claim to originating that one.

The safest way to do a till is for three grafters to go into a shop separately. One goes up to the till to buy something very cheap. It doesn't matter what you buy, as the intention is to win a bit of confidence from the person working the till. Then the blagger will throw in a line about something he might be interested in buying, but say that he needs some advice. Normally the shop worker will blindly co-operate and escort the blagger over to whatever he has asked about. One of the other two will then move in to cover the worker's line of sight to the till; there are many ways of doing this, such as holding up something nearby like a pair of pants or a jacket, while keeping your eyes out for other people who might clock what's going on. This is called blocking and it's as important to block Joe Public as it is members of staff, as they love to catch a robber or put the scream up. The other grafter will ask the blocker covering the till if it's sweet or safe to move, and when he gets the nod he'll hit the 'total' button while both grafters cough loudly to cover the sound of the till opening. The one who has banged the Jack will catch the drawer that has opened and wait for the blocker to give the all-clear before he takes the money out.

Depending on the situation, it's normally wise to leave a couple of notes in the till, as an empty draw is likely to bring on a steward's inquiry straight away. Even when you have the till open you sometimes have to close it before you can take the cash as someone's on to something going on. This happens more often in the small stores but isn't a massive problem. Even if the staff run over, you can always blag that you dropped something that must have touched one of the buttons and stay there while they check the takings. Often when this happens the worker will even go back away from the till if the blagger is good and so give a second chance for the Jack to be banged.

Back in Skegness, we sussed out the tills on the High Street and decided to go for one of them using the blag and the block. It worked a treat and before anyone was the wiser we were on our toes back to the Butlins camp. We jumped the fence and went straight round to Gagzy's chalet. It felt good splitting up the money whilst Gagzy went and got us a weed. After a smoke we went out to get some scran and ended up banging another till in the camp supermarket. There were six tills in a line at the exit to the shop and so we waited for one of the checkout women to go for a break. Three of us went to the till next to the empty one to pay for a bottle of milk I'd picked up. As soon as the checkout girl pressed the 'total' key on her till, one of the lads pressed the same button on another till with us covering him. I started to talk to the girl about something or nothing, allowing time for the other till to be cleared out. As the girl closed her draw, the Jack we'd banged was closed at the same time. It might not sound it but once you've done a few it's easy. Gagzy had also been on the rob and had screwed a few chalets. They really were so easy to do but it was very risky, as you could imagine what a full family of Yorkies would do to you if they caught you, before handing you over to the Dibble.

That night we all got off our heads in the bierkeller. Gagzy was drinking champagne out of a pint pot. I told him to stop, as even the proper drinkers were gobsmacked that he'd had three bottles to himself, but he was on a roll and was surrounded by some of the best girls on the camp. A bottle of champagne cost more than the weekly wage of most of the staff and there were a few daggers flying round, so we decided it was best to move on. We did another till in the camp and one in Skeggy and then headed down to Bognor for the last bit of summer sunshine, in high spirits and fully wedged up. The football season was due to start in two weeks and by the time the first game came around at Wolves we'd blown every penny we'd robbed, with the help of the Mickeys.

United beat Wolves comfortably and after the game we got away from the mob and jibbed a train in to New Street. Maca and I had arranged to meet up with a couple of hooligans for a piss-up: Malt (he loved whisky) from Birmingham City and Coke from Aston Villa, who'd travelled all over Europe with them. But we forgot the names of the two pubs they told us to meet them in and instead found a mean-looking pack of local thugs looking for aggro. Maca surprised me by taking me round all the sneaky back and side streets, then over to a cheap bed and brekkie where he was staying with his dad and uncle. His uncle had one of those mics that goes over your adam's apple so people can hear what you're saying; I think he'd had part of his windpipe removed because he had cancer of the throat. Still unable to remember where we were supposed to meet up, we decided to get out of Birmingham, but as we were making our way back to New Street we bumped into Malt, who was on his way to meet Coke. And so we had a top night out with all the same thugs who would have kicked the shit out of us given half the chance.

United's next away game was a midweek night match at Birmingham and Maca and I took a few of the Scousers with us. The last time United had played in Brum the police had cancelled all the trains to keep the mob away, so this time more Reds than normal travelled in a kind of protest, to say you'll never keep us away. At half-time, we went into the main bar and helped the Scousers zap a few wallets from the older fellers. They made it look so easy and nobody was any the wiser. As we came out at the end, a huge mob of Brum was waiting for aggro on this massive wasteland. I'll never forget the look on the Scousers' faces when we all charged over towards the

Brum brutes, as they had to make a quick decision: stay with us or try to make it back to New Street alone. They made the right call and stuck with us and were buzzing off the fighting all the way back to Bognor.

When we got back to the camp, Irene, who had sorted us out with chalets, told us she was going back to Glasgow, so was no longer able to keep us in digs. She'd also heard from the office that the police were preparing to do some swoops. Maca said he was back off to Manchester for a few days, but I didn't fancy it, so when Scouse Mac said he was up for a bit of travel, I suggested going over to France, as I had the address of a work agency in Paris who'd sorted out a friend of mine with a job a while back. So we went down to the station and bought two single tickets to Gay Paree for the very next day.

* * *

We rode the train to London, then to Dover for the ferry. Only when we tried to board the boat did we notice that our tickets were for the hovercraft from Ramsgate, not Dover. Typical. We finally made Paris nursing monster headaches after necking a couple of bottles of duty free Pernod – which I've never touched again. We then tried to score a Denis around the Gare Du Nord train station and almost got cut up by the French Algerians who grafted round there – they were real bandits. Mac said that hanging around for two more days until the work agency opened on the Monday was a no-no and suggested we get out of Paris while the going was good. He reckoned there was plenty of work down south grape-picking on the vineyards, so we jibbed a train to Bordeaux, which took almost two days. The conductors in France are sharp and don't see the funny side when you haven't got a ticket; we were thrown off a few trains.

We arrived to find that the grape-picking didn't start for another week, so we looked around and spotted a till in a bookshop that the woman owner kept leaving – but she always locked it and took the keys away. I suggested we just carry out the Jack, but after we had looked around for something else to rob, I noticed the same kind of till in a few other shops, one of which had the keys sweetly nestling in the lock. Mac blagged the worker's head to the side, while I leant over and took the keys. Then we went back to the first shop and waited around until she left her till again. By now we were worked up and even had a massive bag in which, if the keys failed, I'd be putting the till and taking it as it comes. We couldn't believe it when she went off for her break and the key fitted like a dream. It was a bit noisy when I banged the total button but Mac was down her end of the shop and dropped a load of books while coughing and spluttering away, which covered the noise. I cleared out the lot. We jumped in a taxi and could hardly keep down the excitement, feeling the size of this French wedge. It was almost £300, a bumper amount for us. We figured out we could have 2,000 pints and five ounces of weed if we got on the train and went straight back to Bognor.

Instead we went back to Paris and round to the work agency, who thought I was taking the piss when I asked if they knew where my friend was working now. They did sort us out with a job to start the next day in Dieppe, which was only a couple of hours away on the north coast. The job was apple-picking on a massive farm; we were over the moon when we got there, as we were among the first to arrive and could choose the best beds in a huge dorm. Within a couple of days, other young travellers arrived for work. We were not the only ones who liked to smoke a weed and we all enjoyed coming back after a long hard day in the fields to chill out with a few bottles of red wine and get stoned. After a week or so, Mac started to get careless with his work. When you had picked a certain amount of apples you had to put them into a huge crate, but it was important not to be rough with them because if one bruised, the full crate would. The gaffer had to use these bruised apples for cider, which meant the worker got only half the amount of money for picking them. This got right up Mac's nose, so he tried to get everyone to go out on strike with him: typical Scouser! This backfired and we both got the bullet, but not to worry as we still had most of the money left from the Jack and some wages to come.

We got on the booze and slept in a hotel with spot-on ham and eggs and French bread rolls for breakfast, then sailed from Dieppe to Newhaven and decided to head back to Bognor, where Miriam the Geordie let us put our things in her chalet. We mooched around the town and soon found out everyone had gone back home as the season was finished; only a load from the Salvation Army were left on the camp and a Scouser had robbed a few of their chalets the night before. He was one of Mac's mates and I bought the stuff off him, which was more to help him out as he needed the money to get home.

A friend of Miriam's from Doncaster, who'd just come down to see her, took a shine to me and let me stay in her room. So when the police burst in I was grateful for the night of sex, as I knew my time was up and it was something to dwell on when they put me in the cell. Yet amazingly I got bail, charged with handling the stolen stuff I'd bought from the Scouser. A few people had also stuck my name in over the screwing of the fashion shops and I'd broken my suspended sentence for the Post Office books. I had to be back in Chichester Magistrates Court in two weeks' time, but it gave me the chance to go back up to Manchester for a fortnight.

I met up with Gagzy, who had just left Lincoln jail after a few weeks locked up charged with robbing chalets at the camp. Maca and a few more had been nicked as well. They all got suspended sentences and fines. Gagzy and his dad had moved from Southern Drive into Burnet Close, one of those new, shit modern flats in which you can hear everybody and everything next door. Gagzy was telling me how he watched the bulldozers knocking down Southern Drive and was in tears, and I could fully understand, as those Flats were our own castles and everyone who lived in them was proud of how close it made us. It would take a couple more years before all the Flats were demolished.

That night we went to see Roxy Music at Belle Vue and what a top night we had. It was the first time we'd heard 'Love is the Drug' and I got a snog and a hip-grinder from a girl from Heywood called Denise, who said she'd keep in touch if I didn't go down for too long. After the concert we went to the Cotton Club, where we bumped into Smiler with her new boyfriend Colin Kelly. We ended up going for an Indian over near the newspaper office on Great Ancoats Street and I had a load more booze and a 'suicide' – a lethally hot curry – which was always a mistake. We used to call it a Johnny Cash, from his lyric 'burns, burns, burns like a ring of fire', for its effect the morning after. They even sold tee-shirts saying 'I Survived A Suicide'.

The week before court, I helped our Jimmy with his window cleaning. He had a steady round on the Racecourse Estate in Sale. It was his nice little earner on the side. I kept thinking about the film *Confessions of a Window Cleaner*, where the window cleaner sleeps with loads of different women, but after a full week's work I had not caught a blip of a woman, let alone anything else. On the last night before I was due to go back down to

Chichester, Scouse Mac came over and tried to reassure me about what was round the corner. He said Kelly, who I did the Post Office books with, was due out soon so maybe I'd get six to twelve months and he was sure I'd end up in Lewes, where he knew some Scousers who could sort me out. So at court I was gutted when the magistrate recommended a trip to borstal.

Chapter Eight

Banged Up

THEY SENT ME to Ashford youth prison near Heathrow Airport for borstal reports. This meant six weeks of being asked questions by the staff, who put you through it to assess if borstal was the right place for you. The jail itself was alright and the food was spot on, so good I'd happily have paid for it on the outside, though I'm sure the porridge left over from brekkie went into the soup.

A few kids were in for killing a tramp. They'd done it after seeing the cult film *A Clockwork Orange*, where in one scene a group of thugs out looking for aggro end up all kicking a tramp to death in the rain. The film got banned a few weeks later. I had two cellmates. Dave from Saint Albans was a young kid who wagged school and robbed a big house with some older kid. It came on top when the owner walked in while they were forcing open a briefcase with a screwdriver. Dave used the screwdriver on the owner so he could get away and the fella ended up dying, so Dave got Her Majesty's Pleasure, which meant his sentence could be from five years to life, depending on how he adapted to prison life. He was waiting to go to another youth jail, then he'd have to go through the system.

The other kid was a dread from Brixton in for drugs, who backed me up when I had my only bit of trouble in there. United played Arsenal and we watched it on the communal television. The priest had just been in to tell me my nana had died, and United were getting murdered 3–0; the Doc had dropped Alex Stepney and put in Paddy Roche, who was almost punching the ball into his own goal. Then out of nowhere Pancho Pearson scored a beaut of a volley in front of the Clock End, and all the Reds in the TV room reacted as did I. The trouble was, I was the only kid from the north and immediately got a couple of slaps from behind. It was coming on top when the dread stepped in and so the Cockneys left me alone.

In that first week my mum sent me a small parcel with soap, shampoo, a bit of backy and a box of Jaffa Cakes. This was her way of reminding me how she fed me Jaffa Cakes under the table while visiting me in Foston Hall detention centre five years earlier. She put in a letter saying she hoped I enjoyed my favourite toffees, Opal Fruits, but it wasn't until I opened one of them and found a nice piece of hash from our Mark that I realised what she was talking about. So the dread and I both looked forward to bang-up, as we were very much on the same wavelength and would make a nice joint to see the night out.

I went back to court in a taxi. We passed the billionaire Paul Getty's house and the man even had his own traffic lights at the bottom of his road so when he drove out they'd stop all the traffic; he never even had to think about braking but drove straight out and away. I got my duty lawyer to put up some kind of battle to get me a youth prison sentence, not a stretch in borstal, as it would mean less time inside and I wouldn't miss out on next year's summer season. The lawyer tried his bit but after a few words it was clear it was a waste of time and as he sat down they sent me to borstal for between six months and two years – your release date was determined by your behaviour inside. Because I got boxed off early I was able to get my head down for a few hours before we went in the van on a tour of all the courts, picking up and dropping off other prisoners, including two women we left inside Holloway, to cheering from us lot and shouts of 'lock up the broomsticks'.

It was late when we arrived at Wormwood Scrubs. The size of it was something else. It even had a full-size church in the middle of these massive single blocks. One block was only for very long-term prisoners and in there was some kind of IRA protest going on, so the reception area was full of screws slagging off the Irish. When it came to be my turn to go through the motions, changing clothes and giving your name and details, I got a few snide comments for being called Blaney. So I was well pleased to get over to the youth wing, where a few hundred others were waiting to get sent to different borstals. I was even more chuffed to find out we had our own individual light switch, so I could read for a while to tire myself out.

Next day at breakfast I was gutted to find out I was the only one from the North but happy to get sugar with the porridge. After a couple of weeks I asked to see the senior officer and put my case forward for a move up north, as I had been told I was going to Rochester, which was even further south than London. This would have made it almost impossible for people to visit me, plus plenty of goons from the Home Counties were starting to get on my case, giving it the 'Ay up lad, how's the black pudding?' and other bollocks. So I was well pleased to be given the nod for the next transport out the following week.

I was lucky to get the window seat on the coach. We got stuck in the early morning traffic because there was some kind of siege going on, so we could see all armed dibble creeping around getting in good positions. We reached Winson Green in Birmingham around dinnertime and everyone laughed at the screw who opened the main gate and allowed the coach to pass through: he was Asian, with the full turban wrapped round his head, yet he took all the stick in his stride, giving us lots of funny reactions. The scran came next, followed by a couple of hours waiting for another dozen prisoners to arrive for transport up north.

We drove down Princess Parkway into Manchester at teatime, which was excellent timing as the traffic was all backed up and we could look at women in cars and at the heads going in and out of the Moss Side shops. I recognised a couple of City fans. Facing the old Reno was a massive pub called the Big Alex and in one of the large entrances were three local dealers going about their business, with a queue of punters. It was one of the busiest hotspots in its day. Whenever Maca and I went to the Moss to score weed we went to see Black Lincoln or Smokey Joe, who was the original funky white wheeler-dealer, accepted on all the front lines in the Moss. Joe – who supplied coke to some of the world's top snooker players – and the likes of Tall Boy and Lincoln broke down the barriers for white guys like us from the north side to enjoy the late-night places in the Moss without hassle. But most white guys from the north side who liked the weed went to the small frontline at the bottom of Queens Road in Cheetham Hill, a shebeen called Banjo's.

Through the gates at Strangeways and they split us into two groups, the main lot being cons and the rest of us under-twenty-ones. As I walked up to the block, the first prisoner I saw finishing off his outdoor cleaning duty was Gagzy's brother Kevin. Now I knew I was home. He shouted that he'd see me in church, which made me feel good, like one of the boys, particularly as the kids I was with were all from outside Manchester. I soon saw a good few more familiar faces: Oggy from Salford, Steve Dale from Monsall, Bobby McCurdy from Burgin Drive, and Mark, a tall half-caste from Miles Platting who was in for some trouble up at Belle Vue, where he'd put an axe over a skinhead's bonce; the skinhead got up, wiped the blood off his head, grabbed the axe off Mark and chased him halfway round Gorton. Mark said he was so relieved to get nicked, as the red mist had descended on the skinhead and he couldn't run him off. He introduced me to his mate Tet-T, a dipper from Wythenshawe who was his crime partner on the out. Both had got their first borstal as well, so all four of us soon hung around together.

The four of us were told we'd be on the first coach out in the New Year to Stoke Heath borstal in the Midlands, which was rumoured to have a new wing with toilets in all cells. The borstal wing at Strangeways was bollocks, as you had to make up a bed and kit pack and leave it that way all day. The screws could creep up on you at any time and if they caught you lying on your bed you were in big shit. I got a job preparing and dishing out food from the kitchen and cleaning up after meals. We got all the choice food, which was a result, as generally it was the worst I'd ever come across. Everyone used the soup for gravy and they made the stalest bread you could imagine; the rock buns we gave out with the mug of tea around seven o'clock at the cell doors were often knocked back as inedible. The stew was known as boomerang because it came right back through you.

Because our dorm was downstairs next to the kitchen, sometimes the screws would leave us alone and we played cards for hours. It's not always easy to get on with screws in the nick, but they seemed happy with this arrangement and one of them used to tell Mark who the nonces were – the prisoners locked up for sex with kids. Mark had a spell as the landing cleaner so he had a lot of free time to move around and crack the nonces whenever he got the chance.

Lads on the block spent hours tattooing each other. I tattooed tears coming down the face of one Geordie lad; I didn't want to do it but he insisted and even paid me a few cigs. Many kids tattooed their borstal numbers or the borstal spot high on a cheekbone. Some put three small dots between the thumb and finger to let people know they'd done three months in a DC; if they'd done six months the three dots were on both hands. Another one popular down south was five dots on the same part of the hand, the five standing for: find 'em, follow 'em, feel 'em, fuck 'em and forget 'em! The Geordies were the worst of all for homemade tattoos and all said how proud they were that lads from Newcastle used more ink on their bodies than anyone else. The ink was smuggled in in condoms. The worst tattoo of all was the 'borstal glove' made up of hundreds of black dots covering the hand; it looked a pure black mess, but the Geordies loved it.

A few days before Christmas, my mum came in with another little treat from our Mark and also brought me in a little radio with earplugs, which made life more bearable. The big tune was 'Bohemian Rhapsody' by Queen and I was able to get right into the sport as well. We got to watch two films, one of which was Bruce Lee's *Enter The Dragon*, which had everyone making chicken noises and launching high kicks back in their cells.

Shortly afterwards they bussed us out to Stoke Heath, which is in Market Drayton in the West Midlands, and the rumours turned out to be true: they'd built two new sections, E and F wings, and they were the dog's danglies. They had first-class showers and a TV room with a dartboard at the back, a table tennis room which I dreamed of and even a room with newspapers, magazines and a record player. We were allowed five albums each, so I got sent in the first two Roxy albums, a couple by the Beatles and *Band On The Run*, the big one from Paul McCartney's Wings. Bobby got a cushy number on reception while me, Mark and Tet-T were sent to work in the manufacturing workshop, making cell doors for jails in the Middle East. The job included bits of everything: filing, cutting sheets of metal, painting and welding. For a break, a lot of kids would take off their face shields to get what we called a flash, which burnt your eyes so badly that you'd have to lie down for five or six days with special ointment. It was agony and no kid ever did it twice. One of the Scouse zappers from Kirkby called Fitzy, a little carrothead with a massive LFC tattoo on his dipping hand, started to rob the thinners and the hand cleaner to sell to kids to sniff.

My pad mate was Ken Senior, or Sen, from Barnsley, the black pudding capital of the world. He'd never been outside his home town until being sent down for a motorbike accident that killed his best mate. Sen had steel pins in his legs to hold them together, which gave him a wicked limp. He worked down the coal pit and every weekend he'd get into fights, but until the accident he'd never been involved with the dibble, so when he arrived on the second coach from Strangeways he was a big pussycat, without any knowledge of the scallies, bullies, drugs and screws that made up the borstal system. For weeks he was bullied. I kept telling him he'd have to throw his hammers about, otherwise it would really come on top. Some bullied kids slashed their wrists so they could get shipped out, but Sen's head was not in that state yet. Eventually he took my advice. The first guy who copped for it was a Pakistani kid from Moss Side; Sen flipped and properly shed blood. He then did a Scouser at breakfast and no-one fucked with him again; we put it round that he was the Daddy and that's how it was all the way through our sentences. Sen loved to work out every night and would pose in front of the mirror and ask me to punch him in his six-pack belly. Fair play, he never flinched no matter how hard I hit.

We had a big kit inspection on Saturday mornings and most people worked hard to get their pads spotless, as they gave prizes for the cleanest cells, which everyone chipped in for on a Friday. The cleanest pad got an ounce of Old Holborn baccy and the second cleanest got a massive cream cake covered with fruit. Sen and I won second prize a few times. On Saturday nights everyone from the wings went to the gym to watch a film. This was the best time of the week, with many of the lads being high on a blow of weed. The smoke situation was grim during the week, but Saturdays were almost a cert to score a Denis as visits were allowed in the afternoon and some kids were let out with their families to Market Drayton village for a few hours.

Many of the other lads hated wings E and F, mainly because we had individual toilets and each pad had a separate light switch, but the lads from D wing in particular had the raging hump because most of the older heads were put there and they thought they should have the best pads, although they did have a snooker table. These were older kids who'd broken the terms of their release licence and were back for their second whack; some were in for a third lot and a few had spent four or five years doing borstal training. A way of giving out stick was to grab hold of a kid's nose using your strongest fingers, give it a real good old squeeze and a shake and then twist it as hard as you could. Budgie, one of the older heads from D wing did it to me because I captained the team that took the monthly sports shield off them and God it was painful – my nose looked like someone had bitten the end.

I had my first visit over Easter and it was my old feller, who walked into the visiting room doing his boxing moves, catching me all over the place with punches and saying how he could have made a decent boxer out of me. He said he was doing all right and gave me a few tips about playing draughts, like always play from the left, which really did improve my game. He slipped me a pound note under the table and said not to worry about writing, as he knew himself it can become very boring as a youth in borstal. Rather than try to write letters when you have nothing to say, he suggested I make postcards with pictures from magazines to send to the people who were in my thoughts, to let them know I was thinking about them. It was great advice and made keeping in touch with people much easier.

Letters arrived from Scouse Mac and Kelly. They were talking about going back down to the camp for the summer season. Our Mark also penned a few lines to say how the Sale Reds were geared up for the FA Cup quarter-final at Wolves, which United won 3–2 after being two goals down. United got through the semi against Derby at Hillsborough, beating them 2–0, and played Southampton in the final. I was glued to the radio and even Sen was right up for United that day, so I was gutted when Southampton scored the winner in the last five minutes. I got a letter from Maca a couple of days later describing how he'd watched the game in the pub with the lads and when Southampton slotted the decisive goal home he'd smashed a bottle of whisky on the floor.

In the evenings we all had a choice of night class: weightlifting, which was most popular, rugby, with a proper game once a month, or learning German, which I tried and which was a waste of time. I also took art lessons and thought the woman teacher was interested in me, as she was always saying if I behaved I'd be given work outside, where they give you a bike and a packed lunch and you work on the screws' houses, sweep the paths or clean out their fishing pool. I was baffled by the thoughts that kept coming into my head every time I spoke to her and I was right: she did have a soft spot for someone, it just wasn't me. It was a kid from Wakefield who we all hated, as he was always sucking up to the screws. They got caught at it in the classroom and she was either sacked or moved on to another place in the youth system.

In May 1976, just after my twentieth birthday, my mum brought me a birthday parcel. The probation woman from Sale drove her up so the parcel wasn't checked and contained boxes of Jaffa Cakes and the top Opal Fruits from our Mark. At the beginning of July, I got a visit from Maggie and Sue from the camp; they were working at the Amsterdam Hilton and were home on a fortnight's holiday. They kept in touch with loads of people down at the camp and were full of stories. Scouse Mac and Geordie Miriam were now a couple and Glasgow Irene had been promoted to supervisor. Maggie and Sue had called through London on their way up and got free haircuts from Vidal Sassoon, so they both looked like top darlings and when Maggie kissed me at the end she passed me a piece of hash she'd been keeping in her mouth. They were both going off to see the new big film *One Flew Over the Cuckoo's Nest* and the next week they sent me the book to read.

At the end of July we all got our release dates and for the lucky ones there was home leave. They dropped you off at Crewe Station on a Thursday and you didn't have to be back until Monday. I was due for release in the middle of September but we were all more interested in who was getting home leave. Sen was the first, then Mark and Tet-T were told they were not getting any, a real bummer. Bobby was down the block ready to get shipped out, as he'd been sussed selling prison-issue striped shirts, which were in demand as they were heavy duty cotton, lasted years and looked even better when faded. I got the thumbs-up for the week after Sen and was jumping up and down thinking about getting on the razzle back in Bognor. That night Sen asked me to tattoo a star on his ear; he'd never spoken about wanting a tattoo before but I think the occasion got to him and he wanted something to show for his time at borstal. When Sen came back from leave he was buzzing, showing me new moves he'd learnt on the dance floor and describing all the girls he'd seen. He had also sunk a fair few pints in Crewe Station before being met by the screws. Hearing all this made me gate happy, particularly when I got a letter from Scouse Maca saying Irene had gone back to Glasgow but had spoken to her mate who worked in the chalet office and she had sorted me and Collyhurst Maca out with a chalet for three days, with a staff pass so we could use the canteen and pass through the main entrances.

It was a sunny day when I got off the train in Sale and straight away our Jimmy took me for a few pints in a Boddingtons pub. I gave him a baccy tin that I'd been making for weeks out of matchsticks; a kid from the art class painted two Red Devils on it with a Celtic crest on the top. I then headed round to Syl's for a big fry-up but she had bad news: all my best stuff that I'd asked her to wash and get ready for my trip to Bognor had been robbed off the washing line. I was gutted. I called round to see Grandad and then headed for Ardwick to meet Gagzy in a new pub by the Apollo Theatre. Eric and Maca came in and we all went to Papas, better known as 'Snappers' in its heyday, and bumped into Smiler, who gave me a picture of my son Lee.

Next day, Maca and I jibbed the train to London, then
the tube to Victoria to get the rattler, which is what we
now called the train, down to Bognor. Over the camp
fence we went and straight round to the staff lines. The
first person we saw was Miriam. Before I had a chance to
give her a hug, she burst out crying and almost collapsed
as she blurted out that Scouse Mac was dead. We went to
her chalet and she told us he'd gone out on the town and
taken some speed and when he came back he'd collapsed
on the bed, out of it. Miriam put the scream up and a
couple of people tried to give him mouth-to-mouth but it
backfired and gave him a heart attack. That night was
very sad, with all kinds of people coming over to me with
sympathy and doing my head in, so the next day we got
the rattler back to Manchester. I stayed up on the
Racecourse Estate and got hammered day and night. I
saw my grandad for dinner on the Monday and then
headed for Crewe, where the screws were waiting to pick
me up. My head was so cabbaged I forgot I'd told my old
feller I'd go round to see him, but I had only another
month to do so I figured he would understand.

When I got back and went through reception they handed
me a new set of clothes; they'd changed what we wore
from the old thick itchy army stuff to horrible bright
colours, though the fabric felt much softer. Sen and Mark
understood that my head had gone west and gave me space
and a few days to get over the disaster of my home leave. I
got a boost when a screw came in and told me I was to be
allowed to work outside. So in my last few weeks I would
go over to reception after breakfast each day to pick up my
bike and a packed lunch and then go out doing odd jobs on
my own. This was what I needed to think straight. I
decided I would not return to Bognor and also thought it
might be an idea to rein in travelling with the Red Army
and all the nickings that came with the territory.

Still, as soon as the chance came I went to Old Trafford. All the lads now stood up in the top corner of the Scoreboard Paddock, which had a bar. I felt part of something when everyone started singing and bouncing around on the wooden decking. There was now a proper little crew of grafters: Maca, Marshy and Tommy Gun were all making a bob or two at the matches. Some would do dips at our end, others would do sneaks and tills in the town before the game, then pickpocket at the match and after.

Before games we went for a few pints around the Piccadilly area, generally downstairs in the Mitre Bar, the Brunswick or the Waldorf near the approach. After the game, we'd meet in the main bar below Piccadilly Radio station – we called it the Dive Bar. They had a decent select bar upstairs with a rounded corner and a nice interior from which you could see endless people running for buses. There was never any trouble in this part, even though downstairs was full to the brim with Cowboys, Cockney Reds and Lancashire boys. I often met Geoff the Greaser from Nottingham in here; we'd been in Foston Hall together and he was always rat-arsed. The Dive Bar was the kind of place a mob could take over, which worked both for the people running the place and for us punters, as we'd spend a lot when we were all out on a bender and on Saturday nights lots of the lads' women would meet us there.

I was determined to stay sensible and decided not to travel away with the Red Army, although I still went to the big home games. I was also cutting out the booze in midweek and keeping my head down. I went back working at Clean Walls and was able to save a few quid, helped because I'd cut down on the weed too. I saved enough money to buy my first sound system, a Rotel with Wharfedale speakers, and got right into Bob Marley, the

Brothers Johnson and ELO. But at Gagzy's twenty-first I let myself go. He had a full freemans spread and a disco and I ended up rolling round on the rug in his living room with Denise from Heywood. She had hinted earlier in the evening that she wanted to spend the night with me so I'd gone off and had a few extra pints with chasers to calm the nerves. I passed out on the floor next to her and was woken the next morning by the front door slamming and her stiletto heels running down the driveway. When I got my senses together I realised I'd slashed in my kecks and that was the end of that.

Chapter Nine

The Salford Lads

I WAS PISSED off. After a long talk with Gagzy we decided to try our luck and wrote off to the camp at Bognor, asking for a job that Christmas. We could hardly believe it when a week later we got the green light and a free coach ticket with a start date in a fortnight.

The night before we were due to head south we got steaming in the Manhattan, then nipped over to the Electric Circus on Collyhurst Street. This was the old Palladium, with Scotch Steve and Hughie on the door. It was a mad gaff: sometimes when you were sat on the toilet the door would be flung open by a Hell's Angel or a biker wanting the space to crank up drugs. We got to know Kevin O'Brien, a Gorton Blue who worked upstairs serving hot pies with one hand and holding a rounders bat in the other to keep everyone in line. 'OB' spoke well, was clean and fit and could handle himself working in a bearpit like this. He was a grafter too: he used to steal the pies that he sold from Marks and Spencer, and would knock out wraps of whizz with them. He would also do the top gold shops; because he looked the part, after his bit of patter they'd get out the best tray of diamond rings, which Kev would snatch as clean as a whistle. The problem was, he forgot about one thing: he'd tattooed the symbol of *The Saint* on his hand at approved school and when the police burst in on him early one morning they grabbed hold of his right hand and said, 'You're nicked, Simon Templar!'

That night Gagzy decided to take some strong speed that was being passed around and when we came out of the Electric Circus he was still full of life, giving it, 'What's our next move chaps?' He decided to rip down a huge poster from a billboard – his bedroom was full of posters he'd taken from walls and boards all over. This one was way up above some exit doors. He started to scale the wall and managed to get onto the ledge below the poster, but as he tried to edge along he froze. Before I had a chance to stop him, he made a bid for freedom and leapt off the ledge, trying to grab hold of a lamppost on the way down. The noise he made when he hit the ground was sickening. I ran over and he'd busted his ankle in a major way. I got an ambulance, convinced that he had cracked his head when he hit the deck and that he was on his way out. He limps to this day and has never taken any drug besides weed since.

I went over to Maca's to see if he wanted to take Gagzy's forms and to work with me over Christmas at Butlins. Mac had not been with us in the Electric Circus because he was barred – the management put all the purses and wallets that had been going west down to him. When we got to the camp it was good to see Irene, who gave me a key for her chalet, one of the best with a double bed and an inside shower. In Bognor town we met up with some of our Scouse grafting pals, who'd just done a really hairy sneak. One of them, Tommy from Huyton, had a Leo Sayer hairdo and was driving round in a Jag with a nice flat already sorted for the winter, so we drove back there for a quick weed. The next few days were amazing: chalet parties nonstop. How we worked I don't know but we did and with our wages and tips we were right on it again. A few of us started boozing outside the camp and were buzzing, with lots of banter and people letting on to you.

New Year was spent back up north at George's in Miles Platting. George worked at Watneys and brought a few crates of Special Brew home. This was my first ever session with the Golden Can and the next morning my head had a wee fella in it banging away with a lump hammer, the unmistakable leftovers of the Brew. After a coupe of months back with Clean Walls, Maca and I hit Blackpool for Easter. Our first stop was the Yates's on the front and then the Manchester Arms, where we met up with a crew of Salford, with a few faces I recognized from United. Rabbi was a real Brit bulldog, with two MUFCs tattooed on each side of his neck, 'Born Free' on his hands and a borstal star on his left ear. He was small and stocky with a very cocky style of walking and talking and had a huge razor scar across his left cheek. Rab was a top shoplifter in the town and had just had a crazy escape at Lewis's department store. He had crept along a ledge from the stairwell and into the stock room, where he'd loaded up with gear. As he was climbing back out of the window onto the ledge, he got clocked and the scream went up. Sharp as you like, he slung the gear back and turned it into a suicide bid! They turned out the fire brigade and a priest was called, who said prayers and pleaded with him not to jump. Rab lived with his grandad in the old flats off Eccles New Road and told us about all the fights on the cobbled streets and that the police weren't interested in getting involved.

Jimmy Miller looked like Spencer Tracy and wore that same light brown Crombie overcoat. He'd just come out of borstal; they had sent him round almost every one, as he did like to fight and so ended up doing the full whack. He had started boxing at the YMCA but was already switching his fighting to United games, even though his team was West Ham. I later saw him leading the charge down Warwick Road into a load of Scousers, brandishing a massive dildo (it's true), not long before he got a lump of jail for smacking a policewoman at Euston. He got another four for pulling a gun on Market Street and a further seven after the Strangeways Riot. We got to know Jimmy well over the years. When you were out on the rob with him, if you couldn't sneak the money Jimmy would just take it anyway. I once went into a shop on the Salford Precinct with him. The tune 'Money' by Pink Floyd was playing and there was lots of noise from the shoppers and the tills and Jimmy was singing away while banging the jack without asking for any cover or someone to blag the assistant. He cleared the lot and smashed the till shut, then strolled out still singing with the full shop staring and the manager scratching his head thinking it was a *Candid Camera* job.

Then there was Lezzo the Lisp, whose dad was a wrestler, and Freaky Fred, who we'd seen out of it in the Electric Circus. He was very slim with a big mop of blond hair and always sounded like he was stoned. He had a walk like one of the Freak Brothers, which were the feature of a big Yank comic for drugheads. The thing about Fred was, over the next two years he came out with all us thugs and he was the complete opposite, as he was so laid back, which seemed to many people freaky, hence the name. Yet when there was trouble brewing he'd be egging on everyone to get properly stuck in, out of his brains after sniffing glue or gas. Steve Murphy, better known as Spud, was even smaller than Rab with loads of tattoos and a huge mass of blond hair as big as the Scottish defender Gordon McQueen's. He was another United nut. The year before, Spud was nicked over in Belgium when United hit town. I remembered seeing him on the news on his way to the jail with another eight or nine Reds after court. A few weeks later the cameras were on them again when they got deported and Spud did a classic Brit and stuck two fingers up at the lot of them. Spud had lived as a kid for some years over in the States and was telling us how bad it was when he returned to live in Salford with a Yank accent and got his head slapped around at school. Around that time we were all wearing Stan Smith trainers but Spud wore top-of-the-range, leather US All Stars, the first brand of basketball trainers in the world.

This mad Salford crew would become big mates of ours over the next few years and would join us in the grafting game all over Europe.

Suddenly Spud started to shout abuse to another kid who'd just come in; he was one of Salford's most hated City fans. Dicko was always hanging around Piccadilly with a little crew sniping off lone Reds. He had also been seen running into a pub and cracking a pint pot over some Yorkie Red's head. He always wore a donkey jacket with a Kellogg's logo on the back and had all the usual homemade mess on his arms and hands, which he'd done in borstal. He wasn't the brightest and the tattoo across his right, fighting hand had NCFC instead of MCFC! But everyone agreed to forget about things for the night and we started a serious booze-up. After beer and whisky, Dicko told Spud and the rest that he had to get off buses at the wrong stops and make his way back home via crazy routes, as he was hunted high and low round Salford. We couldn't stop laughing.

The next lad to bowl in was Sully, who immediately burst out slagging Dicko, calling him 'Kacky Eye' and asking what he was doing on the firm. Dicko did have a dodgy eye that went funny when he got pissed and some people took offence, as it looked like he was growling at you when he wasn't. Sully and Dicko knew each other from the Oasis shopping gaff next to the Arndale and a neat pub round the corner called the American Disaster. A lot of thieves hung out in the downstairs lounge selling stuff and it was always full to the brim with mad gamblers who blew a lot in the nearby bookies and drunks from all over. One feller in there would draw your face even when you weren't aware and you'd get him a pint. The drawings were first class yet the feller never spoke a word to a soul other than the barman. Sully worked on the Oasis part time for Scotch Steve, who was still in charge of the door at the Electric Circus. Steve's stall sold all the best stuff.

Sully came from Little Leeds, which is what some people called Wythenshawe, as from certain parts of Manchester it was quicker to travel to Leeds than it was to go to Benchill in the middle of Wythenshawe, where Sully lived. He never looked like the thug he was but seemed more like a student from the arty side. Dicko took great pleasure in suggesting Sully looked like a faggot and grinding it down his neck, all in good fun of course. Sully had been nicked a few weeks before with some others in the infamous Wythenshawe War Wagon, one of those big yellow buses that was used to get handicapped kids to schools that was pawned out for the big away games and was always full of timebombs. Sully showed us the newspaper clippings. Later he got stabbed in the back at Wolves and kept the same shirt on for a week so we could all see the holes and blood and where he'd been stitched up.

Sully started turning the key in everyone's back, winding them up saying there were a few crews of Geordies walking up and down the front looking for trouble while we were sitting there getting bladdered. Maca and I were not looking good by now on the cashflow so we went out for an hour but couldn't find anything to rob. In a final attempt we tried our luck in a secondhand shop, but the fella caught me creeping in to the back room, so I twisted it by taking off my leather coat and asking if he wanted to buy it. I said I thought I might be able to sell it and thought the back room was another part of the shop. The feller looked at me and said, 'What a load of bollocks!' but he still bought the coat for £20, even though it was worth over a hundred. It was well enough to see me and Maca through that night.

When we got back, all the lads were up for looking for these mystery Geordies, so we had another few pints and took a walk down the front. A police van drove past and the coppers looked interested in us bouncing round causing a nuisance of ourselves. The next minute they got out of the van so we started running down these side streets and got split up. Sully's first move was to pick up an empty milk bottle and slip it into his large inside pocket, then he took off one of his socks and put a load of change in it, tying a knot so it was a decent cosh. I didn't really see a problem, then he reminded me about the Geordies and somehow had me starting to believe they were out there, so I took off my Levi belt to use as a lash if required. We went back on to the front and spotted a mob of lads coming our way and neither of us liked the look of them, so we slipped into a hotel on the front and sat at the bar hardly able to breathe, sure we were going to get done in. The landlady came over and asked what drinks we wanted and I started to settle down. It was a nice and safe bar with a mega view of the front so we could see Maca and Co. if they appeared. After half an hour, a girl came into the bar fuming. Turned out she was with a group from Chorley, all pissed, and had just caught her best mate in bed with her bloke.

'No way,' says Sull.

'Fucking telling you,' she says. 'Come over here and I'll show you.'

We took our drinks downstairs to a small flatlet where, sure enough, this feller was riding like the clappers with her so-called best mate. Straight away me and the Sull strip, as she's out for revenge on her cheating feller and wants to do the biz. The funniest thing was, Sully's milk bottle rolled out onto the rug.

'What the fuck's that?' she said.

'For that fucker's head if he steps out of that bed,' said Sull.

'No danger, lads,' responded the feller. 'I'm ret as rain here boys, enjoy yersens and give her one for me!'

* * *

Sully and Dicko started coming to the Electric Circus, where punk rock was really kicking off. Although I'd promised myself I'd not travel with the Red Army, it wasn't long before I was also back into all the away games. I was cleaning offices in Sheffield when United drew Leeds in the FA Cup semi-final at Hillsborough. On the day of the match, my boss Alex came to Sheffield to see how I was doing and, while I worked, spent two hours on the client's office phone to his relations in Australia. Alex had not been to an away game for a few years, so I told him that we still all went into the other team's end but that it was not as blatant as it used to be. The police were getting better, though it was still not that hard to get past them in small groups, as none of us wore colours anymore. Then we'd meet back up again around the top area of the terraces so at the chosen moment we could charge down into them. This was Plan A for the next couple of seasons; Plan B meant it was every man for himself.

We made our way to the train station and met Maca and the lads off the one o'clock train. We had a few pints then jumped on two buses down to the ground. We were over 100-strong. Maca and I cut off from the mob to look for a quick earner and caught this local fella unloading boxes of programmes from his van near the main entrance. Maca soon had a load of Reds chanting and singing, bringing them into the path of this poor feller and he lost the lot. Most of the Barmy Army were just ripping them up, kicking them and throwing them in the air, but we got a grip of a few full boxes. We went right into the United end and sold a couple of boxes at the price printed, then went and got hold of one of the many ticket touts – lads like No-Neck Frank, Skinner, Swift Neck and Dirty Neck – to flog the rest cheapo, as it was around half two now and time to get over and into the Leeds end.

We got in but couldn't see any faces we knew, so we went up the stairs to the top of the open terrace. Immediately we heard, 'On then!' and it kicked right off. We always shouted that when we made our first move and then either 'Come on then!' or 'Let's go!' United were to the right of us and what a joy to hear our lot chanting, 'Come on then,' as they steamed right into Leeds. Maca and I slipped to the side and the first head we saw fighting his way through was George Lyons, whacking a few Tykes with a crutch he'd taken off someone. Within five minutes, 3,000 Reds were together in their end, chanting and taking the piss. Alex was soon over, buzzing at the violence, and we all went potty when United scored the first goal.

At half-time Alex strolled down the stairs to the toilet and then went for some pie and chips, but being inexperienced he forgot to keep with the mob. He'd also borrowed my jacket, which had a United pin on the top pocket, so he got a good slap and came back with a bumper lump glowing and growing away. United scored another goal and though Leeds won a penalty towards the end they couldn't save the game and their fans went quiet. Plenty of life came back into them at the full-time whistle and they made a big push from behind. Leeds were now in control of the top of the terracing and their surge had both their lot and our lot falling over each other on the way to the bottom exits. We got split into small groups outside and then Leeds piled out with a full-strength mob. We were on our toes.

I saw a small black fella dressed in a green boilersuit giving a Red a real good kicking; the kid, who was called Pooley, had to scramble underneath a parked van to get away. We all turned round and had a charge at them but Chalkie at the front was stabbed in the shoulder blade by the same green boiler suit. The police started to get involved but had little effect as Leeds got their revenge, pushing us all the way back into the centre and then on to the train station. As we split off to get the train home, up popped the green boiler and shouted to me, 'Now then Beaner!' He'd broken through the police escort and as he got closer I recognised him as Charlie, a black kid from Chapeltown who I'd met in borstal. It was a happy high to wish each other the best and we went for a drink. Chalkie passed off his stab wound as only a scratch but Charlie had the last word: 'Don't worry Manny, I'll refresh it for you next time.'

When we got back to the train station a couple of hours later a few Leeds were still milling about but we just gave them verbal abuse as we were now in party mood. Back in Manchester, Alex got a pull from the police, just the normal run through, but it came up that he was wanted over a shotgun shooting outside the Reno in Moss Side a few months before. So he had a hectic return to the terraces, particularly as he ended up getting borstal for being involved in the shooting.

The 1977 Cup final was against Liverpool, who had just won the League and were booked to win the Euro Cup the next week. 'Only a Red Devil can stop a Treble' was the best-selling tee-shirt in town and United went into that final with nothing to lose. On the Friday morning, Maca and I met Sully in our new HQ and early meeting point, the Blackbird cafe off Oldham Street. We had sorted out a wages snatch from a kid who was going to let us take the money off him after we'd given him a few digs. We waited for him to show up round the corner from the bank but instead two giants collected the wages; he had obviously bottled it when it came to the crunch and turned out to be a total timewaster.

Maca said he'd get in one of the vans that would be going to London around midnight, so Sully and I jumped a bus to Altrincham and got a lift from a load of Devils all the way to Euston. There were trainloads of Mancs and Scousers pulling in all day and into the evening and from one Liverpool train a kid pulled a gun out on the first group of United he saw. The police steamed in but the kid got away – but it revved everybody up. Sully knew Keith, one of Tottenham's main thugs, who lived at Neasden, the nearest tube stop to Wembley. We called round to see him and he was made up and said he would take us out and put us up. I was surprised at the money his mates had – they all had the latest sports cars and owned their own flats and were pure Spurs nutters. They took us on a full tour of all the nightlife in North London, and as Spurs were my second team after United – Jimmy Greaves was the best sneak thief ever when it came to nicking goals – I could hold a sensible conversation on Tottenham, while Sully sang United songs all night. Next day Keith dropped us off at a big pub, where George said he'd seen Scouse

Kelly, the lad I'd done the Post Office books with at Bognor. Kelly had been laughing and claiming Liverpool were certs for a win but we thought different and when United scored the first goal I knew the Cup would be coming back to Albert Square, even when Jimmy Case equalised. Lou Macari scored the winner and it never mattered that it got a nice touch from a Liverpool defender. It was Tommy Doc's finest hour – and his last at United. A few weeks later he was sacked.

After the game, Dicko came over to Keith's and brought a nice chunk of hash, so we had an hour relaxing while listening to all the new funk stuff, George Clinton with Bootsy Collins and Parliament. We ended up in the West End in the Cockney Pride pub; it was ours for the last hour as the staff gave up, with Reds singing draped in flags, hanging off ledges and stood on top of tables. The dibble blocked off the traffic on one side of Leicester Square, then lined up a load of police outside with horses and dogs. It took them over an hour to get us all out at midnight. Finally our mob went down to Trafalgar Square to jump in the water, like they do on New Year, but there were packs of Cockney thugs from every team wanting to have a go. Sully and Dicko kicked it off and started a full-scale riot; the Cockney Reds led the charge and took over the show, as only a handful of Mancs remained by then.

Keith dropped us off at Euston around eight in the morning, where Coco and the rest were still drinking cans. The trip back was spot-on: the ticket inspector left us all alone, knowing not one of us had a ticket, and one lad even copped for a shag on the train. When we hit Manchester the weather was still fantastic so we made our way to Albert Square, where a crowd had gathered to watch the bus with the Doc and the team, all dressed in those wicked white suits. Seeing them made everything worth it, the good and the bad for all those years, even if it was the only thing we won all the way through the Seventies! What a night we had, ending up in a punk hangout next to Foo-Foo's Palace called the Ranch. I fell asleep on the night bus back to Sale and was woken by a young girl called Bev, who'd seen me around and knew I lived on the Racecourse Estate. Her dad was a well-known Nigerian guy from the Moss. I walked with her down the Avenue, a tree-lined street where God's police chief, Jim Anderton, lived, to the border of the estate, where I asked if she fancied a date. She agreed. Little did I know we'd be together for seven stormy years.

It was my twenty-first the following week, so I took Bev out with the lads to a club called Kloisters on Oxford Road, better known as Harry Oysters or Harry O's, where we'd started to go at the end of the night. The first time we went was on a stag night that turned into a full-scale battle with the doormen, but things had settled down since then. Harry's was good every night. It had two big bars with lots of separate places to sit and there was one part where you could sit and skin up a joint. At the back was a wine bar with good deals on certain shorts and the dance floor was a classic, as it had full-sized knights in armour on each side, with their weapons on show. Harry's turned into a pure United stronghold and there wasn't a firm around who could take liberties with any of the Reds in there. But the City fans that came in regularly were in no danger of being jumped, as they used to join up with us to fight the coaches that came to the big club on Oxford Road called Rotters. These coaches came from parts of Cheshire and Lancashire where we knew they supported Scouse, so any coaches from the 'pudding area' were all due a proper dig.

The hardest fights happened in Chinatown, where we sometimes went after Harry's. If we had any money left we'd go for a curry at the Star of India, near Tiffany's, but if we were on our arses it would be the all-night Greek chippie, which sold food till four o'clock in the morning. We'd normally get pie and chips with curry sauce and take a stroll through Chinatown, pissing and gobbing away like young kids. It didn't take much to upset the Chinks. They were all well slippery and we gave up trying to fight them with our hands and feet, as it would take three or four of us to get one of them off us. I always used my big heavy Levi belt to lash them and others picked up sticks or bottles. One Chink who really lost it and chased us into the bus station ended up taking a beating from the dibble, who saw it as the only way they could nick him.

*   *   *

The new football season started as usual at Wembley with the Charity Shield, United against Liverpool. I went down in a stolen car with Maca, and once there we linked up with the lads and saw Dicko. He'd started a bit of ticket touting for Big Carl, so we soon had tickets. Sir Matt and Bob Paisley went round the ground on an open-topped cart waving to both sets of fans, hoping to take the sting out of the hate. It was Dalglish's debut and the game was a tight draw, the only time I've not seen or even heard about any fighting between United and Scouse.

I took Bev down to the Notts Castle pub in Collyhurst for an engagement party. Bev was gobsmacked at how everyone took each other's cigs without asking and the way everyone was pissed and swearing, enjoying themselves. After that we went to Snappers and, well, it wasn't the image Bev was looking for. To show her another side of me, I took her the following week to see the Real Thing at the Kings Hall. Unfortunately they had an offer on cans of a strong malt beer called Breakers, and at the interval I bumped into the Rabbi and Co., who were on top form busting away at these tins. I helped them out and after half an hour went back upstairs to find Bev, as I was really up for a dance. We started dancing but I didn't know that behind me Rab had brought the full firm over, who all joined in around us. This was the first time Bev had seen the Salford lot. I wobbled over to the bar and got hammered that bad I couldn't remember Bev carrying me out for the taxi. She told me I was kippered in the front seat all the way to Sale.

Our relationship would continue like that for the next seven years. We really did love each other but she couldn't handle my lifestyle or how I earned a living, and couldn't stand any of my friends, so seven years was quite an achievement.

I was thinking of getting a flat down in the Whalley Range area, which would be a perfect place to live as Old Trafford was on one side and the Moss and Hulme on the other. For a guy who was always round those areas, I thought I might as well live there, plus Syl hated it when Bev and I hit the bed at hers. Right from nowhere Sully said that Emma, his gran and the number one woman in his life, had a spare room and asked me if I wanted to move in. It was perfect, with a few direct buses to Sale plus it was dirt-cheap. So I packed and moved my stuff into the spare room. Sully went to get a chippie while I wired up the sound system. After a few minutes I heard the door open and shut and Sully's gran popped her head round the corner, gave me a big smile and went straight into the kitchen to make a pot of tea.

Emma, Sully's gran, turned out to be a saint, always cheerful. The best thing in a way was that she was deaf, so the music Sully blasted out was not a problem. Bruce Springsteen and the Stranglers were his favourites and I was now into Dillinger's *CB200*, Burning Spear and the Clash – especially 'Bank Robber'. I lived there on and off for the next eighteen months, and got bang at it on the grafting.

Chapter Ten

Bang At It

WHEN 'MADCHESTER' HIT the music world in the late 1980s, everyone started speaking the Manchester slang. Well, a lot of this jargon came from us, and had been around for ten years or more. Some was adopted from Cockney rhyming slang or the Scousers, but most of it we invented ourselves. For example:

Bugs	Money (Bugs Bunny)
Cakes	Beers
Change	Whalley (Range – an area of Manchester)
Dammed up	Can't get out
Dibble	Police
Gerannie	Sneaking a money pouch or purse
Hank	Starving (Hank Marvin)
Hector	Train guard
Jack	Shop till
Jam	Car (jam jar)
Jocky	Driver
McFees	Ecstasy (Es)
Newtons	Teeth (Newton Heath – an area of Manchester)
Nitto	Don't do
Rattler	Train
Russell Harty	Party
Salfords	Socks (Salford Docks)

Sweet	Get in
Swiss rolls	Necklaces
The Magnet	Amsterdam (also called the Elastic Band)
Tom	Jewellery
Titty	Petrol
Twirlers	Keys
Uri or Uri Geller	Stella (Artois)

All of these words and many more, plus phrases like 'have it', 'do one' and 'top one' developed as we met more and more lads from other parts of the city. I started to booze around Sharston and Benchill in south Manchester and got to know all the Reds Sully went with to away games in the fabled Wythenshawe War Wagon, so I was mixing with a whole new set of thugs, thieves and ticket touts. Bev would come over every other Friday night with a kitbag and stay till Sunday teatime. It pissed her off when the football season started, as it meant I was gone every Saturday, and the times I took her out after the game with the lads were always a big mistake. But we were getting into making money at the games and even started going to other matches in midweek in the Lancashire area, like when Chelsea came to Bolton or Millwall went to Bury.

The Electric Circus had become one of the most popular punk venues in the UK, quickly changing from a shady rock place to pure punk. It was funny to see the first coachload of punks from London get off and stand underneath the arches on Collyhurst Street to get away from the Manchester rain. All the kids were pulling at the safety pins in their ears and noses. The Circus saw week in, week out punk rock, from Manchester's finest, the Buzzcocks, to the Clash and the Damned. We loved it, though a lot of the kids would tone down their dress for games. The fashion on the terraces had turned into adidas trainers, snorkel parkas with massive hoods, Kicker boots and Puma rain tops, which were easy to take off and roll into a small ball.

One night I saw Dicko and he asked why I didn't come on one of the punk tours selling tee-shirts. He was working for Tony Vaise, who was one of the first to trust you with a bag full of swag – you either paid him after you'd sold it or returned the goods. Through Dicko I also met a few City thugs and even went with them to away games, while they came to the odd United game. It started me off working the swag game, and for the next decade or more this became a very good side earner. We bought all kinds of stock – programmes, scarves, badges, patches, tee-shirts, posters, hats – and sold it at concert halls, then later the big stadiums. Our first tour was Adam and the Ants and then we worked legally on some heavy metal tours – Status Quo, Iron Maiden and Kiss. Programmes were always the biggest earner and eventually we moved up the ladder, printing and selling our own bootleg 'swag'. We got termed the 'Pirates' but in fact our swag was better and cheaper than the official stalls inside – most of the time, anyway.

I loved the music scene but football still came first. For Arsenal away I met the Ardwick firm with Coco at Piccadilly Station for the early service train to Euston. There we joined a few Cockneys in the pub, with no big plan, just the basic get there around half two, split into small groups after the Tube, then straight into the North Bank, stay at the top for fifteen minutes while we all spot each other, then give it, 'Come on then, let's go.' Only the police stopped us taking liberties though there was only 150 of us, as the days of half the Red Army taking over someone's end were over. This new way was in a way more daring and showed the other fans what was really the hardcore mob, so the chant of 'Come and have a go if you think you're hard enough' was still on the menu. This was also the first time I saw all the young punks in action: Skinny Vinny, Scull, Witt, Crewy, Young Harvey, Holmesy, Sale's Lol and Eddie Punk.

Birmingham was another potential kick-off. We caught the early service train again, then took over the Yates's and Plan A was put around – we were all going to either jib it or pay in their end around half two. It was a touch late when Sully, Rab and I got in and went up to the top to meet a few Reds, not saying much. We moved forward hoping to join our other lost lot but a few heads turned and we were on the verge of being sussed. Rab clocked it as well, and before the full mob sussed that there was only a handful of us, he threw us a lifeline by screaming, 'Come on then Reds!' like we had lots of others around us. We all hit the high note – 'Let's go!' – and went straight into them, but only to make room for Plan B: every man for himself. We all got busted up but made it over to the spiked fence that split the two set of fans apart; the last one in our group was stripped to the waist as they tried to pull him back.

As we boarded a service train back to Manchester, Maca spotted a firm of Scousers getting on who'd been zapping United fans. We were on them rapid and Maca took the main dipper into the toilet to tax him. He was lucky that Maca left him with most of his wedge. As the train was about to leave, the main thug in the group tried to shove a sharp stick into Coco's face; he managed to catch it but not before he'd copped for a wicked slash that opened up his cheek. There was blood everywhere, but the daft Scouser was nowhere near the exit door and got caught. We left Coco to it: he broke the kid's nose with the first few digs, then went into the body. The other Scousers were happy not to get touched but we knew it would be bad for the future if everyone kicked off, as we'd all be meeting each other on the road. We hopped off at Crewe and Maca got the beer in with the money he'd taxed.

The same week I took a day off from Clean Walls and Sully and I went to meet Rab and Coco in the Blackbird café; Millwall were playing a Lancashire team in the Second Division. We got a bus from Salford and near dinnertime hit a gaff near Bury where there was a few shops and a little precinct. After a mooch around we banged a jack in a supermarket for around £200. It was sweet, as it had been unattended and so the scream wasn't due to go up for a while. We waited a bit offside with the bus stop in sight and when the bus arrived slipped straight on it, not going to the ground but into town. We then sneaked into an office, and as the office worker went to talk to the grafters, I got a grip of the cashbox hidden behind some books on top of the safe. I was careful not to rattle the change as I lowered it down and made sure it went back in the same place, leaving a few notes on the top. We'd robbed over two grand, by far our biggest score.

We got on the bus and sat on the back seats upstairs. A few folk wondered what were we celebrating as we counted the wad and did a war dance up and down, looking like we'd won the Pools. The money went to a trusted pair of hands who was going back to Manchester, as we'd decided to carry on as planned to scout what was about at the game. It was better to get the money offside in case of a pull later. At the ground we clocked the turnstile that was taking most money and took up positions in preparation for a Tony Hatch – a snatch. Just as we were thinking how best to make our move, some Scousers clocked us and came over to make small talk while they tried to suss out if we were dipping, so that we didn't tread on each other's toes. Sully knew one from detention centre and told him we weren't after wallets. We arranged to see them in a pub down the road after the game for a pint and a chat, then both sides went to work. We snatched the pouch containing the turnstile takings and bolted to the pub with £150. The Scousers came in later and Sull gave them the script about the fallout and taxing after the Birmingham game, which they'd been a bit unhappy about. We struck up a truce then took them down to the Frontline in Moss Side, where they bought about an ounce of weed in pound deals and got a fair few thrown in freemans. Then we all went to Harry's, where Sully got so trashed he woke up in Liverpool.

This was the start of some big scores as we all improved our sneaking methods. Not long after, one of the lads took over a grand from the till in a hi-fi shop. They seemed to be taking more money than anywhere else, so soon Dixons and Currys were our prime targets. That jack we'd done in France had stayed in my head a long time and kick-started me studying tills. We soon perfected how to open them, which we called 'banging the jack', and I would eventually become the King of the Jacks, clearing out as many as ten a day, all fully wedged. I really studied locks not only on tills but on jewellery display cases, often in big hotels. We learned to make master keys out of keys from simple shops that had locks but fuck-all worth taking; they often left the keys lying around or even still in the barrels and we would steal them, give them a light file – you can even do it on a brick wall – and ninety-nine per cent of the time they'd fit any lock: full barrels, crocodiles, full and half moons, the lot. When the new electric tills came out we quickly learned button codes and the location of emergency buttons that were normally under the till so you had to give it a wee tilt. They were all easy to suss.

* * *

The derby that year saw us all meet in the Mitre Bar. Our Mark and all the Sale crew came down and within the hour there was a proper turnout, with lads from Hulme, Ardwick, Gorton and the whole of the North Side. This was one mother of a mob, with top lads like Sam Smart, Coco and Eddie Beef. We all knew each other now and it was uplifting – you felt you could do anything. A mob of Cockney Reds arrived just as we caught some City fans spying at the top of the staircase. We wrecked the gaff, cleared the Jacks and kicked the City to fuck.

Three match-day special buses took us to Maine Road, where we walked around the ground and into their end. They were waiting at the top of the Kippax stairs and as soon as they spied us arriving, they ran down to do the first ones in. We jumped over the turnstiles – not one of us paid and we could easily have robbed the fellers working the gates but we were not after money today. This was tribal fighting. The City who tried to stop us were soon shattered and we ran up those monster staircases and grouped in the top open corner. Then straight into City again from their left. A small group of them who later became known as the Cool Cats did make a token effort but today was our day.

At half-time George gave it a solo big-time: 'If I die in the Kippax Street.'

The full mob joined in with a steady, 'Woh-oh.'

George again on his tod: 'If I die in the Kippax Street.'

'Who-oh.'

Then the full mob stamping and banging away, all running on high octane with this same chant but turned into a war cry:

'If I die in the Kippax Street, there'll be ten Blue bastards at my feet, woh-oh, who-oh-oh, woh-oh.'

This was the pure taking the piss and City should have steamed us but in truth we would not have had any problem.

By the second half the police had us boxed in but some of us managed to break away and went straight round to City's social club. There was no mob to fight. We all trooped back into town and the only City fans I saw were Dicko, Bez and Bondy, who'd robbed a massive bottle of charity coins from a hotel reception. We could see there were a few notes in it, so we went over to Piccadilly Gardens and smashed the bottle, grabbing what we could. It was enough to see us through the night.

Soon after, United were due to play in France at Saint Etienne. I had some work in Lincoln with Gagzy but was back in Manchester to sort out my next Clean Walls job. Going over to Oldham Street for a couple of pints before returning to Lincoln, I bumped into Rab, who was already pissed and said how about making the trip over to France? I said no but it didn't take him long to persuade me, so we stole a Van Gils suit, sold it on and got ourselves some shady ID, catching the Post Office before it closed and coming away with two visitors' passports. We jibbed the trains all the way down to the ferry then jibbed the ferry with twenty other Reds and had a fair old booze-up and sing-song. The train took us on to Paris but when it arrived the dibble carted off some of the lads. Undaunted, we jibbed a real top jolly train into Lyons and bumped into all the Reds in the main square.

I called Danny, the boss at Clean Walls, and told him straight I was in France. He was alright about it. The next morning we rode the train down to St Etienne, which took only an hour or so, and the beer and banter flowed. The Barmy Army had taken over the place and everyone was out in the sunshine drinking the local wine, singing and waving flags – it was going to be some day. Rab and

I went out and copped for a couple of shitty purses with barely enough to get a few rounds in, and it wasn't long before we were out on the mooch again. The plan was for me to block for Rab while he shoplifted in clothes stores. He got only the best tackle – including Lois jeans, which were bang in at the time and worn with Kicker shoes – and we decided to wear some of it ourselves, as we were starting to smell. After a quick shower in the train station toilets, we sold the rest of the clothes for about £100, so now things were much more relaxed and we went back on the piss for another hour. We even snatched a couple of cashboxes on the walk to the ground. Lots of United fans were wearing green tops, scarves and hats – they'd robbed the club shop – so Rab and I got a St Etienne tracksuit top each in return for a few drinks.

The atmosphere in the ground was very Continental, with all the klaxon horns. St Etienne were a top team who'd never been beaten at home in Europe. It was a working class city and they adored their team. Even though the ground held only around 30,000 it was tight and compact with lots of passion. A couple of thousand Reds had got into their end; this wasn't planned, it just happened, as they had all sneaked in and this stand was the nearest and easiest to get into. Plenty of French were throwing stupid things like plastic bottles of water and even bread, so United whizzed back coins and things built up. Then it kicked off: Reds were pulling the sticks out of their homemade flags and using them as weapons, forcing hundreds of St Etienne to flee and run to the front, where they scaled the wire fence separating the terraces from the pitch. Some climbed to the top then fell off as the fence wobbled like mad.

The exodus continued even when the game kicked off and the riot police steamed in swinging batons and cracking heads. They chased about 500 Reds out the ground and all the way back to the train station. While the police steamed in the locals also took bits of revenge, with the dibble looking the other way – they didn't give a toss, so there was a lot of bad feeling when the group arrived back at the station, despite the fact that we'd won a famous 2–0 victory. The dibble were everywhere but we took over the bar and waited for the train to roll in. At Dover the press were waiting, but Rab and I were more concerned that we didn't have boat tickets and our ID was snide. We still got back to Manchester okay – and headed straight to Harry's, where we wore the St Etienne tracksuit tops we'd acquired on the way and started a new song that other teams copy to this day: 'Que sera sera, whatever will be will be, we're going to Wemb-er-ley, que sera sera.'

I went back to work in Lincoln but knew I'd soon be off again with the Reds – they were playing Porto in the next round of the Cup Winners' Cup, plus England were playing in Luxembourg. Sully and I and a few of the other lads, including a mate of Sully's known as the Cat, headed down to Euston on the sleeper, sneaking every purse and wallet we could en route. On the boat we got pissed on duty free, then split up and went through some of the cabins, all finding bits of cash here and there. On the rattler at the other end, a couple of the lads again went into the sleeper part of the train, where a load of Japs were akip, but instead of sneaking bits they took full suitcases, cleared them of money and slung the cases out the window. The firm of Japs reported the thefts and the train stopped. While the Dutch police were trying to sort it out, we slipped past them onto a Rotterdam-bound train and split into three groups.

We moved on from Rotterdam to Amsterdam for a smoke, booking into a cheap hostel with massive dorms, where the Cat headed off for a shower. Sully started spluttering, as he was having problems with his asthma and couldn't find his spray. He went through the Cat's jacket to see if he had picked it up and felt a roll in one of the zipped side pockets. He pulled out a wedge of Dutch money that the Cat had sharked away, money he should have put in the pot to share. The Cat held his hands up with a weak excuse that he was saving it in case we all blew our money on the razzle.

We divvied it up and headed out to a Jock bar near the canal, the last pub before the Zeedyk, which was the longest and most violent frontline in the world in the Seventies, with wars between Chinese gangs, Turks and others whose bodies were routinely fished out of the canals. Half the guys dealing were high as kites, smoking freebase coke in the doorways from long glass pipes. Others sniffed smack and coke from the end of long slim knives. Tourists often got done over or worse and as it was near all the action and the main train station, loads of backpackers walked right into them all day long. We saw a big black guy go straight up to a large tourist fella and pick him up in the air in some kind of huge bear hug move, like he was playing, while his partner in crime went through all the tourist's pockets. After removing his cash and cards, the other guy even put the wallet back before the black guy put him down.

We had a walk around, then went back to the Jocks' place. No coffee shops were open in the Seventies so all the business was done in this area. We were lucky that the barman knew the score and told us that if any Jocks got done by the dealers, they would get a firm together and fight them with knives and swords. Most of the time the Jocks came out worse but they never changed, so the street dealers hated having to fight them and pretty much left them alone. I got talking to one of the Jocks, nipped to the corner, sorted out a quick deal with him by my side and was back in the bar ten minutes later with the hash. It was a nice chunk of black but was too strong; we'd not smoked anything this potent in Manchester and were all cabbaged for a good hour or two, hardly able to speak.

In the morning we had a wee mooch around the old shopping area. Sully blagged a fella in an antique shop while I cleared out the money from his cashbox and slipped out to meet the lads on the corner. We moved on into another shop up the road, then heard a shout and saw Sully pinned up against the wall by the feller we'd just robbed – and he had a gun to Sully's head. We swerved back into the shop and kept an eye on the scene outside: the guy almost strip-searched Sully, then charged up the street looking for me, so we bailed. Sully was having an asthma attack trying to tell us what we already knew: 'It's on top!' As we got round the back of the train station, police cars from all sides blocked us in. Guns came out and the feller from the antique shop joined in, pointing his shooter at us.

They took us to the police station and sat us on benches. One by one they led us into a cell to be strip-searched by a copper wearing plastic gloves. I gave him my jacket, then top and pants, and every time he searched an article he'd give it back and I'd put it to the side on the solid, concrete slab beds. Now I was down to my undies and socks and the right sock had this fella's wedge in, so I slipped off my undies acting very shy, then took off my left sock as well, which I wasn't supposed to do, and threw it almost straight after the undies. This split-second move gave me time, while he dealt with the left sock straight after the undies, to slip out the rolled wedge from my right sock and put it into the back pocket of my jeans. The timing was perfect – as his head came up I was peeling the right sock off my foot, though I thought he'd sussed me and was stringing me along. But he wasn't and they had to let us go. I walked out of the cop shop with over a 1,000 guilders in my back pocket. The lads were stunned – and the cops ended up giving the feller from the antique shop a load of abuse for pulling out his gun.

We got into Luxembourg around teatime and dived straight on a bus up to the ground. We found some of the East End's worst thugs smashing it up for no reason. England won with little hassle, so the fans started fighting with each other. We got offside and found an all-night bar that had crates of lager under the staircase by the toilet, so we supped freemans all night. Next day we headed for Lisbon on those trains where you can mess around with the seats and turn them into double beds. We used Sully's Union Jack as a quilt and travelled for twenty-four hours over the French border into Portugal. Under a bright sun we found a great hotel that was very cheap, as the holiday season had ended. We drank all afternoon on the beach then walked to the local fishermen's bars by the harbour and saw not one bit of trouble. The only problem we had came on the train to Porto when Sully got into an argument with the ticket inspector; at the next station the police came on and took Sully off. They handcuffed him to a radiator, beat his legs black and blue, then let him go.

Porto was a culture shock after Lisbon, with streets full of beggars. We headed for the red-light area, found a hotel and went out on the lash. After best steak and chips with a few pints of strong lager for a nicker, we did the rounds in the red-light zone. By match day our banks were smashed, so when the Barmy Army turned up it was time to have a look around. We saw a fella count his takings, put them in a large envelope and stick it in the drawer beneath his till. I crept in, went behind the counter and opened the drawer, but unbeknown to me there was a tricky mirror up above and the fella's wife could see what I was doing. She put the scream up and I grabbed the money, so the creep turned into one big run through all the shady back streets. At the ground we hit the nearest bar and divvied up. A few of the local kids started telling us about the hardest crew of thugs at Porto, the local gypsies, and said Porto had been banned from Europe the year before because of crowd trouble.

We sneaked into the best part of the ground no problem: I showed the guy on the gate a Saver Seven bus pass with my photo on it. We climbed to the top tier and to our right, in the large open end with a big hill behind it, were 1,000 or more local gypos, all singing away. A few hundred Reds had now gathered around us and Sully hung his Union Jack over the tier as the game was about to kick off. I then saw Sully pull out a blade and start threatening someone in the tier below; a pack of young thugs had climbed on their mate's shoulders and got a grip of the Jack flag, which they were trying to rip down. Sully wasn't happy and lost it a little with this blade on show, but the kid underneath pulled out a gun and pointed it at Sully. He let go of the flag and it floated down to the scum below, who wiped their backsides with it.

United were well beaten, and after the game we made our way from the gypo side to the coach park to see if we could jib a lift into town but nothing was doing. We called into a back street bar, where we ate cooked pigeons, then moved on back to the red-light area. We heard lots of music from a decent-looking bar and, thinking it was Reds in there, we burst in singing a United song. It didn't go down well, as we'd in fact disturbed a gypsy wedding. Fortunately we had with us a mad Portuguese Red from Lisbon who had followed United since they beat Benfica in 1968; without him to explain our case and apologise I dread to think what they'd have done. They told us we had ten seconds to get away and the fuckers were firing the odd shot over our heads as we all ran like never before two miles into the red-light.

Next day we pitched up at the British Consulate and told them we'd lost our tickets home. They paid for a decent hotel for all of us and said we could collect our tickets the next day. We stopped off a couple of times in France on the way home and someone copped for a cashbox, which saw us right for our expenses all the way back. At Dover, the Customs took our passports off us and said once we paid the cost back they would return them, but most of us were travelling on the two-day passes, so they had no chance of getting a shilling out of us.

We almost pulled it off in the return leg at Old Trafford, setting about Porto from the start with Steve Coppell flying down the wing. We won 5-2 but went out on aggregate. The Euro adventure was over for the season – at least with the football.

An away game at Villa was our next opportunity for an earner and some bad behaviour. Shortly before half-time, we bailed into the best bar with a big seated area where all the top jollies drank, and after a few minutes it was packed. We downed our drinks, then Rab jumped over the bar and grabbed the main money pouch, but was pinned down on the bar when he tried to climb back over. Pure chaos reigned as we all fought to get out. The money went everywhere and I doubt if we got more than a score.

Back at New Street Rab was fuming and slapped the first Villa head he saw, as the kid was a bit too young to punch. Rab also took his Villa cap. He was still wearing it as we had a quick pint in the station bar when we saw the kid's older brother and a huge mob of Villa villains heading towards us. We all picked up bottles as it looked very bad. The first one of the Villa through the door was Coke, a lad we had worked with at the Bognor camp.

What a lifesaver! He gave Rab a slap and took back the kid's hat – then we all went for a booze in his local. He showed us how to jib onto the train platform through the back way and said to Rab, 'No harm meant over the slap.' Rab was as pleased as us to get out of that one. We often had to keep Rab from losing it but it was his nature, always slapping kids with the back of his hand around their ears. We had enough trouble coming at us and didn't need to attract more by Rab's slapping. He was much calmer when we were not with the mob, as then it was all about looking for money.

One thing that season had given us was a taste for foreign travel – and in Amsterdam we had found a home from home. It was relaxed, easy and on its way to becoming the drug capital of the world. A couple of weeks later, we thought we'd go back over for a good mooch, plus we needed winter clothes and wanted to smoke some more of that Amsterdam hash. It was the start of a mad odyssey that would see us become the most prolific sneak thieves in Europe.

Chapter Eleven

Dambusters

ONCE OUR EUROPEAN adventure started, it wouldn't stop. For twenty years we had the lot, year in, year out, from Ancoats to the Alps, Collyhurst to Cannes, Langley to Lake Como, Miles Platting to Monte Carlo, all Europe got hammered. We went through The Netherlands, Switzerland, Belgium, France, Italy, Liechtenstein, Andorra and the north of Spain, Germany and Austria. We were in Klosters in the same week as Charlie and Di, Gstaad in the same cafes and bars as Liz Taylor and Roger Moore, Davos with the international smart set. In summer we'd switch to the south of France, the Costa Brava, the lakeside holiday regions of Swissy, Lake Como in Italy or Konstanz Lake in Germany. But the Dam would be the hub of it all – so much so that we christened it 'the Magnet' or 'the Elastic Band'.

But that was in the future. On that first trip back, Dicko had just enough smoke left for a last monster joint as we settled in front of the TV on the ferry to watch *Coronation Street* – the big story where Emily Bishop's husband got shotgunned in a wage snatch. We went rooting after the bar closed and acquired a few wallets, and once through customs we decided to miss out the Dam and instead scored in the red-light area of Den Haag before taking an overnight train to Hamburg and a hotel.

We showered, changed clothes and bolted a good scran, as that German food was right up our street, plus they served beer with breakfast. Dicko, the Cat and I said we'd work one side of town while Sully, Skinny Vinny and Coco worked the other. I was surprised that the tills in the big stores were in such easy positions to bang, yet none of the thieves we knew really hit the tills in Deutschland. They even had tills with four drawer compartments, and it was so easy to watch and learn how things worked. I sussed that for the tills that had a key in the side, all you had to do, instead of hitting the total button that caused all the noise, was hold the drawer itself with your left hand while turning the key back once, then forward again, and it opened without a sound. Other tills had a hidden tricky button where the paper till roll was, that if pressed did the same. I also noticed that the main keys were often left lying by the till, so I had a few away.

The first till we banged contained that much money that Dicko and the Cat had to come over and help me out, as I couldn't get anymore down my undies. When we got in a bar we knew we'd hit the jackpot and that the keys I'd had away were going to be a massive help: we christened the keys 'twirlers' and drank to them, then headed to the dockside where a lot of old hippies and bikers had bars and it was easy to get a smoke. We met Sully and the others and could tell by their faces that they'd also had a good day. They had not done any tills, just a couple of easy sneaks on shops where they'd thought the wallets and purses would be slim but turned out to be all well-loaded. They also had a massive bag of clothes each, so it was off to a top hotel for us. We hit the fun side of town and Hamburg was our kind of place, with good Irish pubs and bierkellers close to all the action. The local guys sported homemade tattoos so we blended right in.

Next day we hit Bremen and banged a few top jacks. Dicko got the train back to Holland for a bit of the Dam then home, while we went to Switzerland, better known as Swissy, the Land of the Wad. The money there was even better than Germany. We enjoyed another good day in Basel, then went to Zurich for two days' rest and bought pairs of those massive hairy white snow boots, the only thing that's sensible to wear in the ski areas. Then up to St Moritz. I was strolling round buzzing out of my brain, sniffing Alpine air, and got talking to some guys who were competing in the World Bobsleigh Championship. Because we were wearing football tops and in a crazy way looked like we belonged there in these hairy snow boots, they thought we were part of Man United's youth team having a break.

The bobsleighers invited us to a party where a cook had best steaks burning away, then took us on a tour of the top jolly places. The next day we hired kids' snow sledges from the hotel, rode a bus up the mountain, saw a bit of a slope and asked the driver to stop. We all went for it and soon started to pick up speed. There was no way to slow down and I burst out back on to the road and off down the other side of the mountain towards St Moritz. I think it's the closest to death I've ever come, yet the best buzz ever. I looked for a decent place to crash but the only way to go was into the main square, where tourists were drinking iced tea and coffee, waiting to go up in the ski lifts. I collided with a fence and then some people who had their backs to us; it didn't go down well.

The next day we went ice skating and then looked around the tom shops. It was hard to believe how easy the Rolex watches and diamonds were to have away. We did a sneak, then went for some new clothes: we'd buy a pair of socks or undies that cost a fortune, then fill up with all the cashmere tops when the staff were looking the other way. We robbed a Nikon camera each to go round our necks, to look the part for going back through customs the next day when we burnt back off to Zurich. Sully was a bit twitchy, as he'd given his right name at the hotel and not paid (a year or two later he was fetched back and did six months' jail in the Alps). In Zurich we had planned to stay at the Hotel Italia on the edge of the red-light area, a very cheap hotel with the best value food, but because we had a few bob we went to the Hotel Trumpy behind the train station, by the river. It had these rooms with massage beds and buttons to press to change positions on the bed. Before finally getting off back to Manchester we had a quick look around the airport and liberated a few Longines watches and Dupont lighters.

The journey home was all tom talk, about the shops and how easy it was to stroll in even in a small group, how it was important to look good and how it was harder for black guys, as they were watched by the shop workers – though out of us all, Coco always looked the best, going for the extras like a top designer umbrella and those men's purses they all have in Europe. Coco had so many clothes that he held monthly cast-off sales. Once in the shop you could drift off over to a cabinet or the front window display, which was never locked – some just had curtains with little bells on to alert the staff, and these you lifted up a touch in your palm while opening the curtain.

* * *

When we weren't over at the Dam, I drank in the Parkside pub near Man City's ground, and downstairs at the Grosvenor Snooker Hall on Oxford Road, where a lot of the thieves would congregate to keep up with all latest news. There I got to know the funniest firms Manchester ever threw up: the A and B teams, a mixed group of grafters from all over Manchester. I met them through the Ghost and Budgie, who were working their way up from the B team to the A team.

The teams had around twenty members, all 100 per cent thieves twenty hours a day. Even when not out after a wedge they'd be scouting parts of Lancashire and Cheshire, sussing out things. They soon got onto the things in Europe and helped themselves to parcels of Swiss tom, selling a lot of it to a talented but wayward soccer star of the day who I won't embarrass by naming. As Fagin said, 'In this life one thing counts, in the bank large amounts. I'm afraid these don't grow on trees, you've got to pick a pocket or two boys.'

When you got fresh out jail you were straight into the A team: they'd have all the best cars and moves. There was Irish Suzy (a fella), Mouse, Shoplifter who worked from a briefcase for years, the Deans, Farts the Dipper, Dave Nod, whose head was always nodding, Johnny Newt, Bomber, who loved his black bomber pills, and many more – and all of them knew every trick in town. Being out on the piss with them you met a new member every time.

We started to buy Inter-Rail tickets, which were supposed to be for students but we knew a girl who worked in the travel office so she sorted us out. They cost £60 and you could travel anywhere in Europe for six weeks – and we soon had fake ones made up. We could make two or three separate trips over on the jib in a month and the lifesaver was that we could get night sleepers up to Denmark where the train drives straight on to the ferry and you can sleep right through, no hassle, thus saving on the cost of a hotel.

Visa cards were another next big touch. We found out that cards stolen in England took days and sometimes weeks to report stolen in Europe, so you could smash into them in a big way without worrying about the scream going up. It wasn't long before our pockets were full of stolen cards, which not only bought you all the best scran and clothes but also bits of gold and jewellery and best cameras. Some of the cameras were Hasselblads in gold-rimmed cases and were worth thousands but were very hard to sell on, so we went for Nikons, Canons and Leicas. We had a feller sorted out in Amsterdam who gave out top prices for cameras; as long as they never came from Holland was the deal.

This was ideal because our base for the rest of the Seventies was Amsterdam. It made sense in so many ways, as the price paid for tom was almost as good as in England and it was no problem if we'd copped to wear a few gold chains with coins on and a good watch through customs. If we robbed the parcel from Holland we'd get straight back to England via Antwerp in a taxi using a stolen Visa card. By the side of the train station was an area full of Jewish gold merchants and they would buy off us as well, though the prices they paid weren't that clever. One day while I was doing a deal the plainclothes police came in; the owner's face was a picture when I put the full parcel in my mouth. He knew I hadn't swallowed it but he never stuck me in, just kept up the patter with me nodding my head and mumbling away – and we still did the deal as soon as they walked out.

Our HQ became the Last Waterhole over on the red-light side of town, a big American-style bar with a hostel attached which sold big jugs of good beer. Whenever there was a stolen Visa card around we got to know all the sex clubs where you could put sunbeds, saunas and the rest on the card. Hair Erotic was a small backstreet barbers where the wash-and-blow was a young cloggy bird on her knees giving you a blowjob while her mate attended to your hair. (The Oriental hooker that I first went with in Amsterdam charged me double, told me to trust her as she tied my nuts with a lace like a cock ring, then gave me what's termed a blowjob on the rocks, as she had crushed ice in her mouth.)

On Mondays we would go down to the 'Thieves' Market', where most of our tom went through. I did the biz with a feller called Rudi, who I later brought into Amsterdam centre to meet most of the lads. In future, half of all our tom went through him. If it was a big parcel, I'd go down, give him a wink and let him know what hotel we were in; at seven o'clock that evening he'd turn up with his son, both carrying a lot of money, and we'd strike a deal. Our mutual trust carried on even after Rudi died and left the biz to his son Jerry, with his own son now alongside. The Thieves' Market was an education in wheeling and dealing for hours while looking over your shoulder for the police. Eventually it was pulled down. Everyone of us got nicked or stop-searched at some time and taken back to the main police station to be checked out, but we got to know their liberal laws and what they could and couldn't do, and Manchester's mob of bandits kept flooding into town.

American Bob was another guy we did all sorts of business with. He ran a hire firm called Dream Cars on a few plots around town, so if we needed cheap cars to last a few days before being dumped, we always went to see Bob. VW Beetles and Minis were great for parking and good for snatches in Amsterdam, as they could slip through the stumps that blocked off some of the streets. Bob didn't need all the hassle that we brought and finally the police gave him an ultimatum, but he loved rubbing shoulders with the English crowd in the Flying Dutchman and you could hear his booming, stoned voice saying, 'Hey, you guys you were on the Dutch Crimewatch TV show again.' They had it in Holland years before us and regularly gave out warnings about these new sneak thieves who all spoke very funny English.

Our main pub later became the Flying Dutchman, run by Terry, a Red from Collyhurst. Next door was a Scouse bar, the Three Musketeers, but there was never ever any trouble with the crowd. Hardly a day went by without seeing someone you knew passing through. The Scousers were really the only other grafting firm we met at that time, and they tended to concentrate on Switzerland. Otherwise the field was clear for us – until others began to cotton on.

When Boon, Billy Black (known as 'Thud' for the power of his headbutts) and some other grafters came back from Germany with massive smiles it meant our exclusive little bubble had burst: over the next few years you would get all kinds of groups going abroad to 'work'. Even straight workers began to go on the jib in their summer holidays. The word jib was now used for everything to do with sneak thieving and Manchester's young lads had all copied our way of talking in sly backslang. New thug names were springing up at the football as the soccer casual firms got organised. Spurs were the Yids, Arsenal the Gooners, Leeds the Service Crew, Portsmouth the 6.57 Crew, and many more. Apparently United's lads were called Inter-City Jibbers by some, which I never even knew about until years later.

Half of the grafters in Manchester would eventually head abroad to bring back the best perfumes, clothes and whatever else they could. For many it was an easy way to earn a crust and a lot of the young kids were happy just to get a feel of Europe – it became like a cult thing to do. On your travels you would meet other firms and often pick up new ideas about thieving, like how to cut and shape a strip of plastic cut from a bottle so it could open Yale door locks; once you got the feel for them it was quicker than using a key.

The jewellers would eventually wise up, as would the hi-fi, camera and department stores. Many installed modern alarms and security tags, yet this actually made it easier for us in some cases: when the staff felt they had a foolproof system, that was when they were at their least alert. We spent hours working out ways of getting round the security. One example was on the shoplifting front: you took a roll of silver paper, covered a strong cardboard box with it, then put that in any decent-looking bag and went straight to the best part of the shop. You'd throw in, say, two top-of-the-range cashmere coats, worth up to a grand each, and stroll out without the alarm going off, as the foil foils the system! There were many more ploys like that.

When they started putting locks on windows, we soon found keys for seventy per cent of the locks, and the other thirty per cent we could open with a strong pin or a slim knife. Another way of getting the stuff was 'fishing': there were small gaps at the edges of some windows and small showcases where we'd push through a thin, strong wire and hook the rings. It was a bit of a nervy affair but we did get some amazing things out: diamond and pearl necklaces, rings, coins and those pads and rolls of chains and bracelets.

When it came to watches, we had the lot: Rolexes, Cartiers, Omegas, Tissots, platinum, multi-coloured golds, full gold lace on the strap, faces edged with diamonds. The latter were called 'Jimmy Saviles' while the nickname for all Rolexes was 'Big Bens'. Most of us only ever wore them to get them out the country, then sold them as soon as possible. Personally I think they are very uncomfortable: too heavy and the top of the winder is always digging into your skin. Plus it's a dangerous thing to have on your wrist in Manchester, as people will do you in for one. Ask Jimmy Beard: he got done with baseball bats by a couple of thugs early one dark morning at his own front door for his full gold one. I only ever kept a stainless steel one which was so I'd look okay in the tom shops, as the shop workers knew it was a real Rolex. We rarely looked flash, as it attracted unwanted attention; we would adopt an 'office worker' look, with navy blue the favoured colour.

When we returned from abroad we'd stop at London, where we'd get the tube to Sloane Square and then head down the Kings Road. First stop was the shop Kickers, then all the rest for the latest clobber. Back in Manchester and looking like a million dollars, I'd spend a week picking up twirlers in the shops. I even started to file certain ones down, then spent days testing them in shops that sold tills and it was well worth it, as we had a mega set of keys that could open half the town's jacks and the other half we could still bang when it came to the crunch. So we started to work just on tills, with a few sneaks and tonies if there was nothing going down.

Of course, we didn't always get away with it. Dotch, Simon Charles and Renno copped a good few grand in the Flatlands area, the tourist stretch of South Holland's islands and the north-west Belgian coast. They were seen almost every day driving around town in a black cab with a crate of beer, off their heads. But when they got a flat back in Chorlton, Renno was nicked over a tin of beans and got borstal. Then Simon came out of a nightclub and went sneaking round a hotel; there was a naughty scene and he ended up getting ten years. While he was in Strangeways, two kids came in for running a young kid down in Moss Side. Simon cut one of them up pretty bad and got a few more years put on his sentence.

Skinny Vinny was next. He was also known as 'Big Bird', after the *Sesame Street* TV character, because of his looks. A newspaper report of one of his crimes said something like 'the money was snatched by tall, weird-

looking youngster with a very long, prominent nose.'
When he finally got his borstal the *Manchester Evening
News* wrote how this young kid was addicted to watching
United away in Europe and got dragged into crime to
support his habit!

Then a bit of trouble came my way. I was walking
through the Oasis shopping centre when a couple of
dibble pounced on me. I had a nicked suit in my carrier
bag and ended up being charged with handling stolen
goods by a policewoman who used to live round the
corner from me in Collyhurst. It wasn't nice getting turned
over by one of your own and at court I got bound over to
keep the peace, with a big fine.

* * *

That christmas I stayed in Sale and on Boxing Day was on
the train to Lime Street to watch United at Goodison.
Everton were on their best roll in history, with so many
games unbeaten, but United destroyed them. I jumped a
lift back and as we set off up the main road I saw a lone
Red at a bus stop with his full United outfit on. We were
going to pull over and have a word but were too late and
the first-timer got thrashed by a mob of Scousers and
thrown onto the road, where a bike ran over him.

On New Year's Day we played Coventry away and
were all after money at half-time in the bar. Someone hit
the light switch and the drinks went west while I jumped
over the bar and gripped the cashbox. The police burst in
knocking heads and caught me halfway back over. They
took me out to the van but it was full, so they turned me
round and started escorting me back down to the holding
cell in the ground. One had me in a headlock, but on the
turn I slipped out of it and saw that the electric gate that
let the bus out was still open. I bolted through and down

the road, with all the top of the open end shouting for me to keep running, as two dibble were right up my arse. We did a full circle of the stadium before I hit the side streets. I was making headway but at the bottom of a street I bumped into a few local thugs, who forced me down to the ground, where the cops caught me. Lots of reporters attended the court and I thought I'd be looking at a jail sentence but my story that I jumped over the counter to get away from the trouble went down alright and I got a silly fine.

Time, I thought, for another trip to Europe. Dicko and I met Keano and Manny in a bar at Piccadilly, then jibbed the rattler and the ferry over to the Hook of Holland. In the morning I dipped a feller's wallet for 3,000 guilders. He worked in the money exchange and as we passed through customs I saw him reporting it. Dicko was a few people in front of me in the queue and got a tug; they ran his details through and found his passport had run out. They were too bothered with Dicko to notice me slipping through but as I was about to get in a taxi I heard, 'Hello,' and they swooped. They said that if I admitted dipping the wallet they'd put me on the same boat back with Dicko, so I did and they didn't even charge us for the return ticket.

On the way back, Dicko told me a new firm from Old Trafford was working big concerts, where they could sell merchandise like tee-shirts, sweatshirts, scarves, badges, hats, patches and posters. The two guys that ran it, the Dinks brothers, knew a fortune was round the corner if they played it right and wanted good working lads who didn't mind the travelling involved, so I told him to put me in for the next tour, which was Status Quo in Europe. Dicko had already worked a few shows in the Midlands.

At the ferry bar we got talking to a big ginger-haired lad from Old Trafford, who was known as 'the Grid' because he'd take anything. A whisky head with an infectious laugh, John McKee was the original Dambuster – he'd been in Amsterdam before any of us and soon got a taste for the good life. He graduated from selling pancakes on the dreaded Zeedyke to ripping off Germans and French who were in Holland looking for kilos of hash. The rip worked like this: the tourists would get a nice deal to begin with, then would come back asking for a bigger amount. One of the guys would agree to this and take them to his car parked round a corner. He would hand over the bag with the hash in it and take their money while they were still in the car. Then the ginger lad would turn up, open the car door and show them a police ID card. The lad who was onside and in the driver's seat would get out and run away, leaving the tourists and a huge bag of hash. The ginger feller would give them a hard time and eventually say that because they were not criminals he would let them go, but would have to confiscate the hash. All the Grid's mates said he looked like a copper, so he thought he might as well make the most of it.

Soon enough we were all back over in Holland for the Status Quo tour and met the bulk of the grafters in the Last Waterhole in Amsterdam. Most of them we already knew and they were all top chaps, including the Cavanagh brothers, who would later break away and run their own merchandise business. Dicko and I were weighed in with a load of swag and started banging it out around the area where the punters caught the trams for the concert hall. After a couple of hours we got on the tram and sold a lot more stuff outside the hall, then restocked from the stall inside with more gear to sell later. Near the end of the show we all took up positions outside, selling for a good two hours more around the car parks until everyone was away, then it was back to the Waterhole to get paid for the day's work.

The first day went really well, but the next day we were working the tram again when a vanload of London Irish shouted us over. One of them pointed a shotgun at us and said bluntly that we had to stop working, as they were taking over. It was a silly move, as there was plenty of room for us all to work, but that's how it went down so we wrapped up and they took over until they'd sold all their gear, then disappeared back to London, where they controlled all the best spots for selling hotdogs and burgers.

We went to Brussels the next day, did another good day's work, then took a day off before the next concert. The Ghost, a lad I'd known for years who was now working the swag with us, sneaked into the back of a café with me and we had a money pouch away. The Ghost was up for going back to the Dam, so the next train sped us back and we spent every penny in the red-light area. Next stop was Cologne, where I noticed a small supermarket about to close; two of the women workers had left their tills and a third was serving the last few punters. The Ghost positioned himself between the woman on the till and me and the unattended jacks. As she hit her total button, I hit the total keys of the other tills at the same time and emptied the lot while The Ghost made a nuisance of himself. We got over two grand and went a bit mad in the Old Town, then headed for a red-light bar near the hotel where we met a few of the other lads. The bar girls saw our wedge of money so when the bill came it was totally out of order and we left, telling them where to get off.

Just as our keys were going into the front door of the hotel, the police were there with guns out. One of the lads lost it and started ripping off his top, doing a crazy Jack Nicholson impression and pointing to his belly, screaming, 'Come on then, shoot me.' A copper walked over, whacked him in the belly with a long baton and dragged us all into the van. Nothing was mentioned about the Jack and after a few hours we paid the bar bill and caught breakfast before moving on to the next town further down the Rhine area.

We did a sneak and a jack, then the Ghost sorted us out with another hotel while a couple of the lads scored some hash. It took them hours and when they came back they were both scratching and pinching their noses. They'd bought some smack and coke, which they said was better than hash and sex. After getting myself ready I called into their room and found them both cooking up drugs, putting liquid from a spoon into needles and saying again how it was the best rush in the world.

'Let me try it,' I said.

They strapped me up and stuck the needle in my vein. As each second passed, it felt warmer. Then I hit the deck and spewed up fountains of sick; my head went and the vomit kept coming. However much was in those needles, it was way too much for a first-timer like me. They dragged me into a taxi and took me to a bar that had stunning women from Asia and Africa, but I kept throwing up over the big rug. This cost me dear, as the pimps were gangsters and rolled me for all I had. I never touched my veins again. We got the first train back to Amsterdam and bought some Nepalese hash, the strongest I've ever smoked, but the other lads kept hitting the powder as well – a sign of bad things to come.

We needed to get away from the Dam to where they sold only hash and weed – which, we soon found out, was everywhere. The smoke was three or four times dearer than the Dam but it sounded good to us, so we first hit Hamburg for a day on the tills, then ferried over to Copenhagen, where there was a big hippie commune on an old army camp. There we got a smoke. Next we had a result in a tom shop and four of us – me, the Ghost, Andy Chips and John the Grid – took the flying boat over to Sweden. Customs strip-searched Chips and the Grid and found strong morphine tablets and some major sleepers, as they were both on cold turkey. They wouldn't admit anything and claimed they got them in Belgium for flu. The officers confiscated the tablets, which was bad news for their withdrawal.

We booked into a nice hotel. John was hit bad by cramps and the sweats, so he did both mini-bars in a couple of hours to knock himself out and get that necessary sleep. Just before dinner we copped for two tills and had to wait around for a couple of hours before getting a train to Stockholm. After finishing a day's graft we smoked a couple of joints and went into a massive music shop. Normally it was me and the Ghost who liked the hash, but as the other two were rattling they got stoned to take their minds off the pain of coming off drugs. We all had a play on the drums and electric keyboards, then I blew a sax to the Average White Band's 'Pick up the Pieces'. I noticed how near the door was and, without thinking, walked out with the sax in my hands. I went a little way down the road before the scream went up and I was dragged back to the shop, which they locked until the police arrived. The Grid tried and failed to jump through the glass door and we had to stop him trying again. They found tom on the Ghost, hash on McKee and twirlers and tom on Andy and me. They added the two tills we'd done that morning to the charge sheet and banged us up.

The first four weeks inside were bad, as we could smoke only one cig a day and were allowed only ten minutes' walk on the roof in a small wire cage, with a copper sat in a cabin to make sure you didn't shout any messages over. We were all on total bang-up in separate parts of the police station and it was especially bad for

Andy and the Grid. We could hear them banging and screaming for hours until the coppers would rush into their cells and stick a needle into them with something to calm them. Eventually they received a liquid knockout every night – they didn't even have to bang the door. In court, the shop staff testified how they'd been blagged to the other side of the shop whilst the money went. As for the music store, I started to say I had the sax because I was learning music but this blew up in my face, as the feller from the shop had me talking bollocks, which the judge soon had enough of. He gave us three months each – so we had two more to do – and banned us from entering the country for seven years.

The jail in Malmo had four wings. One was for Swedes, one for remand prisoners and one for Western Europeans and Americans – which is where we all should have gone, but they had room only for Andy and the Ghost. The Grid and I copped for the fourth, armpit wing, with the Turks, Moroccans and Eastern Bloc criminals. It turned out sound as they said we could have a double cell together and we soon got talking to the main guys, who were all Yugoslavian and in for robbing tom shops with guns. Part of the reason there was little trouble was the way the punishment block in Malmo worked: they strapped you to a slab twenty-four hours a day and fed you with a spoon. This cut out almost all unnecessary fighting – we didn't once have hassle.

We were amazed at how easy their prisons were. We had TVs in the cell with a top radio built into the wall, with all the knobs there to get even the BBC. The shower rooms had a massive sauna, which you could use twice a week, and there were lots of sports. For our work we received more money than the dole gave out in Manchester. Paid sex was legal and you were allowed to pick out the phone number of a brass you fancied from the newspaper; she'd come to the jail and you had an hour together in a nice room that you took your own clean sheets into. Local fellas who had a woman got even more time, twice a week for one hour, and one fella whose wife was on the women's wing was allowed to stay with her every Saturday night! The biggest fish was Pete from Amsterdam, who ran all the best sex clubs around Europe; he was going out with Miss World, who was Swedish, and her Rolls-Royce was there every week. After the visit he always sorted us out with hash she had smuggled in her knickers – what a top buzz smoking that! Even on our last day he came round and give us all a bit for the trip home, which saw Andy and the Ghost on a plane straight to London from Malmo.

They handcuffed John and I and put us in a small van, then on to a ferry for a couple of hours over to Denmark, where they kept us for an hour in the cells at the airport. Then they marched us up to the plane, but John wasn't having any of it until they took him to the duty free for his bottle of whisky. They finally unlocked our cuffs on the plane and we got blitzed, even smoking a joint. When we got off, I saw this moody geezer looking over his newspaper at us, like they do in the spy films – he even wore the obligatory cream Mac. He tailed us, and as we neared customs, John saw a few Stretford CID moving towards him. One started saying, 'John, don't worry, you'll get bail tonight,' but he didn't hear it, as by now he was Jack Nicholson in *The Shining*: his face was purple with fury and his chest pounded. He necked the last bit of whisky, then smashed the bottle on the floor. I saw this as a good time to slip through, but the whisky, the joint and other effects of the day had the better of me and more plainclothes police dragged me down. John did get bail but I went over to the Central Detention Centre on top of the courts. I'd been nicked months before with Rab in the town, both pissed and singing, and had forgotten all about it, so they wouldn't give me bail. I got a nice visit from Syl and our Jimmy with papers and cigs and when I eventually got out the lads took me for a drink on Oldham Street and I got all the latest football news.

Chapter Twelve

The Swag Game

BEV AND I rented a place up in Partington, a time-warp overspill estate out to the west of Manchester, and I started doing a bit of work with Ernie, one of the massive Burton family of gypsies from the site at the back of our flats: Hughie Burton, the boss of the clan, was a champion bareknuckle fighter and known as the King of the Gypsies. Ernie sold carpets to anyone daft enough to believe a word he said yet he found punters all day long. I was rarely in our flat until the night-time and Bev soon tired of all the activity, so we moved down into a high-rise block off Chester Road. Andy and John moved into the flat next door with Roufy, who was just back from DJing in Spain and had been offered a job over there for the next summer season. We had a spare room that Coco rented out. We were all skint and needed to get back into working the swag game, so I gave Danny at Clean Walls my month's notice.

Cutting through town to meet Gagzy, I bumped into Dicko and the Ghost, who had bought a massive chunk of hash from a sauna round the corner. They were going down to catch a coach to Torquay, the English Riviera, and asked if I wanted to go.

'Does the Pope wear a funny hat?' I said.

We spent all our dosh in three days but still had two ounces of smoke left. We jibbed the train to Reading where there was a big three-day event on and Status Quo were playing, so all the lads were there selling the swag. They sorted us out with a shopping trolley full of gear and we got to work. We took speed and kept working for three full days. I got home with a nice few quid, then went up and did the Glasgow job, which was easy as I enjoyed showing Mark around, though the pair of us were worried about our Jimmy's drinking.

On the Monday morning we went to work at Blackburn Royal Hospital. Jimmy told me and Gagzy to set up the scaffolding while he nipped over to outpatients. Next minute the loudspeaker blared away, 'Can one of the Blaneys please come over to the emergency unit?' Jimmy was laid out – he'd had a heart attack. Yet as soon as he saw us he started shouting for us to bring him some cigs and newspapers. They kept him in the special part where you can't smoke and after a few days he discharged himself and came round to the site as we were packing up to leave. 'Hey boys, wait on and give us a ciggy,' were his first words.

We went back to the Racecourse Estate and Jimmy was out as soon as he saw the pub. 'Tell your ma I'll be home with a chippie,' he said, banging his chest like I'd never seen. We both said he should take time off but he was back to work the next day. Not long after this things became very bad for my mum as Jimmy really lost it. He began to take lots of strong tablets with the booze and would pass out for days on the couch, or walk round the house nude trying to set fire to the curtains. He was always falling asleep with a lighted cig – all our quilts and blankets were burnt. He tried drying out but it just sent him on a bender and he ended up nicked for screwing the local off licence for the umpteenth time. He got six months in Strangeways. (Jimmy would eventually return to County Armagh, join Alcoholics Anonymous and become a leading spokesman for them – a great man who drank way too much yet came through it.)

I finished at the Walls and went back at the swag game with the Cavanaghs for a tour by the glam rock band Kiss. We jumped on a boat from Harwich to Gothenburg and got sorted out with our gear. The Cavanaghs had brought a few heavy guys from Dublin and Manchester, as they'd heard the Cockney Irish were due to turn up again and they wanted to be ready for trouble. Harry Cav was hoping to be able to talk them round but we all knew this was doubtful, as this was a chance for the London Irish to get a good early foothold in this business. I was willing to back the Cavanaghs up but if guns came out I'd be the first runner.

We all sold out before the first concert even began, so we started to get a few beers down, as we were expecting big trouble to kick off: Harry had heard from a Cockney that the Irish had left London in two vans and were due. The selling on the out was even better than before the gig, so we were all in merry but nervy moods back at the big hotel where the band were staying when someone phoned to say there'd been a dust-up on the boat over and all the Cockney Irish had been deported. Everyone could relax and enjoy the perks – often the guys who worked as roadies invited us up to the parties with all the best young girls getting gang-banged. Many a time even the group would invite us up to the main party, which would have piles of coke for people to sniff. I know they say it's good for sex but I always thought it was bollocks: it gives me heartburn and worse still you can't taste or enjoy your beer, so sniffing coke soon passed me by.

There were always plenty of women around who were ready for anything, as they thought the likes of us were well connected. What the fuck: even if we were just the pirates (which is what sellers were called), we could shag as good as anyone else, and we never went short. We worked them all: U2, the Rolling Stones, Pink Floyd, Madonna, Michael Jackson, Bruce Springsteen, David Bowie, in the best halls and stadiums in Europe – though sometimes you could work a small tour in smaller places and do just as well financially if there were not too many workers. Harry, Kev and Tony Cavanagh said we could be the main workers for as long as we wanted, which in my case was for a few months every year right through to the nineties. The rest of the year I'd be on the jib or on a short holiday, as that was one thing I did more than most thieves: treat myself to well-earned breaks.

After Stockholm with Kiss it was Copenhagen, Germany, Holland and then home. We worked two Status Quo gigs in Manchester, then I started to rob video recorders, which were then worth £6–700. I tried to nick one every other day; they were easy to get, as most shops just had those stupid chains attaching them to the display stand. I also got to know all Dicko's mates who lived down on Dickinson Road in a massive house converted into flats. Hash and weed fumes came out all day long. There was Derek, whose dad was an inventor, Vernon, who made the best speakers around Moss Side for all the shebeens, little Danger Mouse, who was a cat burglar, and Jamie, a mad City fan. All of them bought hash from the Asians in Chorlton, so I asked them to see if the Asians wanted to buy any videos. Word came back that they did and we couldn't supply enough of them. They were shipping them out to Bombay and a certain amount of hash came back to Manchester in return.

After a few months the Asians wanted to pay me in hash. I earned more selling it than they'd paid me before but I wasn't cut out to be a dealer. Dicko, Jamie and Danger Mouse, however, all started to fly out to Morocco and Pakistan to buy big amounts of hash. It was the first time we'd invested serious money in drugs and it didn't take long for the wheel to come hurtling off. Most of those involved got nicked in London and Manchester, and Danger Mouse was caught in Karachi Airport with a suitcase full of hash. He was a pretty boy and only sixteen years old, and at the first jail the governor wouldn't take him in, as he said there'd be a riot just for his arse. The next jail did take him but the screws raped him bad for near on a year. When he came home he had to spend four months in hospital, as he'd picked up some bad things.

This was a big lesson to me. I had many chances to make easy money from drugs but knew that thieving was much more up my street. I went back on the jib in Europe.

* * *

Sitting in Bonn train station that summer, I remembered that Roufy was down in Lloret De Mar doing his stuff on the twin decks, so instead of going home I kipped in the station and bought a ticket in the morning. With a few hours to kill, I stole a nice camera for some photos in the sun and flirted a video recorder from the shelf as I walked out. It was mid-afternoon when I arrived in Lloret, so I parked myself on the beach and soaked up a few hours of sun on my tattooed, pale white body. I sold the video for a top price – they were all mad for whatever I could nick – and blew the lot and more with Roufy as he showed me round all the best places.

I stayed for two weeks in the old part of town, eating at the fishermen's places or at an old-style Spanish eaterie with low prices that cooked their meat, rabbits and chickens on a spit over a wood fire. The best nightclubs tried hard to keep the English beer monsters out, but

Roufy got us in alright. The two main guys for smoke were Van, a Dutch all-round gangster with a big name in the prisons in Holland, and Cockney Frank, an East End fella who was a top-cat sneak thief. He'd done a nice one the week before I got there by nicking a full locker from behind the counter at a big hotel; they used it as a safe deposit for the guests, so it was full of money and passports.

At the end of my stay in Spain, Roufy got a few days off so we went down to Geneva. A long day's graft saw our pockets and bags full with cash, watches, tom, vids and cameras – we copped for everything we had a pop at. We bought those long, fold-up sausage bags and it must have taken us four hours to get it all in order. Next day I hid our bags on the bus while Roufy blagged the driver, slipping them into the wrong section for bags going back to England and putting one in the back trunk. If it came on top we could deny all knowledge. We would go back this way and by train countless times over the years, and in cars which were hired or stolen or bought, and not once did we have any problems.

Back in Manchester I soon put all the lads on to the opportunities at Lloret De Mar, and Bev and I packed our bags and spent the rest of the summer in Lloret. Coco said he'd look after the flat while we were away, as Bev was like a sister to him. Lloret became our main place besides Amsterdam to call into. The only thing that wasn't worth selling there was top-of-the-range tom, as they couldn't afford it. Yet now and then we'd get a parcel of shit gold called 888, which is the lowest carat gold in Europe, and in Barcelona they'd give us amazing prices for it and would even buy silver and pearls, which we'd normally throw or give away.

* * *

I spoke to Dicko about calming down at the football and he agreed. We decided to concentrate on making money at the match by ticket touting. We knew trouble would still come our way – it always did – but we'd try to give up playing the thug, or at least wouldn't be running in head first. Let the new ones try their hands at it.

Dicko took me down to meet some of City's main faces before a big game and it came out that they were all now following the National Front, going on marches in London. This was crazy to our lot, as we'd always been mixed and the NF wouldn't have lasted two seconds at Old Trafford. It seemed even stupider at City, which was in the heart of Moss Side, and it wasn't too long before the NF hardcore got slapped by the City's black gang, the Cool Cats.

Sometimes I'd go to City games with him. We jibbed the train to one at Leicester and a big mob of Cool Cats went into the away end, giving out a few digs before the police escorted them back to the City section. At the same time, Dicko asked this feller in his cafe cabin for a drink while I was after his money, which was in an open till tray with all the notes stacked together. I could see a heavy clip on the notes; the rest, in coins, was almost overflowing. I ordered and paid for a hotdog, then as he was giving me my change, Dicko knocked the ketchup off the counter with his elbow. I asked for it, which meant the feller would have to take his eye off us for a split second.

This moment in thieving is rare but I've had it on tills and tonies in the past: they know 99.9 per cent that you're up to no good, but still fall into the trap, and it's that certain helpless look on their faces that stays with you. As the feller bent to pick up the sauce, Dicko leant over a touch, put his full weight on my back hip and gave me the leverage to reach over without having to jump and grab the tray. We couldn't hold the change but that was okay as we scattered it for the City fans, causing more disturbance and giving us that bit of space to get offside. We grabbed a divvy cap and scarf each and looked like real goons for the rest of the day. We binned a ton. City, after grabbing all the change, then pulled down the feller's shutters and locked him in. All through the first half they rocked the cabin from side to side until the police got him out. They had him with binoculars looking through the City crowd, who all threw back dozens of coins on his and the coppers' heads.

November 1978 found Dicko and me in Köln in Germany, banging two jacks on the first afternoon to get us back in the swing. The next day we were prowling a shop when a woman worker left her till. I was straight into it when all of a sudden I felt a right crack across the side of my head from some feller who'd dived on my back screaming for help. I threw my cards in straight away and told the police how the woman walked away leaving the till open, so I was weak and couldn't resist. They searched our bags in front of us but failed to find the huge bundle of German notes in one of the side pockets of Dicko's, as it was partly hidden by the strap. So they had nothing on Dicko but both coppers kept rubbing his full-length sheepskin coat, saying they knew it was stolen. After half an hour of this, they let him go with all the dosh!

I was remanded in custody. The jail was massive, with underground cells built for terrorists. They even had watch towers with armed screws, and police driving round the jail twenty-four hours a day. I was in court just before Christmas. The judge, who had one arm as the other had been blown off in the War, sentenced me to a month in jail. With time served on remand, I was free to go. I headed back to Manchester and surprised Bev on Christmas Eve.

In 1979 we all spent most of the summer in Spain, then back to Manchester in October and on to Brighton, where a friend of Roufy's who had just got out of a Moroccan jail sold all our tom. A few weeks before Christmas, I was asked to work on the Supertramp tour and agreed to join up with them in Berlin. We had to pick up a connection in Köln and had a few hours to wait, so Roufy said he was up for some robbing. I told him I wasn't, because of the nicking I'd had the previous Christmas. We met a couple of hours later at the station and Roufy had two bags full of stolen stuff. He was putting them into a locker when we both got swooped on again – and they enjoyed sending us to jail, as they knew we'd be missing Christmas.

They put us on separate wings and we didn't see each other for three months; it was pure bang-up with long days and only a few minutes in the morning for a walk and a chat. The priest gave us both a Christmas parcel with a bit of food and some books. Roufy pleaded guilty and I pleaded not guilty to the same one-armed judge. After a few minutes of offering explanations, my lawyer told me to be quiet and listen to the judge, who was waving his stump in my general direction. He said he was going to send Roufy home but would send me back to jail on remand, where I would wait six months to be tried in a higher court. So I changed me plea to guilty and when we walked out of court they gave us tube tickets to return to the jail to collect our stuff. As if. We were buzzing like kids and both in need of a drink, so we robbed a good-quality bottle of brandy for the night train home, then necked another full bottle and went to sleep.

Back home I found out that Dicko, OB and Noddy had been nicked in Blackburn and were in Strangeways, while Coco, Scull and Pooley had copped for twelve months in Swissy. I decided to cast my net a bit wider and started grafting in Yorkieland, as some places there were still in the Dark Ages – so much so that the Chief Constable over there started moaning in the press about gangs from Manchester and Liverpool using the M62 to hit the easy pickings on his turf. I banged a till in sunny Scunthorpe, the exact same till I'd done the previous year, but three building workers jumped me as I made my way out and one sat on top of my chest until the dibble arrived, saying, 'Hey up youth I say, that could have been my bloody wages.' In the police car I had two other problems: a snide driving licence in my pocket and a bag of weed down my trousers. I was handcuffed from behind with a copper on each side, but managed to get the licence down the back seat and they never looked for the weed.

At magistrates I asked for a crown court hearing, as I knew they'd be requesting one anyway, and when they asked me what I was pleading I said I wasn't entering a plea until then. This meant that when I got sent to Lincoln Jail I'd be put with all the fellas pleading not guilty, which was a much easier regime with three visits a week, parcels and even a small bottle of wine or can of beer. We'd save them and drink them all on a Saturday. We could buy a newspaper every day and life was very easy, with a bit of part-time work sewing miners' vests. I had Dicko and our Mark post my 'Opal Fruits' and baccy straight from the Dam.

Bev took a live-in job in Walton-on-Thames as an auxiliary nurse. Once down there, she more or less admitted she'd shagged a guy who was working in Spain and had stayed in contact with him while I was in jail. The simple fact is that Cowboys on the road like us should never have strong relationships, but like everyone else we do and not many women can cope with the stress and hassle that comes with it. I never pushed her to admit to cheating on me, as we both knew it had gone down.

Our Manchester flat had been a bit of a party zone and became known as the 101 Club after its number. When I got out I cleaned and fixed it all up, and just before I went back to Europe I went for a booze-up in the Midland Hotel when in walked Sully with a new firm of Wythenshawe. They got pissed, then Sull and some others Tony'd a nightsafe pouch, so they all had a few bob. They bought the 101 Club off me there and then for £1,500, fully furnished. Even though it was a council gaff it was well worth it for this firm, who all said they'd be seeing me over in the Dam soon. They all soon became heavy drug users. Gordon was one of the first in Manchester to die from Aids, while Bingo caught it doing time in Germany and also died.

Our Mark now was fully on the firm; his Clean Walls days were over. Dicko was back from Swissy and took us out on the town in the Dam for a couple of days, then we stocked up with the best hi-fis for a trip to Lloret. Spain was still emerging from the years of General Franco's dictatorship and you could not get decent hi-fis or ghettoblasters there. Walkman pocket systems were amazing; the money we could get for a bag full in Spain was bounty and so easy. Every now and then the Customs went on strike. Up to ten days was normal and this was the only time I would ever smuggle. Once on the train it was hilarious how many would be off to the toilet coming out with big grins. I always got off after a few stops and straight into a taxi.

Unfortunately we missed the last coach from Amsterdam because we were on the piss in a late-night bar and had to wait until the following morning for the next one. We stayed out all night, then snorted two big lines of speed to keep our heads together before getting on the bus. The journey took twenty-four hours and neither of us slept, so when we arrived we both got a sunbed out on the beach, splashed on some oil and fell asleep – for eight hours during the hottest part of the day.

I felt like death when I woke up and we both spent three days in bed with sunstroke, though once the lobster colour had subsided I had a great tan. We headed back to the Dam and I bumped into little Ronnie the Scouse zapper, who was running with a new firm into buying smoke and coke. Ronnie was still the same, loved his dipping and was now living in London. I saw him off at the airport and bumped into Sully, who had a new lad with him from Wythenshawe known as 'Fletch' (from the TV series *Porridge*). He turned out to be an asset on the firm as he was only into the beer while almost everyone else had got into the Class As in a big way and was sniffing coke before grafting.

At this stage we had the firm running like a military unit. Twenty of us would come out every day after our egg and bacon and head for the Flying Dutchman to plot up. The beauty was that we never knew what we were doing, so if the Dutch plod were watching us there was no way they could have known. Britain might have been in the grip of mass unemployment but we went through cash like water. Money was always split down the middle. If anyone tucked a wedge down their socks they were off the firm, but it never happened. You were working with good people and you knew it would never happen.

It finally came on top for us all down near Rotterdam. We were in the car checking out a getaway route for a planned snatch when Chewy from Chorlton, another new recruit, inhaled a couple of full fat lines of coke, ran straight into a shop and came out with a bag of money. We were gobsmacked, even more so when a few of the local cloggies clambered onto the bonnet to stop us driving away. They soon jumped off when I put my foot down but as I turned a corner onto the first decent bit of road the police got right behind us. I cut across two lanes of traffic and onto the motorway but it was blocked off by police with guns. Chewy was still counting the money and when he looked up, said, 'Drive through them and then it's every man for himself.' Instead I pulled over, put my hands in the air and let the police do their thing.

At the nick, Chewy, not knowing the ways around Dutch law as well as we did, shouts up that we might as well throw our hands up and admit it – I think he wanted the company in jail. No chance. We told them we were visiting friends in Rotterdam and had stopped to find a café and use the toilet when Chewy was on drugs and had jumped out and snatched the money without warning. We spent thirty bad-arse days in police detention, where they even took our mattresses at seven in the morning and gave them back fourteen hours later. No cigs or walks or books or writing, just pure bang-up. Yet the court in Rotterdam listened to our story and found us not guilty. Chewy got six months and the rest of us were deported. On the ferry home we got talking to a group of bandits from Stockport who'd smashed up the customs room before the cops put them on the boat. They'd been grafting in Turkey on Visa cards, then with the proceeds had toured Europe before swinging through 'the Magnet'.

When we got home we bought a car at the Salford auction under the arches for £100 without tax, insurance or MOT. We'd had a bit of a rethink and had decided to travel by car and say we were Brit workers on the lookout for work. The car was a dream, a poor man's Rolls-Royce, a top Rover with a spare tyre outside on the top of the back boot, a three-litre engine, inside leather with a mega dash and a magnified rearview mirror. It had a few holes in it and we had to pull one of the wings out and back into shape, but it would do for us.

We drove to Camden Lock in London to meet top City lads the Gillett brothers, who were down for the FA Cup final against Spurs. After they drew we decided not to stick around for the replay (which City lost) but to cross the North Sea again. Sully got a pull for something to do with bent passports and was sent back up to court in Manchester while we continued on. We drove to the north of Holland, to Groningen, a nice old town near the German border with lots of student parties and small concerts by well-known bands. After a great day, we crossed the border into Deutschland without being spun or having any hassle from customs – it appeared our new identity as Brit workers was holding up. We copped for a tray of diamond rings, then nipped back into Holland and stopped in a village for a scran. One of the lads went into a shop to buy a pair of shoes while I sneaked round the till area and liberated the full money pouch, slipping out of the back door. We got a bit lost and after an hour or so ended up driving back through the same village, where the police were waiting. I don't think they could quite believe it.

That Sunday the police took me into a big office that had the Wimbledon tennis on the TV. I had a smoke while one of them brought up a tray with one of those jolly silver lids on – and when I lifted it, there lay all the diamond rings we'd nicked across the border. They sent me to Zutpen jail for thirty days. I was probably safer there than at home – when I phoned Bev she said riots had broken out in Moss Side and the police station was under attack. I pleaded guilty to the money but said the tom came from selling my arse in a Swedish porno film! The cops couldn't prove any different and had to let me have it back. After another week they let me out and I drove the Rover to Amsterdam, where I let Dicko take her over and he used her for a full winter around the Dam without having to spend a penny on her. Our Mark and I got a limited edition BMW touring car from American Bob and drove it down to Lloret, where Roufy, Coco, Rat and a full contingent were in town. We had a good three weeks, the only trouble coming when a few Dutch doormen baseball-batted one of the City lads. In revenge, we followed them home at the end of the night and gave them a shoeing.

We decided to have a drive round France with another car full of grafters including Cid and Divvy, who had a three-litre Ford Capri. We reached Marseille around five in the morning and parked in the square, waiting for a café to open. We drifted to sleep and were woken by the Div, who'd clocked a kid grabbing our Mark's wallet from the glove compartment. We got out of the cars as the kid ran down a back alley towards some grim-looking flats towering over the Square. None of us were up for chasing him, as the wallet held only around £150 and some bits of Spanish money and a passport. Instead we had a few beers and were soon joking and wishing the kid luck.

When I got back to Manchester, Bev and I found a flat in Whalley Range. There was an approved school for girls on the same road and I watched a few of them scaling the walls to prostitute themselves round the corner. I had a couple of brief trips abroad working the concerts again and became friendly with a Cockney called the Jackal, a lone grafter we met on the boat who would come up to Manchester and hang around all week waiting for any kind of work, armed pull-ups being his speciality. He suggested making a few grand turning over some Asian drug dealers he knew well and who trusted him. The Jackal was going to tell the Asians I was a mate from London, in town to buy a few kilos of hash and a certain amount of powder, with £10,000 to spend.

He arranged to meet them at a curry house. When I pulled up round the corner, the Asians clocked me and told me to wait in the car, as they'd only do the biz through the Jackal. He walked into the eating area, then up the back stairs into the attic, where they were going to count the money. This money was the worst snide you've ever seen, so what we'd done was count it out the way they do in drug deals, with £90 in a bundle the normal way and the last £10 note creased over it to make a £100. We put ten £100s folded up this way into a plastic bank bag, so the Jackal had ten such bags in total. The Asians opened a couple of the bags and never once unfolded the top creased note, which would have exposed the Rip, as they trusted the Jackal so much. I kept my engine ticking over outside, waiting for the scream to go up, but it didn't and we drove off not quite believing we'd got away with it. The Jackal knew the Asians would kill him if they got hold of him, but neither of us gave a fuck. Once we'd sold the parcel on it was happy days, even though the car ran out of petrol round the corner. I promised myself I'd get back on the jib in the Alps as soon as I could.

Chapter Thirteen

The Wide Awake Firm

IN MAY 1982, I crossed the water to see a couple of Middleton lads who were in jail in Den Haag. Driving away afterwards, I was heading to the main road when a truck pulled out in front of me. I tried to swerve but it hit the passenger side of the car with such force that it sent me through a wall and into a small pond. There was a photograph of the crash in the local paper the next day, which I saw as I lay in my hospital bed with a busted hip. I had to lie flat for weeks, but the hospital was like a holiday camp, as they'd wheel my bed out on to the big balcony and the sea and the sun were right there. I watched Ipswich win the European Cup Winners Cup with a few of the lads who brought a TV into my room and the staff said it was alright for us to drink cans and have a couple of joints.

Once I was better I headed for the Alps with our Mark and copped for a couple of tills straight in, even though some of the shop owners were getting wise to our game. As with any crime, methods evolve. Some of the gaffers told their staff to empty the till two or three times a day and to count out the money, then put it in bundles underneath the till tray. Yet this made things even easier for me, as they wouldn't notice it missing until the next time they counted the dough. They also started using counter cashboxes – or 'countie cashies' as we called them – for the bigger notes, so a lot of the time these became better to rob than the till itself.

At dinnertime, our kid and I walked through a side door into a flower shop and could see the two staff in the back cutting up and arranging flowers. They'd left the keys in the till, but as I was sliding the cash tray out a woman appeared in the doorway facing me with a big dog that started barking. I jumped back, startled, and the tray crashed out of my hands. We ran out but the snow was up to our knees and we were lucky that the car was parked round the corner. We drove away up into the mountains but it started to snow again, which soon forced us back down. We knew the police would be looking for us, so we parked out of the way and a few hours later slipped through a farmer's road – right into a police roadblock. The cops were not at all happy and I could tell they wanted to hurt us. They started digging us in the side and twisting our hands when we were cuffed but we kept our cool.

The cop shop was tiny, so small that at certain times when the air vent went quiet we could whisper to each other. That was a lifesaver, as we knew they'd split us up very soon. The police were not even interested in the till; instead they started asking questions about a tidal wave of sneaks in the area and a blag where ten grand had gone. They knew they were all down to us. After two weeks of grilling they sent me to jail at Chur. I lay in my cell listening to the radio and was elated when it came through that United had reached the League Cup final and were playing Liverpool. That final became infamous among the lads for a £50,000 smash and grab on a tom shop in Swiss Cottage, north London, by a load of United.

The first morning I got out to walk round the small yard, I heard:

'Now then, Beaner!'

Fuck me, here was I looking up at the snowy mountain tops and there was Tony Cav's head at the barred window of his cell. Tony was doing a few months for not paying tax on his tee-shirts and posters the year before. His cellmate Dave, a Yank, was in for shooting someone over a bent card game.

Mark came a week later but was on the punishment wing, with twenty-three-hour-a-day bang-up and solo exercise. We each got taken back to the police station every other day for three months for more questions. This got to the stage with me where they'd take off their watches, place them on the table and then say, Right, you've got four hours to make up your mind to admit to at least the £10,000 theft with your partner and you will be banned from Swissy for so many years and we'll escort you to the German border. They never knew until near the end that we were brothers, so when they got the info from Manchester police and presented it to us they were shocked that we didn't throw in the towel and tell them the lot. Instead we blagged that we had snide passports because the dates of birth made us younger so we could qualify for cheaper flights!

Eventually the police put up the white flag and let us go. We went straight to Zurich to get a smoke at a druggy haunt called Needle Park, then went to see if the British Embassy could sort us out with a ticket to the UK (so we could see United play Brighton in the FA Cup Final the next day). The guy on the counter more or less told us to fuck off. So we thought we'd hit the Dam to watch the game in the Flying Dutchman, and drove through the night, slipping through customs in France, Luxembourg and Belgium and going through the back door into Holland, as we had only a snide slip of paper from the Swiss police as ID. At Eindhoven the car started to lose power and no sooner had we pulled over than the motorway police were behind us; they drove open-top white Porsches that looked like something out of the *Wacky Races* – the cops even wore those helmets with ear muffs and long white scarves. They checked our names in the bad book and deported us that night.

* * *

It wasn't long before we were back, with the added attraction of watching United play in Eindhoven. We'd had to dump our car in the Flatlands after a bit of business, so instead of getting on the ferry as planned with the car, we jumped on the train to Eindhoven, where we met Binzy and Toby. Plan A was to run into a tom shop and go for whatever, as there was now more than twenty of our lot all ready for it in the White Horse pub with another 200 or more Reds getting pissed, stoned and coked-up. But there were armies of police about, clocking us all day, and we all kept thinking that if we made the final it would be played in Basle in the Land of the Wad, so we left it and instead joined in the singing and drinking.

The game was a tough 0–0 draw. Afterwards the police did well to get 90 per cent of the Reds into the train station area. They had a special train all the way to the ferry but not a soul got on it; police with dogs had to stand there for over a hour with all the trains going up to Amsterdam bursting full with Devils shouting over sarcastic comments. Me, our Kid and Spud went back into the bar where the Benchill lads were on form till well after the midnight hour. The return at O.T. was equally close but we got the winner via a pen.

The build-up to the quarter-final second leg at Old Trafford was huge there as we'd been hammered in Barcelona 2–0. Reds flew in from all over the globe for this one and I managed to get a top-of-the-range seat. The crowd that night were at their peak – 'Maradona, you're a wanker, you're a wanker' – and it was United at their Euro best as Captain Marvel and Frank Stapleton led the successful fightback.

We all hit the Gallery, which was now Manchester's number one club. It was a small wine bar just off Deansgate. Pete opened up the downstairs, then next door and finally a massive function room that had parties and concerts, with a good gallery upstairs, and Roufy was the main DJ for all the time it was open, bar the year in jail where he got not guilty in a big drug case and the times spent in Spain. Later on it became a notorious gang haunt but back then it was a great night.

It all ended in the semi against a strong Juventus team with that man Rossi the killer after Big Norm had banged in an equaliser to give us all hope. Truth was United could not win the big trophies for love or money in this period so FA Cup runs were our chance for glory. We played West Ham in the quarter-final of the FA Cup in 1985 and the thugs from West Ham's ICF came down to Old Trafford and slipped out of the ground early to seize the initiative – or so they claimed. More likely they were trying to get back to the train station in one piece. They bumped into the main United boys who busted them up bad, chasing them all the way from Warwick Road to the Mancunian Way flyover at the bottom of Chester Road.

The semi-final was at Goodison Park, against Liverpool. Four carloads of us got into a pub on the outskirts with Snap, one of the main Scouse swag workers. We reached the ground a bit late and settled in to see Robbo put us in the lead. Coins were thrown and from out of the Scouse ranks came a loud bang and a couple of flares. The dibble steamed in and nicked a load. The Scouse pulled it back to 1–1 in the last few minutes and Ian Rush should have put them in the lead. We all started singing our song 'Ian Rush, Ian Rush, Ian Ian Rush, he gets the ball and he does fuck all, Ian Ian Rush!' with the odd 'Gonzoo-oo, Gonzoo-oo' thrown in. It ended a 2–2 draw and we all went back to Snap's pub, where he was giving North West Malc plenty and we all downed a raft of ale and got involved in football talk with the locals.

The match was replayed the following Wednesday at Maine Road. We met in City's social club very early. The game had everything, including McGrath putting into his own net in the first half. At half-time we took over the bar in the social club and decided to stay in there for the start of the second half. Not a one of us paid for a drink. Robbo equalised and Sparky scored the winner, so at the end we all dived on to the pitch and carried Robbo on our shoulders. The dibble were just as happy, as they knew it was all in fun.

* * *

Not long after, our kid and I had been driving overnight from the south of France into the Geneva manor of Swissy when we came across a shopping centre. It looked a likely place so we stopped for an iced lemon tea and a quick freshen-up in the khazi, then checked out a decent-sized store that had lots of people buying stuff, so the till area was busy. Right behind it was an open door with the peter (safe) on show. Mark glided in, found the twirlers, gave me the wink, then picked up a couple of pairs of jeans to slip in the back with – we did this a lot, just a silly blag in case staff barged in while you were mooching around, so you could say you were looking for the changing room.

Mark closed the door, so I strolled over ready to do the block and blag. Then right out of the blue, this huge woman walked in with a bag full of breakfast for all the staff. In this position it was cert to be on top – I knew she'd be heading straight for the staff room where Mark was with all that scran. As Bobby G used to say (and the Happy Mondays later sang), 'Call the cops!' I tried my best to stall her but she burst into room with the food. Mark had managed to lock the peter back up but had no time to put the twirlers back in place and had slung them to one side. He'd not managed to take a bean but the scream was soon echoing all through the Winkel as we gave it legs past the security feller. We legged into the car park and were about to hit the pedal when the guard took a full jump and clung onto the windscreen. After wheel-spinning in circles we finally sent him flying into the main entrance and sped off.

In minutes a lone copper was up our arse flashing but we almost took off in our turbo Golf. I saw a slip road off the motorway but unfortunately it was on the wrong side. Undaunted, I did the best – or worst – handbrake turn ever and rocketed across oncoming traffic right onto a clear run, so I gave it even more gas. It all went to cock when we hit the roundabout at the bottom, shot into a massive advertising board and came to a sudden halt. Then it was offmans into the fields, heading for some farms. We shouted as we split to blame each other for the driving if we were nicked, as we both knew the guard we'd launched off the car wouldn't know for certain which of us it was. We both got nicked coming out of the field.

Now the dibble were on our case, as the feller was in a bad way and being a security guard who was viewed as being like a copper, so after five bad-arse days doing pure twenty-four-hour dub up and getting loads of grief from the older bulls it was a result to get sent to the local jail, or Holiday Inn as it was nicknamed. Mark went to the block where he got fuck-all except a thirty minute walk alone every other day, while I was on menus for dinner and main meals, fridge in my cell, TV, tunes, coffee machine, toaster, the works. The main boys in there were grafters who lived in France and came over the border once a week to steal cars. The screws kept out of the way, communicating via loudspeaker with cameras at the electric gates.

After thirty days, they charged us with attempted and organised theft with forced escape. My lawyer did have one bit of good news: we'd be up in court the following week, so there was a great chance the dibble wouldn't suss out our snide ID, as it normally took six weeks for them to send and receive fingerprints and details to and from the UK. Sure enough we weren't sussed but for some reason my brief never showed for the hearing. I shouted out that I'd take Mark's brief but the court clerk told me to shut the fuck up.

That was it – I was over the dock and out of the court in seconds. I didn't plan it; I felt pushed into a corner and reacted. If I'd known the layout of the building I'd have made it out but I ended up running up and down in circles, then into some coppers with batons. They didn't hammer me, just gave me three or four sharp whacks on the shins to hobble me.

After a break for lunch, they came to take me back to court. I refused point blank. No lawyer, no Blaney. Their heads were kippered but they went ahead with the trial. In our police statements we'd said that a kid from the Dam was driving but pulled over and got a bus. The court had a break which went into a couple of hours; I knew my storming out had got them thinking if it was worth the cost, as the case now looked like having to go to a bigger court. They just about got away with finding Mark guilty of being in a private area without permission, as Mark said he thought it was a changing room and a couple of pairs of jeans were found there. He apologised and said he should have asked a member of staff, but pointed out that there was no sign and the door was ajar. The security feller, as we suspected, had no idea who was driving so they had to drop that charge against both of us. Mark was told he'd be deported for five years, with a six-month jail term hanging over his napper, while I was found not guilty and got 500 Swiss francs for my troubles without even sitting through the trial.

To avoid arousing suspicion as much as possible, we did lots of graft wearing Italian navy blue cashmere coats, so much so that it became a bit of a tag. We'd sell our parcels to the Quality Street Gang in Manchester and Bev used to take the piss wicked when we met the likes of Mad Barney and Killer to do the deals, as they were well known for wearing that sort of clobber and she reckoned we were copying them. I also got murderous stick if I went in the Gallery nightclub dressed like that but I'd often just have flown in from doing some airport and didn't have time to change. Anyway, for the yuppie mid-Eighties this kind of dressing got us massive results – you looked mega smart and they were great for blocking because there was so much coat. Smart reversible jackets were another favourite, to be turned inside out once you'd pulled off a job, and we would also have manicures and wear polished, expensive shoes – many shop staff, especially women, will look at men's feet. But leather soles were a no-no, as they slip when running.

We were all in the cashmere when we hit a big jewellery fair at a posh Cheshire hotel. Terry Corrigan had told us about this fish tank full of diamond bracelets and necklaces. It only had an old fella in uniform standing over it but it did have a few live scorpions in the tank. So we got thick leather gloves to wear, our Mark had a steel bar up his sleeve to smash the case if need be and I had a stun gun. Now we were rarely violent on jobs but someone had told me you could shoot these into the hip area and the person would collapse without suffering any harm – though sometimes in the panic of the moment they'd end up firing into the neck and giving people heart attacks, which was why we eventually moved to CS gas. We had a stolen car and a jocky ready outside.

Just as we'd woven through all the stalls and moved into position to strike, all these strobe lights exploded, music came blasting out and a load of people crowded into the hall to see this woman having her photo taken next to the tank in a £50,000 platinum bikini! We all separated, our heads up our arses, and got the fuck out, but we couldn't help chuckling and saying what a mess it would have been if we'd struck.

Then Corrigan piped up, 'Don't get too down about it all. Look at this.'

He whipped out a tray of diamond rings that he'd slipped from a nearby stall while the staff were distracted by the show. That's what was so good about being in a gang: we all looked out for each other and often surprised ourselves with what came our way.

* * *

Bev told me she couldn't cope with my lifestyle, plus she hated football. She hadn't fully got over what happened at Lou Macari's testimonial, when United played Celtic. Through our Jimmy I knew there'd be a load making the journey, and when I went into Chorlton to get Bev a paper the place was full of Celtic. Not a one of them could get into a boozer. I got talking to a vanload outside the newspaper shop and instead of taking Bev her paper back, I jibbed this lot into a pub, the script being that they all took off their Celtic stuff and when we first got in they all hit a corner while one of them came to the bar and helped me as I shouted the beers in. After an hour the landlord was okay, so the scarves and songs came out.

I phoned Bev to explain I wouldn't be coming home but would be going straight to Old Trafford, and being cheeky I asked if there was any chance of a lift, as it was now last orders. She came down in the car and as she pulled up there was a line of them outside the pub, all having a piss and singing away at the same time. Bev was not happy when four of this lot jumped into the car with me. Bev is black and when they started calling her 'a wee pretty choco hen' she got angry, even though they were only joking because they didn't know any better. Maybe I should have said something but I was now not with it at all and was trying to learn a new song. She dropped us off right outside K Stand, which normally you can't drive anywhere near unless you're on the team, but Bev wanted rid of us. All around the car was a mass of Celtic who'd been in Blackpool the day before and had robbed lots of huge green, yellow and gold umbrellas that were now open and spinning in rhythm to the bagpipers on their firm. When I got back after the game I suggested to Bev that we should try living in Europe and we agreed to give it a go after the Cup final.

The lads got a coach to go down to Wembley; it was due to leave at ten o'clock from the Old Cock near Stretford shopping precinct. The back door of the pub opened at seven o'clock so we were in there early and I'd bought an ounce of weed, so we started to get amongst it. The trip down was brilliant: I'd never been on a coach to a match before and it was great not having to worry about anything. The coach had a toilet and we watched United videos on the TV and pulled over at a couple of service stations for a stretch. We stopped round the corner from Neasden tube, the nearest to the ground, and walked up Wembley Way singing 'Only a Red Devil can stop a treble', as Everton had already wrapped up the double in Rotterdam. I felt a sharp crack on the side of my head from a Scouse flag, but it was just a little shithead who had already given it serious toes. At the bar in the ground I got a few brandies and pints and two Moss Side Frontliners helped me carry them right up into the top part. All around us people wanted a go on my joint that was burning away like a bonfire. The guys soon twisted a few together and it was all smiles through the game, everyone going mad when Big Norm netted the winner.

We all met outside the big hotel facing Wembley and managed to blag a couple of passes to get inside. By six o'clock, twenty of us had used the passes, including our Mark and the Sale Mob. We soon had the waiters pissed and on our side. One of the lads nicked a couple of room keys from the main desk, so we ran up a huge tab on the rooms, getting endless bottles of the best wines all night.

As we left, one of the lads gave the keys to the flunky in top hat and uniform, saying, 'Would you be so kind and drop these off at reception?'

The flunky replies, 'Certainly,' and says to us all, 'Have a jolly good night.'

Ha! We got back on the coach, stopped off in Rugby for last orders and took over a pub. The landlord took our money, then called the dibble, and when they arrived the coach driver said he was getting off. When we got back to Manchester we found a pub on Chester Road that was open for the entire weekend. A couple of the lads missed the coach at Rugby and got a taxi back, before doing a runner at the first set of lights on Chester Road. Bev was not happy when I rolled in at Monday teatime.

When I'd sobered up a bit the next day we decided it was time for a change.

*   *   *

We hired a van and moved to Rotterdam, where we rented a room. It would be my base for the next two or three years. Bev started work nursing in a private house and came home for the weekends. I used a Brit bar called the Boozer, where a mad Red from the Isle of Man was the governor; he'd run a bar in Lloret and I couldn't believe it when I saw him pulling pints. I also started to work the swag game for Renus, whose minder was a bad football thug for years. We would meet in a bar near Feyenoord's ground called Spot The Looney, which wasn't that hard to do as it served a real strong beer and a big smoke. We spent hours playing darts and listening to good music and Barry soon let me and some of the other English lads have a tab that we paid every other week.

I befriended two English guys living over there and when I got hammered they would let me crash at their flats. Paul was from Chorley, a pure United fanatic who'd travelled round Europe with United, and his flat was a real armpit – you had to breathe slow for the first few minutes after walking through the door to get used to the stale air, otherwise you'd gag. Dave was from Hull and a Man City head who kept his massive flat spotless, so I preferred staying with him, if I was in a fit enough state to make a choice.

United played in Rotterdam in a weekend competition, beating Stuttgart on the Friday night, then losing to Feyenoord on the Sunday. I went with Irish Tommy, who had started grafting with us. He was the spit of Barry McGuigan and all his family came from Belfast before moving to Ancoats. The best thing about Tommy was he loved the blagging, which suited me as the blag is more stressful than the sneak – though to be truthful he was up for anything. He always robbed expensive, funky lighters that he'd take back to Manchester and impress the girls with, and when he got hammered on weed and lager he would start writing IRA all over the place, but what a game little feller he was – fearless.

We flew over to Lloret and we were straight into it, on the mooch looking for the next few quid. Tommy had a wander around an amusement arcade and got caught round the back in the office where the money was all on show. He ran out of the back door and over a nasty spiked fence that cut his hands up bad, so we lay low for a couple of days in the sun before heading back to Rotterdam, where we had a good run on the safes in the big supermarkets – we went for the smaller safes in the wine departments, which always contained around £10–15,000, sometimes more. The money was stored in a compartment that we had to bust open with a small crowbar once we'd located the keys. On our first job, we copped for close on £20,000 and went potty, buying a BMW that blew up just outside Amsterdam.

Tommy and I also spent a lot of time at Black Lincoln's: he was now married and lived in London, just off Wandsworth Road in the Stockwell Flats, which were the spit of Colly Flats where I'd grown up. We drank round the Elephant and Castle in a club called Arches. It was quite hard to get into so I always said I was with Factory Records, a blag which opened doors all over Europe – though strangely never in Manchester. Tommy could be a bit of a liability, mainly to himself – he hadn't learned how to handle London. He was forever losing his lighter and as we walked out of the Stockwell tube station I saw him asking a black guy for a light and then disappear round the corner. I was a little way behind Tommy and as I turned the corner myself I saw Tommy with blood pumping out of his head and the black guy running away. Mad as fuck, we chased him with a brick each but he disappeared into the flats.

Next day we went to meet all the Reds at Euston before heading over to Stamford Bridge to watch United win with a power volley from Sparky. We stayed on the piss with the lads, then met Lincoln in a shebeen run by a black guy called Jonesy. He was a Moss Sider who loved United, so I gave him my programme and got a joint going. We were just blending in as the only white guys there when a voice boomed over the microphone, in rhythm with the music.

'See you white boys in that there corner, you'll no get out of here alive tonight, me tell ya!'

It was the guy we'd chased from the tube station, with his full posse behind him. We ran into the back and Lincoln and Jonesy had to lock us in, then call the police to get us out.

Tommy and I also went to see Northern Ireland play England; if the Irish got a result they would be going to Mexico for the 1986 World Cup. At half-time I noticed all the funny looks Tommy was getting from the Paddies, as he was wearing a Man United hat with Celtic on the other side, which wasn't going down well as they were all prods. So in a silly Lancashire accent I passed out a few cans, saying to Tommy that he should burn the hat he'd just stolen. He clocked what was going on and set it on fire. Pat Jennings made two world-class saves in the dying minutes and the goalless draw was enough to send them to Mexico, so at the final whistle 15,000 of us erupted and then it was out on the lash. Tommy was on his biggest high ever and we partied the night away at a club in Camden that had boxes around the top tiers with full-size *Spitting Image* puppets in them. It was one of those sweet nights.

* * *

Back in Manchester for Easter 1986, I bumped into Eric and Gags on Oldham Street. Eric was still doing the acid-washing and sandblasting while Gagzy was not long back from Hamburg, where he'd been sandblasting at the docks. That kind of work was no longer what it had been, though, after Maggie Thatcher cut off the Government grants and killed off some of the big companies. Gags had been through a bad time; his new wife turned out to be a real moll who ended up all over the papers for having sex in a police station with a supergrass. Gagzy's head was cabbaged. He knew the beer was killing him, so I asked him if he wanted to come on the road with the 'Wide Awake Firm' – a nickname we had adopted from the kids' morning TV show *The Wide Awake Club*. Of all the names people called us, this was the one that best summed us up.

Gagzy was up for it, so we took off to Rotterdam, where the Manchester Taxis football team were over for a weekend competition. One lad had taken a line of speed before the game and was trying to take every throw-in and free-kick; another got punched and had to go to hospital for stitches. When the game finished we all hit the boozer, then went to another bar where the Taxi lads got into a big fight with a load of Turks. The dibble turned up but nicked only one, beating him black and blue in the van then kicking him out. The others piled into a hired minibus and headed for the Dam for the night, which was lucky, as the Turks returned with a proper firm, going up and down the pub area looking for them with guns.

We all went up to Gothenburg to work the UEFA Cup final between the Swedes and Dundee United and were joined by Rab, who'd got out from doing four years in Hull and was now back on the staff. Rab had never been to Scandinavia and, having been out only a few days, treated it like one big holiday as we all jibbed the boat from Harwich. There were now lots of other grafters from everywhere: the Zulus football mob from Birmingham – black fellas who were not to be pushed around, the Southend Crew, the Wilmslow Firm, and lads grafting for the Donnellys, whose dad Jimmy the Weed was a well-known old-school Manchester face. There were also a couple of Geordie ticket touts who nobody could understand and loads of Cockney touts. Dicko was married to a girl from Crawley and was living down there, and all the London grafters called him Jack Duckworth.

The minute we arrived, Rabbi went on a shoplifting spree. He first prize was some leather All Stars baseball boots, which then cost over £100. He never had them off his feet. The Grid was arrested on day one in a toyshop trying to nick the takings. The rest of us stayed for three days and made excellent money. (McKee had two operations for piles, known as Farmer Giles', and put us all on to the best cream, Germoloid, as we all suffered from what we termed 'grafters' arse'. It comes from the beer, food, sweating in and out of the car all day and the pressure of life on the road. Same with heartburn: we all have it wicked.)

I copped for a girl who worked on the ferry from Gothenburg to Kiel in Germany, and on the way back she booked us in a first-class cabin with a shower for next to nothing. We hit the duty free for a bottle of Absolut vodka and a full pack of Elephant Beer to chase it down, then went to our cabin. The door was open and we had Linton Kwesi Johnson blaring out when a Miss World blonde walked past, then popped her head round and said it was boring upstairs. We were soon swigging the last of the vodka from her shoes, then hit the disco for a dance. We all thought we were in with a chance with her until Rab potted a kid and gave a few others a slap for trying to muscle in on our Miss World. Rab and I got locked in the brig for the rest of the trip, leaving the way open for Dicko, who had been at the bar and missed all the action. The brig was in the worst position on the boat and it was the coldest cell of my life, with no blankets. When they opened the door the next day I felt ill. They brought us out and there was Dicko with the blonde, both telling the police that it was the others who'd started it. This was a pure lifesaver as the girl was a straight person, so they let us out. We said goodbye to her and bought another bottle of vodka for the train to Rotterdam.

I went to see John the Grid, who'd been sent down to the big jail near the coast outside Den Haag because he'd had a little accident. When he was in the police station, one of the dibble opened the hatch on his cell door to pass him a meal and left it open. John wanted a kip and tried to close the hatch, which was a heavy slab, to reduce the noise but slipped and it took his finger straight off. I talked to him about working for Renus, a Dutch contact of ours who was one of the top ten earners in Holland, pure rich and a mad thug as well, but he said a kid called Toby had all the new moves up his sleeve in the swag game, so when I got back to Rotterdam I met up with this Toby and started banging out his gear as well as the swag I got from Renus. Toby turned out to be perfect in the tom shops too, because looking at him no-one would ever think he was crooked. He had a major spinal problem and his feet didn't move properly, as his heels had been dead from birth. He'd had to learn a tricky way of walking but the feller was a real bandit and had just come out of a German jail for Rolexes.

One of Toby's sidelines was to copy staff and VIP passes for concerts, which cost a few bob to put together but were worth it. First he would fly to the place where the tour started, wait around until the end of the show, then ask one of the workers to sell him his pass as a souvenir for a young kid at home. He would then have snides made up in different colours, as often they would change the colour of the passes at each concert to try to stop the scam. We were well on top of the game and the only time it came on top was for Dicko at a Bruce Springsteen gig in Stockholm – he spent thirty days in police detention then got deported and banned for a few years. In court they had the copied pass blown up and it turned out Toby had spelt 'Springstein' wrong.

We worked the books at Ibrox for a Simple Minds concert and afterwards hit a bar for England's first World Cup game against Portugal. A few of the lads couldn't take the defeat or the stick the locals were giving out, so they headed home. The rest of us went to a big pub called the Mucky Duck where some Rangers fans showed us their tattoos. This soon turned into one big drinking session and the next day's work passed me by. I headed back to Rotterdam, then on to Barcelona, where Terry Venables was the coach, to watch a game. We went in the social club and all the young fellers were smoking El Tel cigars; fact was, Barcelona got beat and Tel got the bullet the next day.

That summer, Bev came with me to sell tee-shirts for Renus at the Rock Am Ring in Germany. It was a massive racetrack in the middle of nowhere, so everyone brought a van or tents. We had to go through all the campsites very early in the morning selling our stuff, which is a touch harder than normal and Bev was making my life even harder by demanding a hotel by the middle of the second day. Eventually she put up the white flag and insisted I escort her back to Rotterdam, after which I joined Rab and Dicko working the books in Belgium for a week with U2 on their Joshua Tree tour. Two days' break followed before the next concert in Rotterdam. We drove up there and I booked into a hotel with them, as it was one o'clock in the morning and I didn't fancy waking Bev up. Having driven the whole way, I hit the bed early.

At four in the morning Dicko and Rab brought back a street brass who they'd just given a small packet of coke to smoke. We all ended up having a go and the next day when I went to the toilet something was not right. They checked me out at the hospital and said I'd caught a dose; I was more concerned about what I was going to say to Bev than anything else. She accepted my story about staying in a hotel so as not to disturb her; what she didn't accept was Rab telling everyone the full story in the bar later – he forgot Bev was stood next to him. Once he realised he'd put me in Shit Strasse he tried to placate Bev by saying, 'It's a man thing, it happens now and then.' Bev promptly attacked me with a glass, then a bottle, and later smashed up the flat. It was the end for us; she packed her bags and cursed me as she slammed the door. We'd been together seven stormy years. She soon found a Dutch guy who ran a record business and had a kid to him.

* * *

I lived in Rotterdam for another year. Around the end of the summer, Skinny Vinny turned up from Manchester. Apparently he was now a full-time gangster. He said he

needed bullets for this stupid gun he'd brought with him,
as he'd seen some post office he wanted to rob. I took him
down to see some Dutch thugs who almost burst out
laughing when Vinny pulled out his gun; it was only a .22
and they called it a pea-shooter. They didn't have any
bullets for it, but sorted Vinny out with a CS gas gun,
which looked the business. The post office raid never
came off and Vinny ended up staying with Dave from
Hull, the Man City head who kept his flat spotless. He
was there a month and didn't pay him a shilling, then on
the Friday when Dave came home with his full month's
pay, Vinny was waiting on the stairs, sprayed CS gas in
his face and robbed his wages. The next thing I heard
about Vinny was that he had held up a post office in
Amsterdam at gunpoint, then to get away kidnapped a
young tourist couple from Australia. He took them to a
field where he raped the girl and made the fella strip, then
forced him to swim across a lake whilst he fired bullets
into the water. He got seven years.

My own life flashed by in a blur of booze and smoke.
Days turned into weeks, weeks into months. I had no
roots, no base – I was adrift in a crazy world of scammers,
blaggers and good-time Charlies. Had I stepped back and
looked at myself I'd have seen I was heading only one
way – but there was no time to stop, no time to think, just
seize the day and fuck tomorrow.

In the winter of 1987, Gagzy bought a decent Ford
Granada from one of the lads and we had a drive out to
the small islands on the Dutch flatlands near Belgium.
Out of nowhere came the boys in blue, who took us to the
local police station for questioning. I had a tin of CS gas.
The main copper took it off me, sprayed it all into one
cell, then made all the young coppers go in to feel the
pain! The best thing to do when you get gassed is not to
put water on but to get straight into the fresh air without

rubbing your eyes. All the young coppers started rubbing their eyes and wailing in agony, while the top cop, who had one of those massive walrus moustaches that he must have been growing since he was a teen, roared with laughter. He loved it, standing back in a safe position peering through the glass. I told them I'd bought the gas in the red-light area for protection, as at concerts we sometimes got jumped by Hell's Angels or skinheads – and they believed me.

They had pulled us because Gagzy's car had featured in a Tony Hatch by a few Mancs on a tom shop, so they took him over to Eindhoven for two weeks for further questioning – then gave him the car back. We did a bit more work for Renus, then boarded the last boat possible to Dover for Christmas. Customs took my passport to check, then started giving me the eye, and I knew it wasn't going to be good news. They locked me up on a warrant for failing to appear at court for a drink-drive charge in Scotland; I had forgotten about being nicked when we were grafting up there in the summer. They told me to get my bag and I told Gagzy to enjoy my Christmas dinner in Sale. He went out and brought me back a Chinese takeaway, into which he slipped a nice chunk of hash.

So I spent Christmas Day in a police cell. The police canteen served me a hot dinner with a top apple crumble and three cans of strong Belgian beer, knockout stuff. A few days later I was on the plane back up to the Bonnie Land, handcuffed all the way. I arrived at a police detention centre full to the brim with Aids cases, all shouting over to each other asking who'd shared a needle with who or who'd slept with who lately. A couple of lads lost it when they found out there was a massive chance they'd been infected. In English jails we always called the screws 'boss', but here the cons were calling them 'turkey' – because of the festive season, I thought. So I called one of the screws turkey and he looked at me and said, 'It's turnkey, not turkey, ye English bastard.' I swear all the lads had been waiting for this, as it cracked up the full block. They made turkey noises all night.

I spent the New Year banged up, got a few points on my licence at court and walked out of the door relieved to be going home. I trawled back to Manchester and went to see Gagzy, who was in the new local for beer monsters, the Grey Mare. Inside were a few faces I knew: Billy Elvis, Tommy Bandage and the rest of the Monday Club, a load of United thugs who were barred from most pubs in Collyhurst, Miles Platting and Ancoats and who earned their name for sacking off work most Mondays to go on the piss. After taking the corners off the day with a fair few pints and chasers, Gagzy suggested a curry in town, so a load of us piled into his car. When we got to Piccadilly, a police van pulled up at the side and asked Gagzy to pull over, which he did. Everyone then bolted straight through the bus station with all the coppers after them. I was too pissed to run, so I moved into the driver's seat, thinking I'd park his car round a few tricky corners I knew, as we needed the car for graft. I turned the first corner and drove straight into another police van. The young copper couldn't get the bag out of his pocket quickly enough. I drew a three-year ban, as did Gagzy, but it didn't make any difference – we all carried on drinking and driving.

Later I was told that if you put a copper coin in your mouth, it beats the machine because of the zinc or something. One night Jeff Lee, another grafter, got pulled over and as the dibble was fiddling round with the bag, Jeff slipped four coins into his mouth. Unfortunately they were all silver coins, so the trick didn't work, but it was so funny seeing him trying to blow into the bag looking like a chipmunk. We started telling everyone about the copper coin trick and discovered that though it might not work when they breathalysed you at the car, if you carried on sucking away it was a cert to beat it back at the station. It used to blow the dibbles' heads to bits, seeing as how pissed we all were.

I was in the Hat and Feathers pub when Gagzy told Donna Vickers the way to beat the system, as she was always on the piss and driving. Donna then turned round and started telling her older friends and family how to do it.

'The way to beat the drink and drive laws is simple ladies: just suck a copper.'

The old lady sat nearest to her pipes up, 'Yer dirty git, our Donna.'

Another scratches her head and says, 'Can't you just give him a hand job?'

Gagzy and I were in tears and poor Donna was kippered trying to get it all over to them again.

The swag game was now worth serious money. Most of the stuff coming out of Manchester was controlled by either the Wards from Middleton or the McPhees from Salford. We grafted for both, but they fell out and went to war with each other. Guns were getting pulled on a lot of workers. I told the Wards I was a free agent but they insisted, 'You're only working for us.' So when I was up in Heywood sorting out some stock with the McPhees and they showed up, I had to get on my toes. I left my diary behind, and in it they found a number for Salford CID – and decided I was a grass working for Salford Police. The truth was that when I came back from Rotterdam, I'd left my clothes in the boot of the car and gone on the bevvy in Snappers nightclub, with the car parked outside. It ended up getting towed away, and because it had Dutch plates, they gave it a thorough going-over. I had to ring the dibble to get my belongings back, hence their number in my book.

Anyway, I got a call at home telling me to go to the
Heywood pub straight away. When I got there, Dave
Ward, the head man and a former boxer with a legendary
punch, had already knocked one of the lads cold as a
show of strength. A kangaroo court was convened for me
in the vaults and they sat me down and surrounded me
while I had ten minutes to explain the phone number. I've
never been so scared. Things were looking bad until
Rabbi showed up with Paula, a Miles Platting girl they
knew and respected, who verified my story. They left with
the words, 'You'll be working for us on the next tour' but
in truth I only ever did bits for them. The story went that
not long after, Jimmy Swords, a legendary face, called
both sides to a meeting in the Cheshire Cheese pub and
calmed everything down.

                    *   *   *

The next summer saw the whole world explode. Ecstasy
hit the Hacienda and half of Manchester descended on
Ibiza. The bad lot were suddenly in demand for all the
partying that was kicking off, and it wasn't only the
Hassy. The Thunderdome in Miles Platting – the old
Osborne Club where my mum had worked behind the bar
– was turned from a rock club to hardcore house and all-
night acid parties were thrown in tower blocks on the
North Side. Local pissheads in their forties started taking
E and acid and would all be there digging away in tune.
Even the football thugs chilled out. We were soon all on
the VIP list at the Hacienda and worked the full shout
with the Happy Mondays, Stone Roses and New Order
and all the warehouse parties in Blackburn and elsewhere
– until the police and the Salford gangs stepped in big
time.

We got on the road again for the last leg of Michael

Jackson's BAD tour, which was in Barcelona. The tour, which lasted sixteen months and took in fifteen countries, had been a major earner for us. Jacko didn't do badly either – it the biggest-grossing tour of all time. We were well on it, with a contact of Toby's actually getting hold of the master disk in America from which the official tour programmes had been printed. We copied them exactly, with just a slight change to the cover, and followed the tour all round Europe. Equally snide ID got us into the venues and if any legit programme sellers sussed us we'd slip them a few quid to keep quiet. We made bundles.

My brother Mark flew to Barcelona the day before but got a pull at Gerona Airport; they looked at his suitcases full to the brim with books (programmes) and he told them the usual, that they were for giving away as a promotion. He handed over a few for their kids and through he went. We all got the same treatment at Gerona and all sailed through, minus a few books each. Mark booked us in a top transport cafe that was open round the clock, with good clean rooms. We used snide passes from Toby the Jug to get in and out and all made a nice few quid.

At the stadium, Dave worked the scam where he has a walkie-talkie turned on, walks up to the main VIP and staff gate with the snide pass half showing. As he gets near I'm about fifty feet behind with another walkie-talkie and as soon as he gets to the gate I shout through mine in my best Yank accent something quick so they can all hear it and he then replies in his best American accent.

'Right I'll be backstage to sort out that problem straight away, and I'll borrow one of these fellas here to help with some of the carrying' – which might be a box of our books. The lot of them fell for it and we were in and out all day and night. Gibbo sold out every time on the pitch. Same again the next day, where we smashed it, selling out and getting lots of punters into the concert as well. The official books went for £5 and we would often get the same, sometimes less.

Once we'd sold our gear, we went for a rest in Lloret, which was only half an hour away, and traded some Es for as much beer as we could drink. Roufy had going a top idea which made him a mint when the Jacko Bad tour was at its peak. He made up thousands of sun visors and charged £1 each, made 70p a time and could go out working with 500 just in his pockets, never mind what he could fit in his bag. Because he didn't seem to be carrying piles of swag he was left alone by all the wankers who look for people working like that, jump you and take your gear. All tour he grafted car parks, doing all the coaches stuck in the traffic around the stadiums. He was soon copied by the workers inside but by that time Roufy had done the biz.

Everyone had heard about Ecstasy in Manchester and was mad for trying it. We served them up and sat back. It was a spectacle watching the kids getting off their heads for the first time, jacking and pumping away like the clappers, stood on podiums and table tops. On the last night Jeff, a kid who worked behind the bar, wanted to try one, but we told him to wait until he'd finished his shift because they were so strong you needed to be with proper people in the right place. It was too late – he'd already taken it and within twenty minutes his eyes were alive and he was working his bollocks off behind the bar. His head was soon cabbaged and he locked himself in the stock room with the pure horrors. In the end our Mark busted the door, got him out and walked him up and down the beachfront.

When we got back to Manchester the kids were taking

Es by the handful, but we had seen the look in Jeff's eyes and showed these pills top respect.

Chapter Fourteen

Bangkok Wedding

I RENTED A room at Roufy's house in Old Trafford. Soon there were four of us who'd all split up from our partners – Bev and I were now history – and we jokingly named his house the Home for Battered Husbands. It turned into a non-stop shag pad, with the Terrorhawks girl gang from Miles Platting all over us and mammas from Moss Side banging on the door at all hours. We got a Staffordshire bull terrier called Charlie who started coming to the pubs with us drinking beer out of ashtrays. Unfortunately Roufy owed some Scousers a bit of money and when we were out one day they came round to the house, sprayed a fire extinguisher in Charlie's face, nicked him and later put him in one of those dogfights. He was a big pussycat who had never even had a fight, so I hope he wasn't ripped to pieces, but we never saw him again.

Early one Sunday morning I was woken by stones hitting the window and heard Rab and George shouting that we had to get over to Old Trafford to blag our way onto one of the coaches. United were at Liverpool and there were big delays on the train. Roufy went mad at me to get up and fuck them off so he could get more shuteye, and on the way out I grabbed a coat, only realising once down at the ground that it was Roufy's fave leather. In the inside pocket was a bag of Pink Champagne speed. We all had a dip and got on one of the coaches.

Then it went pear-shaped.

The lads on the coach were all United season ticket-holders or official members – and they didn't want us on board. It still took them half an hour to get rid of us, so Plan B was up the road to get on one of the unofficial coaches. We got on the third one and were told to give the driver a good dip into the whizz and instruct him to keep the other two coaches in sight, as it was vital that we all mob up on arrival. The strategy was apparently to drop off on the Liverpool side of Stanley Park and then steam one of their pubs near the Kop.

As soon as we got on the motorway, all the lads were having a dip of the speed, then spliffs were out and the tins were bursting open. The driver got the songs going and, no surprise, we ended up on the Albert Dock. Before we got on it, we'd lost the mob and maybe fair to say the plot, and had a police escort over to Stanley Park. We stashed the billy down the back of the driver's seat, which was just as well, because when we got off the coach the police had us all up against the wall giving us body searches. Only George had a blade taken off him and he was going mad, as June had bought it him on holiday in Mexico. He didn't make it any easier when asked why he was carrying it on a match day; he said it was for stabbing.

The noise we made when we reached the ground soon brought on a Scouse lot shouting to another firm of Mickeys, 'The Munichs are here!' They made a massive mistake when we came to clash, as the front boys all had their hands going to their inside pockets as if to pull blades. We'd had countless battles with Scousers over the years and had learned that when they used a Stanley or a knife they came at you from the side or behind; hardly ever would you actually see the metal. So we knew this front lot were bluffing. It was all over within a minute as the Wythenshawe lot came steaming in from behind them and we chased them round to the Kop, before the police got a grip and sectioned us all off in small groups, then escorted us back to the United end.

The game was a classic, with us being 2–0 down then on comes Stormin' Norman Whiteside and soon puts it about, leaving McMahon, their main man when it came to the brutal stuff, prancing round like a fairy. We went down to ten men but the goal by Strachan right into the Kop to make it 2–2 will be remembered by many for his taking the piss by lighting up a pretend cigar and doing a Groucho Marx stance before the United players jumped him. At that point we all burst into 'You'll never beat United' and this carried on back on the coach all the way to Manny, with the lads now swimming in the bag of Pink Champers.

By the time I got back to Roufy's, his jacket was in need of an industrial-strength dry clean and I'm sure you can picture his head when I had to explain the missing bag. My voice, as always after a big game, sounded like I'd swallowed a frog and somehow this made things worse. In the end it cost me a good few hundred quid – but it was worth it!

* * *

Roufy, Toby and I went down to the Students' Union and paid nearly a grand each for an open ticket around the Far East. We felt we'd earned it after working the Jacko BAD tour, plus the Olympics were starting the following week in Seoul, South Korea. We flew to the Dam, then on to the biggest tax-free airport in the world, in Saudi Arabia. It has a counter in the middle with the best Rolexes – a piece of piss to rob, but they'd cut off your hands if they caught you. We next flew into Taiwan, where we were told not to leave the hotel. We ignored them, went down into the local markets and had a good night.

The next day was a classic. Going through the duty free area I saw a big Texan with a Rolex on and had him off royal. We had a quick peep at the wedge before we boarded and knew straight away that we'd more than covered the money we'd spent on tickets. Toby clocked another Yank and slipped an envelope out of his briefcase at the bar; it had almost four grand in American travellers' cheques with ID and a few hundred in notes.

In South Korea they treated us like English gentlemen, even though as soon as we got to the hotel Toby started using the room as a ticket office. Seoul was full of a humid smog and the traffic was nonstop 24–7; no matter what time you looked out of the window, there was endless traffic. The locals all wore face masks and the local custom was to share taxis. The food was a nightmare; even though we all loved Asian food they cooked it in very strong garlic, worse than the French, so we stuck to the Pizzaland and McDonald's. The main nightlife was around Hookers' Hill, where lots of Yank soldiers hung out; it had neon lights everywhere and at the centre was a massive disco pub called King Billy's, where the foreigners congregated. We met a black guy in there from Old Trafford who'd gone to Roufy's school and he told us it was very difficult to get a smoke, so it was lucky I'd brought some from the Dam. The locals called it Happy Smoke. All the pros on Hookers' Hill were cheap but we headed for the proper red-light area called Moon Village, round the old fruit market and got stuck in. Truth is they had to send a kid over to the chemist to buy bigger condoms for us – may I drop down dead if that's a porky.

Chaos surrounded the stadium on the morning of the opening, with crowds and TV people all jostling. NBC even interviewed us. As Toby started banging out tickets,

I heard, 'Fucking hell, what's all this bollocks?' and when I turned round it was Chink, Keano, and half a dozen other grafters. The usual greetings meant we were a touch late getting to our positions around the main stadium, but there were people everywhere looking for tickets. We soon finished serving up and went to the best hotel in Seoul. Its downstairs bar served awesome steak and chips and became our HQ. We were also running the snide ID scam: Chike sorted me out with a blazer with all the right badges and passes, and I escorted groups of Yanks into the stadium. We all went inside and spent a few hours watching the day's events in the sunshine. We made up a flag with 'Come on Daley' and were cheering on Daley Thompson until it all went wrong when his pole snapped in the vault. The best move we made was taking the police chief and his wife to a bar and them walking out with a ticket each for the closing ceremony – that kept them sweet.

At the end of it all, Toby wanted to go over to Japan via the overnight ferry from the south-east coast, but I discovered we could jump on a plane that same day to Hong Kong and we all agreed it was a sensible move. Before leaving we had away a tray of diamond bracelets from a showcase, but they turned out to be worthless fakes so we hung on to them to give out as gifts.

The view coming into Hong Kong is amazing: as the plane slowed down to land we could see people cooking in their small kitchens in the tower blocks, and the view of the harbour was stunning. We'd been advised to stay in an enormous block of flats called Ching Kun Mansions, where families rented out top cheap rooms right up on the twenty-fifth floor and above – the floors underneath were offices, tailors, cafes, and so on. We soon sorted ourselves out with a flat but found the lifts were a problem: there was a huge queue of people, carrying shopping, holding rolls of silk and trying to control their kids. The local nickname for the flats was 'Stress City', but we soon had it worked out – we bought a few bottles of San Miguel beer, joined the queue and enjoyed all the goings on as people lost their cool. They even had a copper standing there at busy times to keep people in line.

We had a wander and I got an Oriental woman tattooed down my leg and Toby got a crocodile on his chest, then we headed for Happy Valley, the big horse track, then the Suzy Wong bar and finally the Pussy Cat nightclub. We sussed out from some of the Europeans where to go for a proper drink and landed in the Peninsula, which had a happy hour with jugs of beer. We spoke to a few lads about business and they put us on to buying snide Lacoste patches for tee-shirts and shirts that cost nothing and could be posted back home without a drama.

The next day we caught the Star Ferry, then a bus round to Recluse Bay, where it was so calm and quiet you soon drifted away on the white sandy beach. I called my mum and told her I was in Hong Kong and she asked me to go and visit the church where she and dad married. The memories flooded back to her: leaving Southampton on a luxury liner, passing the Bay of Biscay, seeing the dolphins playing in the clear blue water of the Suez Canal, venturing into the mountains where the rich people lived and where the Catholic Club nestled high up above the harbour, serving cocktails and tomato soup with croutons. Toby and Roufy came with me to Saint Teresa's Church, which was rammed full with baskets of flowers, and the old priest gave us some top noodle soup.

A taxi took us to Kowloon, where the driver told us not to eat any of the food served up in the market area, as it would be a killer for bods like us. The area was a city within a city, a daunting warren of streets and flats that even the police were scared to patrol. The middle of the market was called Regents Square and the tiny streets all passed each other there. Rats ran round and the narrowness of the streets blocked out the sun. We went looking for a smoke. To get into the shops you had to crawl through what can only be described as holes, to find the shopkeeper's family living in the same room, with bed, furniture, the lot all tucked away in neat places. Having crawled in and out of a few places, we bought some cans, then got into a local bandit who took us to the shop we needed.

We manoeuvred through a particularly tight hole in the wall into a dingy, dark room where old men and women hung half-dead out of hammocks. The Bandit took our money and came back with a ball of white rocks that he said were very good to smoke. Roufy said they were crack coke and Toby said there was no way he was touching them, so he went off and bought us all a few more cans. The Bandit disappeared and came back with some smack and a sheet of 'Joe Royle' (tinfoil). Toby put most of the smack on the Joe and started to burn it but it ran straight off and disappeared into the dust on the floor. We were back to plan A. The Bandit took over, twisting the foil into a long thin stem and reshaping the end into a small cup. He dropped one of the white rocks into it and burnt it, sucking in as he did, then took a deep drag on a ciggie straight after. We all did the same, then took a wander outside.

I felt ten feet tall, and thought the constant plane traffic above was getting nearer and nearer to the top of my head. I felt detached and my heart was banging against the wall of my chest. It was the strongest thing I'd ever taken and made me feel aggressive and keen to catch the eye of a stranger walking by. It turned out that it wasn't crack but a local thing called yabba, which was a super-strong speed. We were off it for hours and walked the miles back into town without thinking about it. We got back to the hotel and all realised bed was the best place to be. I had the longest dream of my life.

On our last day we went shopping and got Ted Baker shirts copied in silks for ourselves. The Bombay Bazaar was the best place, with lots of bargains – one shirt that cost me a fiver would have been at least fifty brick in Manchester. Then we flew to Bangkok.

First night we hit Pat Pong and bought a weed that was what we needed after that yabba shit. It was a mad place, with hookers and ladyboys propositioning every foreigner: 'You want fucky fuck or sucky suck?' In a place round the corner from the main open market we found girls squatted on the bars holding bottle openers up between their legs, whipping off bottle tops, while others fired ping pong balls or blew smoke rings. We pulled two darlings and went back to the hotel in tuk-tuk taxis – three-wheeled motorbikes with a seat on the back for two. The traffic was mad, with whole families hanging off open-top wagons. The tuk-tuks carved their way through, though I felt ours was going to topple over for sure.

We moved from Bangkok up the coast to Pattaya, a tourist resort and also the main HQ for Thai boxing. An English pub called the Red Lion had a disco upstairs and we sat outside it and smoked our first joint of the day, then went off to the beach for a massage until about five o'clock, when we were ambushed by mosquitoes and other bad-arse flies. Roufy was mad for the local food and had duck eggs, garlic soup and developed a real taste for those huge locusts that they fried up in the woks. Toby and I had steak and chips outside the Red Lion, which cost much more than anywhere else but was the best in town.

We went to the Thai boxing and Roufy saw a top darling pull up outside and park her bike. The women's fights had just finished and she went over to see one of the fighters, who'd won the final bout. Her name was Nok. Roufy almost collapsed at her feet. She could hardly talk English but smiled at him as she got back on her bike. The next night Roufy waited all night outside the Red Lion until Nok cycled past and for three days we hardly saw him. Then early one morning he walked over with a huge grin and declared that he'd been up to Buddha with Nok and got married. Even though he knew it wasn't the real thing, it was for her and he said he'd be coming back over for her.

The village held a wedding do for Roufy and Nok, with a Thai and Indian spread laid out on big wooden tables. They both cut a lovely cake, lit joss sticks around a Buddhist altar and placed fruit and fresh drinks at a small Buddha, a reminder to keep your house in order every day. The matriarch of the village was asking me why I didn't like Thai women, as I was not with one and all the lads were. Truth was I was having a wee break from the shagging, needing to recharge, but being polite I said the truth that Thais are the best looking in the whole of Asia. I soon had women all over me, which wasn't really what I wanted. I managed to extricate myself and sat next to Nok's business partner. Her name was Tum and she was the woman we'd seen at the boxing match. They ran a small business cleaning people's clothes, as Tum had a big washing machine, so I asked her if she'd wash my gear. I went back to the hotel on a motorbike to collect it and got back just in time to say goodnight to Mr and Mrs Rouff. My clothes came back next day all ironed and I gave Tum a nice Manchester United 'Scouse Buster' top. She came back a few days later and took my stuff again. Before she went off we had a few beers on the beachfront and got talking, as her English was good. Her family was from way up in the north, Chiang Mai, and were all Thai boxers – even her sisters and her parents. On the night before we flew back to Manchester she stayed over at mine and got on the Thai whisky. Tum could more than hold her own and she was a mad card gambler.

* * *

Despite all the good times, trouble was around the corner. We had been going to the Reno and the shebeens in Moss Side for years, pulling up in our Dutch cars, going in to smoke weed and chill out. A lot of mixed-race lads like big Melvin started working with us. But the gang culture began to take root in the Moss and the atmosphere changed.

The Talbot pub, known as the 'Roots', was the territory of a new gang called the Gooch, the first drug firm to organise properly and not rip people off. Soon white people from all over the north-west were heading to their manor to score. The Gooch were also the first black gang to cash in on rave, which wasn't really a black scene. The Kitchen in Hulme was a main after-hours venue but there was also a shebeen round the corner from Gooch Close that used to play Sade and funky music and a lot of the Ecstasy crowd would go there until 10 A.M. It became known as the 'E blues'.

But after six months you could feel a change. The rival Pepperhill gang were pissed off at how the Gooch had expanded. Stray bullets started coming through the windows. There was also trouble between Moss Side and Cheetham Hill, partly because Cheetham Hill didn't like them dealing with white guys like us, and we would always cop it being in the middle. These guys were armed robbers and gunmen and out of our league – they shotgunned Melvin in the legs and would think nothing of blowing someone away.

I went for a drink in the Gallery with my young brother James and bumped into Dicko, who was at the bottom of the stairs full of stories and lager. A black guy came to go up the stairs and bumped into Dicko, which wouldn't have been a problem except for Dicko's wonky eye – the black guy thought Dicko was giving him the serious evil eye. The guy came back with a firm of other wannabe gangsters; none of them looked best pleased. The black guy started taking his overcoat off and it looked like Dicko was going to get filled in until the top black doorman, Roger, who later ran the door on the Hacienda, took hold of Dicko and did the only thing possible – threw him out. But the guy's mates had followed directly behind Roger so it came right on top for Dicko as he hit the pavement. After they had busted him up, one guy bent down and bit a big chunk from his ear. Even a young girl outside by the door got hit for saying something. The firm came back inside and started looking for me and our James, as they'd got a taste for it, but we were already heading for the back door and gave it toes out of the fire exit. We found Dicko back at the flat in Old Trafford, out for the count on the couch with the bitten-off part of his ear stuck in matted blood in his hair.

Sale was also getting moody – it was the first place in Manchester you could score smack on the streets. Lots of lads from the Racecourse were doing jail all over the UK and word soon got around that you could score on the estate from cars that pulled up at certain times and certain places. Before long the crowd was huge. Heroin would soon get a grip in other areas of the city and people started to get ill. We didn't know why at the time but they had Aids through sharing needles. One lad I knew went blind before he died; another who had his ashes sprinkled on Old Trafford. The estate even had Scousers and Yorkies looking for a score.

One night, driving back to Sale from the Moss with Roufy and a couple of other lads, we were tailed onto the estate by a car full, right on our bumper. I pulled over, thinking it might be someone we knew, but as I approached their car I noticed some shifty movements going on, so knew it was cert to be a firm who wanted trouble. I dived back in the car and we did lots of tricky turns to get some distance between us, then ran straight into the flat and grabbed some big knives and a bat. We could hear bangs and smashing glass and by the time we got back to the car it was wrecked and the guys were screeching round the corner out of the estate.

Someone tried to tax us for door money at the Reno and put a blade to our Mark's throat, while the Cat had a firm come through his front window wearing helmets and swinging bats and chivs – they busted and cut him up bad in front of his baby. The Roots pub, where we'd drunk for years, started to see the odd bullet flying past, so we moved HQ to the Dry Bar on Oldham Street, run by Leroy, who'd put us all on the guest list at the Hacienda and let us smoke a joint downstairs. The Dry Bar was at the heart of the new Madchester scene and hosted a lot of pre-Hacienda parties for all the Factory crowd – New Order, the Happy Mondays and the rest. But Salford heavies and protection racketeers were also moving into the rave scene, especially at the Hacienda, and it was becoming more hairy all round.

I was still doing the swag with Gagzy. We went to the Preston Guild Hall for a Pogues gig and were heading out of the town afterwards when the police pulled over Gagzy's Ford Granada with Dutch plates. They searched us and took us in for a drill. Half an hour later, they came into the cell with a load of stolen Levis that Gags had bought cheap from a grafter. No big thing, we thought, yet they charged us with stealing them from an unknown person and an unknown place. We were in court the next morning and given a date for trial at Preston Crown Court.

When the day came, I'd been out all night and had fallen asleep downstairs on the couch. I was woken up by the phone ringing: it was Gagzy, who was at court and said they were about to put a warrant out for my arrest. It was almost twelve o'clock. One of the other lads had been asleep on the floor and I asked if I could borrow his car. He said yes and pointed at his jacket, so I picked up the jacket and ran out of the door. I met Gagzy in the Yates's and we downed a quick few, then rolled into court, where the judge said he was remanding us in custody to Risley overnight. It was only as I started to walk down the stairs to the holding cells that I thought, Fuck, what's in this jacket I'm wearing?

Whenever I think I'm going down, I always check my pockets before I go to court and make sure a little piece of hash is stored where the sun don't shine. But this was a borrowed jacket and as I slid my hand into the inside pocket I felt a cigar tube that rattled when moved about. Pills! These alone could get me a couple of years, as the press at that time were going mad about E's. We were locked in the holding cell with a few others, where I shoved the drugs up my arse and got through the strip-search okay at Risley. The guy on reception was Brian Connolly from Collyhurst, better known as the Colonel because he walked in a military style. He told us all the latest jail news and we got boxed off with a scran. Next morning in the big holding cell, all the Scousers were smoking joints but we wanted to avoid any trouble as we knew we'd be back in the Yates's for our dinner. Our lawyer came down and we went over the facts. Gagzy was holding his hands up so I knew it would be over and dusted. Gagzy got three months – and I got three for travelling in a car with stolen goods in it. The screws enjoyed it, saying we'd copped unlucky as the judge was on Liverpool FC's board and hated Mancs.

They put us in Walton. John the Grid was in for something else and he and I were up on what's called Skid Row, the armpit landing on G wing on the fifth floor, all unemployed. I didn't see John for a week or two because he'd been chasing the dragon and was on a bad cold turkey with all the sweats, lost lots of weight and looked terrible when he emerged in the exercise yard one morning. Walton's exercise yard always had dead rats in it, kicked into the corners. Gagzy was soon well liked and they gave him a landing cleaner's job. He used to tell everyone how his landing was the cleanest in the jail and that was true – though all the other cleaners claimed it too. The landing cleaners did all the wheeling and dealing in smoke, mainly for other cons, passing magazines and papers or the odd drop of brandy or homemade booze. He brought the main Scouser up to see us, who wanted to know about the Ecstasy pills I had, as there was no way in the world would any of us take them – we just wanted to exchange them for a good smoke. At first he was not really into a deal as they all said Ecstasy was for faggots, which was true at the time – when they first came out they were called Xs and cost around £50 each.

A couple of days later, however, on the yard he came over to me and said he was interested in having a few of the pills. Ecstasy was all over the news, with pictures of people in barns and warehouses at five in the morning, stripped on top and with sweat pumping out of them, off their heads on these pills. I put it to him that later that night would be the best time to take them, because John Peel was playing Acid House on the radio and that would be a way to understand the connection between the pill and the music. I gave him one to share with his mate, as they were that strong, particularly for a first-timer, in a jail. So after tea, he and his cellmate took the pill.

Two hours later, we all opened up for the last slop-out. 'CAN YOU FEEL IT?'

These two Scousers came bounding out, going up to everyone, even the screws, with big crazy faces, doing arm exercises in tune to the massive song that John Peel had just put on: 'Can, can, can, can you feel it? Can you feel it?' They were both getting off to it, singing and dancing; at that moment they were somewhere else and didn't care who knew it. They were even shouting to us four landings up: 'Manky Mancs, can we feel it?'

The next weekend there were a few more bobbing heads. The screws turned a blind eye to it all – and we got a decent smoke out of it.

I looked in on Gagzy on the way to the gym and he had four pillows around his bed. Up on Skid Row we had none, so being top friends I asked him for one, knowing in the back of my mind he'd say no. He burst out chuckling, saying pillows were a perk of the job, and kept reminding me of it all day. A few days later, my cell door was opened up by a screw with a few new young cons on their way to the youth wing. 'This is Walton,' said the screw, and threw a pillow into the cell to let them see me and my two Welsh cellmates fight it out for possession.

John and I were eventually shipped out. John went to Haverigg and I went to Kirkham, the open prison near Preston. On reception was Jan Molby, the Liverpool player, who was in for reckless driving. Lots of press snappers hung around in the daytime trying to get a photo of him, and a kid from Wythenshawe did a deal with one journalist, who threw a small disposable camera and £50 in fifty pence pieces over the fence. The next day he threw over another £50 and the kid gave him back the camera saying he'd got a photograph of Molby playing football indoors. He'd actually taken twenty-four shots of his own bollocks.

I had a visit from Roufy. He'd just got back from Thailand with Nok, who was now officially his wife. He'd paid a good few grand to get her over, as he'd stumped up for the wedding, which had to be done through an agency, then had to pay for the official witness, then bung her family a grand, take her to the hospital and pay for a health check-up, then pay for her visa at the British Embassy, then pay for his ticket and Nok's, which had to be an open return on Thai Airways – and they were well dear. This was to ensure that if a Thai woman wanted to get home she could, as Thais were being used as sex slaves in all the major European cities. Anyway, it was good to see him. He said he'd come again on the last visit before Christmas with a weed and a bag of 50p coins.

I was due out the day after Boxing Day but figured out that the night I'd spent in Preston police cells and the one in Risley had not been counted by Walton when giving me my release date. I put in to see the governor and he agreed and let me out the week before Christmas. Three of the lads came to pick me up and we drove to a big club in Eccles, where the McPhees were throwing a big Christmas do for all the Cowboys and Pirates. Bernard Manning was on and it was a full slap-up steak and wine job, all freemans. As soon as I got in the club I phoned Walton Prison and, with the whole crowd listening, got them to release Gagzy for the same reason. When the screws told him to pack his gear he thought it was a wind-up until finally they got him to the gate and opened the door. His visitors were outside ready to go in and he frantically whispered, 'Don't say fuck-all, get to the nearest pub.' They couldn't get their heads round it until I explained it later.

I was straight on the Special Brew the next day and then went to the bar in the Britannia Hotel where I met Roufy. He said Nok was missing Thailand, as she couldn't speak English well and had no-one to mix with. We discussed the possibility of me sponsoring her mate Tum for a three-month visa, if I could show all the right things to the British Embassy, like having a decent place for her to stay and a reasonable job. I sorted out some moody paperwork from a lad who managed a bar in town and from that got myself a building society account. Roufy offered to pay for Tum's flight, as he said it would make Nok feel a lot better, and I sent all the documents for sponsoring her. They knocked me back within a week. Plan B was for me to go to Thailand and marry Tum. Roufy offered to pay for Tum's open return plane fare, so I agreed. What the hell.

I was dropped off at the airport after staying up all night smoking and drinking Brew in a flat in Hulme – I still had Voodoo Ray ringing in my head. I necked a few brandies and boarded the flight to London, then to Brussels, then Romania, where we had to wait for a couple of hours. The plane was dire and the only food they offered on the whole journey was one bit of cold chicken with shrivelled salad – but this was the cheapest route.

I landed in Thailand at nine in the morning. We were due to marry at lunchtime that day. Tum turned up with all her documents, then we had to do the same script as Roufy and Nok. By the time we reached the stage where the official was asking lots of serious questions, like where would I get Tum work, I had fallen asleep in my chair. Tum woke me up, explaining to the guy that I had a bad case of jetlag. The fact was, I'd bought a bottle of whisky at the duty free and done the lot. Eventually everything was sorted and he okayed the marriage, then we went to the British Embassy to hand over Tum's documents to be checked and passed on. I took her to the oldest Buddha in Bangkok and while she lit joss sticks and prayed away I nipped to the corner vendor and got a few cold beers. We had some food at the fish market, where you picked out the fish you want to eat from those swimming in the tanks and told them how you'd like it. We watched some Thai kids boxing, then hit the hotel. I spent a few more days on the mooch and I was really surprised how much whisky Tum could drink when she wanted to, which turned out to be every night. Finally I left, saying I'd meet her in London when she arrived in a couple of weeks, as I planned to stay at Lincoln's in Stockwell.

Customs were a bit baffled when Tum arrived, but after hours of paper pushing and phone calls they told me to get her over to Liverpool for a work permit. They couldn't sort it out on the day, so we had to go back; Roufy and Nok came with us, as Nok needed to collect her documents. We decided to call into Billy's in Liverpool on the way out to celebrate the wives getting their stamps and work permits. Roufy went into the house and as he shut the door the drugs squad were everywhere: wrong time, wrong place. After a grilling, they drove Tum and I in one car back to Moss Side and Roufy and Nok to the house in Old Trafford for a search. I'd recently moved out of Roufy's house onto the fourteenth floor of a tower block round the corner, and when they searched it they found nothing. In Roufy's they pulled out a bag of speed and charged him with intent to supply. He was definitely going to prison – and he had to settle a huge bill for the speed that was seized.

Things went even worse for Roufy as he got involved in buying a load of cheap hash from some South Americans down at Liverpool docks. He asked a Scouse firm to join in on the deal, which they did, but when it was done Roufy was left with a few bags of shite snide hash – he'd been ripped off. The Scousers weren't interested in excuses, they wanted their investment back, and Roufy had to take out a loan against his old feller's house. He paid them off but didn't make the repayments on the loan, so the bank repossessed the house. Roufy got eighteen months for the speed and when the first visiting order came through I took Nok to see him. The first thing he noticed was that the gold bangles his old feller had bought her after their wedding had gone missing. She told him she'd sold them and spent the lot on a holiday in Thailand, and was now with a Hong Kong fella in Chinatown. Roufy's head went west and I really felt for him on that visit, as his world was caving in.

*　*　*

I got back on the road with Toby and went to Scandy. I had a good cop from a job that wasn't planned so we hit the town and then tried to get into the local club, but the bouncers were having 'no English'. We had bits to say to them, and as we were deciding whether or not to have a kebab the bouncers came running out swinging bats. Toby got away but one of them cracked me over the head and I hit the deck. They wasted me with the bats; I curled up in a ball so only my lips and one eye got it bad, though it always looks worse at the time with the blood everywhere. As I got to my feet I heard a screech of brakes and round came Toby in a car he'd just acquired. The bouncers were high-fiving, saying they'd fuck off the English, until Toby mounted the pavement and ran them over. I jumped into the car and we disappeared, getting rid of it then jumping on a train to Sweden.

It was Saturday teatime and we were on the mooch. I

noticed that the front door of one tom shop had iron bars over the top glass half, but the bottom half was a wooden panel. I gave it a couple of kicks and it fell into the shop. The alarm went crazy so we stood back and waited for the cavalry to arrive. A private security firm turned up after ten minutes, had a look round, then fixed the panel back temporarily. We got pissed, then went back near midnight and I booted the panel in again, dived over the counter and took all the best trays. One of the other lads took the rings back to Manchester while we went back to Norway and copped for a wedge from a supermarket safe, then overnighted on the ferry to Sweden. We threw all the cheques from the safe overboard and got our heads down. Police were everywhere as we drove off the ferry and soon pointed at us and asked us to step out for a search. That was that. In court they gave us thirty days each and we had to repay three grand for the cheques we'd ripped up. The jail was a health farm, showing two English films every day in addition to the top TVs in the rooms. After finishing our terms we were kicked out of the country and banned.

For the rest of the summer of '89 I was caught up in the music biz, selling not only swag but also beer. We'd pay a fella in an ice cream van a few quid to let us put our cans in the back. Every time I came back from Europe I'd buy a load of strong German and Dutch lager and a few bottles of brandy for the ladies and knock it out at the big warehouse parties in Blackburn, at the Kitchen in Hulme and the Green Jockey parties in Chorlton, where Roufy DJ-ed now he was out of jail. Most of the booze was out of date but everyone knew and it tasted all right to us.

I was a regular at Konspiracy and the Thunderdome, the clubs where all the faces were going, and a couple of Salford lads had mentioned the name Paul Massey to me, saying he was *the* up-and-coming lad from Salford. I thought they meant 'lad' as in football hooligan but soon learned otherwise. I had opened an illegal rave out the back of Old Trafford, selling all our own booze and stuff – until Paul M turned up with one of his top henchmen and took over. I knew better than to argue: this was his patch and nothing much got past him. He did hand me back a pack of beer, with the words, 'Remember, this is Salford, Beaner.'

The girls from the Terrorhawks still sold programmes for us at concerts and were unbeatable at handling any young coppers who tried to get in the way, crowding around them, stroking their balls and talking so filthy that in the end the cops turned a blind eye. I also tried my luck as a weed seller and was the worst ever seen in Moss Side, for sure. I drove round Manchester all day with a sack of skunk but most times I smoked the profit away with friends, so I was risking jail for nothing. Tum kept asking where my profit was going.

Tum kept asking what the little pills were everyone was taking and one of the lads slipped one into her hand and said it was a 'happy pill'. She monged out for the night and nearly lost it big time when the lad who was giving us a lift back in the morning fell asleep at the wheel. Tum was ill in bed for a week and never necked an E again. I took her to the Hacienda for the New Year but she soon wanted to go and meet with all her friends who had Thai whisky and a party going in Chinatown.

I got on the Happy Mondays tour, which was one long, wild party. The band took more drink and drugs than all the Pirates put together: it was crazy, doing massive bags of charlie almost non-stop. It was the only tour I ever worked where I ended up in debt. Their entourage was too big and it seemed every scally in the north-west was along for the ride.

After one mad night with them I ended up in a pub at

nine o'clock in the morning. A coach was going to Sheffield United for the third round FA Cup tie, so we got on the blobs for brekkie and Paraffin Pete was up on stage singing 'Danny Boy' when the driver popped his head in to say, 'Let's go.' One lad told the driver we had to pick up Eddie Beef, who lived in this little corner cottage flat right in the middle of a swamp estate in Beswick. I swear the driver lost a stone in sweat trying to get this coach full of singing Reds to Eddie's front door. By the time we got near the ground, the helicopter and heavy lot were on our tail and pulled us over. The dibble removed packs of Carlsberg Special Brew from the boot and put them on the grass. About twenty coppers jumped up and down on them, pulling silly faces at us all, then the head dibble came on the coach and made the driver turn round and go up to Leeds on the motorway. A vanload behind made sure we weren't coming back.

After all our years of plundering, it came as no surprise when the Dutch police finally decided to be rid of us. We'd been on the Dutch equivalent of *Crimewatch* and they had already deported us all a fair few times and banned some from Holland for life, but now they got serious. They started setting up roadblocks, checking out hundreds of people every day around Amsterdam, and eventually developed a book with the names of people who were banned or wanted from all over the world. If your name was in it you were an 'undesirable' and could be kicked out of the country immediately.

Finally they got together with the CID from Manchester and launched Operation Bullseye: the name came from the fact that we were always playing darts in a bar where the undercover officers mingled with us. They had a map of Manchester with all our photos and different pins in it showing where we were from. For all their efforts, the only person they put away was our Mark. A diamond and gold rep had pulled up at a petrol station and our kid burst into his car and got off with the goodies. A year later he was coming back to England and got his collar felt boarding the ferry at the Hook of Holland. In the end Bullseye was wound up but by then it had dispersed us from the Magnet and things would never be the same.

Chapter Fifteen

Cracking Up

MY LIFE BY now was out of control. I acted without thought, drank constantly, lost my bearings. One afternoon in a pub on Oldham Road I met a couple who were going shopping to the massive Morrisons nearby. I went with them and tried to pass through the checkout with a trolley loaded with all the best stuff. Inevitably I ended up back in court. I turned up after a party and was falling asleep when the judge said, 'Time for dinner.' I hit the pub and returned to court late and clearly tanked-up. I got the best thing possible: a two-week lie down in Strangeways. I must have slept for a few days right through, then got a weed and hit the yard. I saw Syl, one of the lads from the raves in Blackburn; he'd been taking Ecstasy in jail and had escaped from the van on the way to court. He looked like he was knocking on heaven's door with his weight loss.

Within days of coming out I had borrowed Roufy's car to pick up Tum from work and been nicked in Chinatown for driving with no documents. The day before I was in court the Strangeways Riot had kicked off and we all went down shouting up to the lads, who were wrecking the Ways good style. Everyone said I'd get a good result in court, as there was pure havoc in the prison. I got six months. It was really bad news in the Central Detention Centre cells, as all the prisoners were coming in from the

Strangeways Riots and they'd been beaten up. The first I saw was Jimmy Miller, who had screws all over him trying to get his clothes off so they could send them to forensic. He was near the end of a four-year term but got another seven added because of the riot.

I was in with two kids from Oldham who had been ripped off for a £10 bag of weed by an Asian, so they drove into his area with a strong slug gun and fired it at the first young Asian they saw. It hit the kid around the temple area and killed him. They were daft as brushes, brains as big as peas. I was glad to get shipped out on the Saturday morning to Doncaster Police Secure Unit. This was built for armed robbers and other groups of heavy cons but the police were nice as pie, even asking us would we like a full fried breakfast or toast, jam and cornflakes? The next week two coaches took us all to Durham Jail. Everyone was from Strangeways so the talk was all stick together as the Geordie screws were sure going to be on our cases. But they were alright and even looked the other way as a few of the lads shoed a couple of local cons who played a trick on them as they came through reception. I saw a few faces I knew. Graham Ross, who ran around with the Gooch Mob, was in a cell with Benny, a kid from Salford who worked for the Happy Mondays. Cam from Miles Platting sent me over the *Independent* paper every day and I went on the working wing, sewing pillowcases. Not quite what I'd had in mind as a career.

When I got out I went straight back to Europe for a few days then came the Glastonbury Festival with the Happy Mondays. I started to work with a firm of younger Salford, including Jay and his brother Paul, better known as Timebomb and Munchen, who got his name because whenever he did a sneak in Europe he always dressed in alpine green clobber. With them were Carrot and Black Henry, who'd just got out of the jail in London for dipping, and Skin and Boz, two real British bulldogs with 'Made in Manchester' tattooed across their six-packs.

Over the three days of the festival, black guys from Birmingham had been given the security job which some of them abused as they drove round in jeeps robbing and taxing everyone who was selling drinks, drugs and tee-shirts. Dicko and I made our money by waiting by the main stage and when the groups came on we'd go right into the crowd shouting, 'Fair deals,' and we'd have £20 deals of hash flying out all ways, as the punters knew how hard it was to get a fair deal with all the taxing that was going on.

I was waiting to get a lift back on the last day when all of a sudden, from the top of the facing hill, a load of gypos on shire horses came charging down into a pack of these black guys who'd taxed one of the gypos. Lots ended up in hospital and the feller who owned the land cancelled the next year's fest because of it.

Everywhere seemed to be getting more violent, with drugs at the heart of it all. Things with Tum and I were not going well, as she wanted me at home – and she wanted a kid. I told her I'd get it together soon. I went to a blues party in the Moss with Skin and Boz and was sat on the staircase having a joint and a talk when a firm of black guys came up the stairs. The leader had a huge stiletto. I got to my feet as he lunged forward with it. I grabbed a firm hold of his wrist and pushed him back and got on my toes past Little Tyson and the rest of them. The full pack was after me and as I turned the corner a lad tripped me up. I felt two sharp stabs in my back. They jumped on me and my knee popped out. I started coughing up thick dark ooze. Skin and Boz laid me flat on the grass and flagged down a lone dibble in a car, but no ambulance arrived, just a van full of dibble. They lined up, putting on their leather gloves, and the one in charge came over to me. He lifted my shirt and told me it was only a nip, then he and the rest disappeared into the flats looking for ghosts. By the time they got back, scratching their heads, an ambulance crew had arrived and told me I had a punctured lung. I was told later by everyone to make a claim but when you live in the fast lane it's all easy come, easy go, plus the thought of having to write down all the facts and seeing lawyers – I'd rather just get back to graft. Funnily enough, a Hell's Angel girl in Amsterdam stabbed our Mark in the back after Mark had decked her feller, and his wound was in the same place: a small deep cut into his right lung.

It took a while to get my health back, and then I went on the spur of the moment to Ireland with Munchen and Malta Fred in an old VW that we bought for almost nothing. The Holyhead-Dublin ferry got us there in time for United's pre-season tour of Ireland. We went to Kilkenny to Munchen's grandad's pub, then to see the Reds in Cork. We scored some weed, kissed the Blarney Stone – not that we needed to – and lit candles in church. The Harp lager was much better than ours in Manchester and they had really large bottles so we sat around supping away. My ancestors were from across the water: the Blaney name originated in the North, though my dad's family came from the South.

We ended up going to score more weed with two big fellers cramped in this old, patched-up VW. They took us on a tour of an estate, then we drove through a gap in a wire fence onto a rugby pitch and over to the posts. A guy was sat on the crossbar, from where he could see if we were being followed. When he was happy he gave a whistle and three motorbikes came from three directions. The guys in our car got out, the big feller jumped down, we gave him the money, he got a bag of weed from one of the bikers and passed it on.

'Wait until we've got off the field before you go,' he ordered.

Fred got the car stuck turning in mud while turning in the goalmouth area and we began to flap a little, with Fred thinking he's back on the Salford Precinct doing handbrake spins. In the end we couldn't shift it, so we had to write it off and walk back to the hotel. We rounded off the day at a big club getting smashed on Beamish and brandy.

Next we went up the coast to Waterford and watched the local Paddies rob all the sellers of their United pins, badges and patches. All through the game, full families were scaling the walls sneaking in with the Garda just watching the football. In the fair that night we copped for the three ugliest girls in Ireland; mine kept asking would I give her a baby, while Fred's had three tits – he took a photo to prove it. We got off to Belfast for the next match and around dinner we scooped some cash and old tom. Then Malta Fred, whose job it was to hold the exes – the pot for all of us – announced that he'd left a smelly sock full of gold coins, bracelets, chains and rings in the hotel, so it was bound to be on top. (When we got big amounts of money we always had what was termed the exes, or expenses – the wedge that was for spending on food and fun. It would be held by each of us in turn and the holder was allowed to lash out and usually had a ball in the local cathouse, or wherever – a perk of the job.)

We flew back to Manchester from Dublin and Tum was not at home. I caught up with her later at work and she said she had left for good – and was pregnant to a feller who worked in the Thai cafe. I didn't blame her and went on the piss even more. I made the biggest mistake of my life in not having the kid Tum wanted and not stopping the life in the fast lane – I blew it good style.

Instead I had people round the flat all the time. It had a

pirate radio station underneath, with music thumping up through the floor, and became known as the 145 Club. OB would turn up, spend three days working his way through a massive bag of coke he'd got on tick, then declare, 'The baseball bats will be out for me now,' as he really did get the stuff on credit from some very heavy dealers. A couple of girls – Mandy from Wigan and an Irish model called Maria – moved into the flat for a while; Mandy was a master at working the Visa cards.

I also got to know a few of City's Young Guvnors: John the Duck, Pill-Popping Pete, Smiler and Big Kev. They told us about Quadrant Park, the warehouse club in Liverpool, so Carrot, Henry, Carol and I got a taxi over with them. We were all a bit nervy, as Henry had had big fights with blades many times with Scousers at games, and being jet black they soon spotted him and us, but Buster, Brian, Paul, Manny and Jeff came over for a chat, which was seen by plenty of the local heads and after that we were safe as houses. For the next six months Quadrant Park became our number one place. It was actually safer in Liverpool than it was for us in Manchester, where gangs were springing up all over the city and the housing estates. Dr D started to DJ there and we'd go before it started with a big bag of beers that we'd put behind the stage.

* * *

On the last day of Christmas shopping, the girls were out working the Visa cards. Munchen, Carrot and Fred were doing a big hotel in Piccadilly, as they'd copped for a master key to the rooms, while OB, Henry and I got a tip that this feller who ran a few jeans stalls in Oldham brought his takings into Manchester with him while he picked up from another two stalls in the Arndale. With it being Christmas, we figured he was sure to have around £50,000. We sussed his BMW, parked in the middle of a small private car park with a feller in a cabin that was right on line with the car, so Henry or Kev would have to block this feller's sight when I made the snatch. Fuck me, the feller came out of the door with the bag of money but in a full rucksack over both shoulders, so I'd have to time it right, as the only one spot I'd be able to have a go would be right at the car door when he took it off. Worse still was the fact he had a big black guy as minder.

I gave Henry the nod to cover the feller at the cabin, then made my move forward.

'Fuck me, Beaner,' said Kev, 'this one looks well tricky.'

Funnily enough a young bird behind us had got on to what was going down and said in that north Manchester way, 'Fuckin' do one, lads!'

That was my cue. Just as I was going to spring out on the feller now taking his bag off, I ducked behind a car inches away. The car had system locking so I stayed down a few more seconds while he opened the driver's door, then opened the back door, threw the bag in and closed it, waited for the minder to get in the front passenger seat, then got into the driving seat himself. As he closed his door, I opened a rear door, grabbed the bag and was clean away.

The feller later told the cops he'd been attacked and even put out money via Billy McPhee to find out who it was. Billy found it funny when he heard what went down. There was over £30,000 and only ten grand was in cheques.

I got in touch with my son Lee, who was about to pass out from army training in Stafford to join the Welsh Guards. Smiler and I went and it was a proud moment. The next day, Dicko, Chink and I worked the England v Australia Rugby World Cup final at Twickenham, then I flew to Zurich and met Little Terry and a tall half-caste kid called Raymondo, who I knew from the Happy Mondays tour. I nicked some top clobber and we decided to blag a tom shop.

The blag was, I'm in a rock band and it's the end of the tour, we're off back to England and the manager is quitting after ten years with us, so all the band have put a wedge in the kitty to buy him and his wife a pair of Rolexes as a leaving present. The posh girl bought the story and out came the Big Bens with the diamonds in a deep tray. When she was relaxed I dropped some papers on the floor and as she bent down to pick them up, I snatched the tray and legged out of the door, swung open by Roy. When we got back to the hotel, Roy started shivering: he was on a cold turkey and had not brought any painkillers or sleepers. Little Terry and I took him to the hotel bar to drink the local strong lager to get himself to sleep. He said he'd be up for graft when he shook off the rest of the pains, so Little Terry and I did a sneak but this went sour and I got a big chase all the way past our car and round the town. I doubled back but my knee started popping out and I only just managed the final hobble to the car.

On the way home Roy said he was feeling better, so we stopped off in Ostende to look for a Tony Hatch. I told Roy not to get excited when he first went in, as the ones lying around on the top don't have diamonds in, so you've got to be a bit patient. I sat in the driving seat and waited and waited. Then Little Terry came legging it round with a couple of people after him. He jumped in the car and we were off. Twathead Roy had snatched the first two Rolexes he saw as soon as he went in and then had run off, leaving poor Terry to fight them off at the door while he jumped on a tram and away.

The football front saw our biggest game for years: United in the European Cup Winners' Cup final in

Rotterdam against Barcelona – on my son Lee's nineteenth birthday. I was going to watch it at home with my mam, as she loves football, but the phone went and it was our Mark, James and Dicko in the Flying Dutchman with all the Reds singing in the background. Syl heard it and knew I'd have to be off.

'I'll just run the iron over a few things for you, Col,' she said.

Aer Lingus came up trumps and on the morning of the final was bursting at the seams, with thousands of Reds all singing. Many planes were held up or late, so to pass the time I robbed three bottles of best champagne and a bottle of best Remy brandy. I necked one of the champers in the airport and the other two on the plane, with even the staff having a swig – opening a duty free bottle isn't allowed but my flight was full of Irish United fans and no-one was stopping them.

Our Mark and some other Cowboys met me at the other end and threw me the keys to a stolen English car. They were even more pissed and stoned than me and not one of them could drive, so I put the flashing hazards on, pressed the horn and made my own lane all the way to Rotterdam. They must have all thought I was a copper or needed to get to the hospital. They all went off asking about tickets so I went straight into the best seats and got up into the staff bar, where I asked Bobby Charlton for the phone code for England, as it had slipped my mind. I phoned Syl and the girls were all round, done up in United gear.

We ended up for the second half beneath the Barca fans behind their net – and up pops Sparky with a goal. We all then went over into the United end and the first person we saw standing on a barrier, chanting and waving a flag, was Lezzo the Lisp. Then Sparky hammered another one in; even Bobby Charlton said he was praying Sparky would tap it in but no, it had to be with power.

It felt fantastic being with my two brothers for the big event. United fans that night had three-quarters of the stadium and 'Always Look on the Red Side of Life' was born. Fuck me, Barcelona has over six million people yet we outnumbered them three to one.

Back in the Dam we ended up all getting barred from the Roxy so went back to one of our old fave gaffs the Ox Off. We were still on the piss three days later in the Flying Dutchman, watching Spurs beat Forest in the FA Cup with Gazza losing the plot.

Next to turn up were Skin and Boz and the Captain, who'd been in the army and was really the only one sensible ever on the firm. He would get up early, order all the lads' brekkies, sort out the plans for the day and change money at the right places. He soon got us all to use CS gas gel, as it sticks, so unlike the gas you never get it coming back on yourself. The gel came in a pouch that hung round your neck for easy access. The Captain's motto was: If you're going to do it, do it right. Yet whenever he took an Ecstasy pill he turned into a mong and wouldn't be able to get into any bar or club but would stand gawping at bouncers for ages, mumbling things no-one could work out, then next day he'd not remember a thing.

Skin and Boz had a tip that this Yank would have a kilo of coke on him when he turned up at dinnertime on a bike at a certain coffee shop. Like most of us, the Captain wouldn't get involved in drugs but I was up for this one, as they were selling it straight to the lad who'd given them the tip. We hung around the coffee shop and the Yank cycled up. Boz and I dragged him off, Boz put a dollop of CS gel in his boat race and we almost stripped him in the street. He had nothing on him, and the feller who gave out the tip later got a good hiding, so we decided to skip the Dam, as that drugs biz soon has people looking for you.

We went to work the Pink Pop Festival in the south of Holland, where the Happy Mondays were playing. The Hell's Angels security almost had us for robbing the main bar's cashbox and we were only saved from a hiding when Muzzer and a coachload pulled up. The Captain was a mega driver and so I was well happy when he suggested working together around the Eindhoven area, where Bobby Robson had taken over the football team and just won the Dutch league. We went back to the Dam and I got jumped by three transvestites, who did me right in outside a club. I got myself a flat in the Belemere area of Amsterdam; Munchen was supposed to come over to live with me but he'd been nicked with drugs and got four years. So Mandy from Wigan and her mate Carol moved in, and I bought a yellow canary called Sparky.

I went back to Manchester for the weekend and was straight on it in the Show Bar, waking up on the pool table at eight o'clock on Sunday morning. A bus took me over to the Swan on the corner of Collyhurst Street, where Dicko and some of the others pulled up in a small van. In I jumped. United were playing Leeds and we got to Elland Road as the main pub facing the ground was opening. My head was spinning and after a few beers and chasers I rolled up to the turnstiles. The fella told me to do one because I didn't have a ticket, so I started yelling at him, tried to jump the stile and got locked up by three Old Bill who were swinging their batons around. I got bail at the same time as a young kid from Blackley so we walked up to the train station to jib home and were sussed by a big firm of Leeds thugs. They chased us down the ramp where we dived into a taxi; the driver figured it out and put his foot down to save his car from being tipped over. He asked where we were going and I kept saying left here, right there and he started losing it. So I said Manchester and he said thirty brick straight in. I offered him my charge sheet as a deposit. He gave up trying to get rid of us and agreed to take me to a pub in Blackley where I told him I could get the money. We both got out at the pub, ran straight through and out the back, and got a lift to the Show Bar where Dicko had some money for me.

* * *

Back in the Dam I started taking heavy drugs, got off my nut and blagged some tom from a casino, then went to a rave and got on it. I came out about nine the next morning and was given the keys to a stolen car, which I drove straight into a fence in front of a copper sat in his car. Back at the police station word came through that my prints had been found inside the glass on the casino job. They took me to the main holding area where life is very grim as it's bed out at seven in the morning and you get it back twelve hours later, so it's just a cold stone floor with no cigs or reading allowed. It was a nightmare and I put the scream up; I needed a doctor and I told him I'd been on heavy drugs for weeks so he put me down for a full three-week methadone programme. Then it was more treatment – very strong sleepers for two weeks – to come off the methadone, then certain painkillers after that. I got a visit from Carol, Mandy's mate who was shocked at how bad I looked; I'd not even noticed my weight loss. In court I said I remembered taking one ring from the glass cabinet in the casino and after my lawyer said I was on the full course for coming off drugs they let me go.

It wasn't long before I was on the Es again and the weight loss got bad. I tried to come off it and instead drank like a madman, but still couldn't sleep with the pains in my back and legs. I was like the lunatic who had taken over the asylum. I kicked out Carol and Mandy and soon the local thugs were all round, using my flat as a dosshouse and crack house.

I took them on a tom job and before it we all smoked crack coke in the car. We were too fucked up to try looking good and no way could any of us blag any staff, so it was straight in, smash open the main display, grab what we could, then run a few yards to the stolen car. Driving back one kid said, 'Suck in,' and I did and got a mouthful of smack from a tube he'd put in my mouth. It felt real good.

Our Mark came over to see me and said if I could just manage to drive on a small snatch in Belgium, then I could get straight back to England to see a doctor and chill out in Sale at Syl's. I flew to Manchester and got locked up, then taken to Leeds for court in the morning, where I got a fine for jumping over the turnstile. In came the taxi driver, who started going on about my attitude. The judge told me to pay the driver his thirty brick fare and then said I could go. I went up to Lancaster to see Munchen, who was padded up with Rab in jail, and sorted him out with a Denis and left some money at his sister's in Salford. I went to see a doctor about not being able to sleep and all this sweating and cramps in my legs but he just said there's nothing he could do, it was just turkey. I tried staying in the house but couldn't so I went out to see Roufy and got some smoke and strong downers and finally went to sleep. The next day I went to see Gagzy in the Grey Mare pub and got the 'Hatty Jacques' big time and not one bit of booze could make me feel better though I just kept throwing it down. Same with smoke and they started to make me feel worse.

I got the plane back to Amsterdam and got what was

left of my stuff from the flat and I went down to stay with Marco in Switzerland. I intended joining Dicko in Sweden, as the Euro football was round the corner, but I wasn't up to it. I had met Marco in the Dam; he'd been a professional goalkeeper until he injured his knee, but he wasn't that arsed as his old feller was loaded and he had the full shout to the family holiday home in Klosters. I thought this would be the place to shake all the shite from my body, but it turned out Marco was on it more than me; he had a full-time habit, so after a couple of days I had to get on the road and decided to head down to Lloret. I saw a doctor who gave me the strongest painkillers possible and I stayed indoors for over a week going through the nightmare turkey again.

After another week on the beach I felt almost human. I went to Berlin to meet my son Lee, Time Bomb and some of the other lads and got properly on the stolen Visa cards. We then headed for Bremen but the motorway traffic was bad so we pulled over in the next town, Oldenburg and got a hotel. It was the town's yearly carnival and the streets were buzzing, so we all got right into the local beer, then Time Bomb slipped into a coffee shop that sold books and I followed. There was no one around, so he went into the back to use the toilet and I had a look round the kitchen until the woman shop owner pops her head round the door and starts going crazy. We gave her a load of verbals on the way out and within a few minutes we were ambushed by police, as the woman had told them I'd stolen her purse. She also said I had pushed her out of the way as I made for the door, so I got charged with violent robbery. I told them I didn't do it but they were less than uninterested. The jail was easygoing; only problem really was the cell I was in was a big dorm with lots of cons all on transport moving to other jails after a few days and more than half were all on cold turkeys coming off heroin. The toilets were a health hazard, with junkies sat on the toilet spewing for most of the day, then at night they'd all be in agony with the sweats and the cramps.

I got three years. I was put up on the main wing, where I shared a cell with a Nigerian called Blessing, who enjoyed a bit of hash at night. I got a job in the workshop and went to a discussion group every Wednesday where the Kurds, Turks, Albanians, Yugoslavians and Russians tried to sort out their differences with each other, but tempers would soon flare over religion and history. I told them I was Irish and they left me alone. I got some magazines and a packet of those Opal Fruits sent by our Mark, and having got hold of my lawyer eventually I decided to put in an appeal. They deported Blessing to Africa and I got a new pad mate called Costa from Athens, who was coming to the end of a three-year sentence for bringing coke over the border in his truck. He loved Eric Cantona and when we listened to United on the radio he'd always join in with 'Glory, Glory, Man United'. Two days before Costa was due for release, a screw came into the cell and said the Greeks had sent a warrant for his arrest over a kilo of cocaine from way back. He was crushed, as a kilo will get you life in Greece. By the end of the week he was in court in Athens and the judge said he had to serve a minimum of twenty-five years before they'd even think about parole.

My appeal came through and, after hearing the evidence, the judge gave me a fresh three years but suspended it, which meant I could get out. I went for a meal with Jana, a lovely girl I had previously met at the Oldenbury beer festival. Then I bought a ticket to the Dam and got right on it, then went over to Hanover to see Toby, Dicko and the lads, who were working a concert. I went back to Sale for a week and watched videos of all the United games that won us the Premiership, then returned to Oldenburg and slipped through the back door into Holland, but got pulled a few miles in. I had a load of tricky IDs with me and got nine months – I was one of the first to get a jail sentence via computer from Den Haag. I ended up in the big new jail at Leeuwarden, where I listened to England losing to Holland in the 1994 World Cup. Then they took me to the Hook of Holland and deported me.

I went to see Dicko in the Smoke, then returned to Holland via Belgium a few days later. I got talking to a kid from Australia who was a big cat burglar and we told each other some of the tricks of our trades. We decided to head for the Alpine winter resorts around Basel in Switzerland and as soon as we arrived I got us a proper good dinner and paid for it on a stolen Visa card. We went on the mooch and the Cat blagged a woman in a tom shop while I had four nice diamond rings away from the main showcase. We rode the train for Zurich, but a local rail cop got a waft of the skunk we were smoking on the train and as soon as the wheels stopped in Zurich they swooped on us. The Cat got deported and I got six months. The judge would have given me more but the local jails were all full and I ended up in police detention, which was well tough: one shower a week, with fifteen minutes' walk by the side of the Rhine every other day depending on how the coppers felt, and twenty-four hours pure bang-up, with the local pissheads thrown in my cell every night. Once a fortnight the Catholic priest came into my cell to play chess and drop off some papers. It was our Lee's twenty-first on the day United were at Wembley in the Cup Final against Chelsea. I sent him what I could, a few United things and a card, though he never received any of it.

When I got out I headed home, back to Manchester where I heard Munchen was out and had a gaff down in the South of France, so I jibbed the train and headed for the sun. On the Saturday night we went to a rave and on the way back got caught up in a police road block. They were picking out cars at random, dragging people out and putting sniffer dogs in. The car load in front of us started to really kick off and as we edged forward one of the coppers waved us through; we were so lucky as under the driver's seat was a cig packet full of Es and coke. Soon after this I went up to Sweden to watch United play Gothenburg and met two new workers from Salford we called the Mac Lads. I got to work with them selling tee-shirts.

We headed for Kiel in north Germany and after getting sorted with a hotel we hit a night club and the Mac Lads were popping pills good style. As we were leaving a Turk pulled a gun out and started demanding money so I put a bottle straight over his head; then it was Plan B.

The next day I was checking out of the hotel when I heard the big scream.

'Hello! Hello!'

I've heard that panic shout all over Europe and it means one thing – it's on top. Down come the Mac Lads with a woman trying to hold onto the safe they're carrying. Then I remembered one of them had the keys for my car – and it had been hired in my real name. I had no choice but to run and get in the car, which now had half the street diving on the bonnet. After a few turns here and there they both jumped out and got into a taxi, shouting that they'd sort me out in the Dam.

I hit the B-roads, trying to make my way back to Oldenburg, but got well swooped in a village and charged with violent robbery, as they knew a screwdriver had been used to force the safe out of the wardrobe. And making a violent escape, as a few have-a-go heroes had had to go to the hospital after the hire car moved them over. I had a week in the dibble shop then got shipped out to Kiel Jail; they put me in a big dorm as the single cells were only for all the local gangsters. I got a reasonable lawyer and he put together a sound defence, saying I had nothing to do with the safe and had given one of the other lads the key for my car, not knowing what he was up to. When the forensics came back and showed I had nothing to do with the safe, the judge dismissed the case having heard from a couple of the witnesses who'd been run over. And I got fifty marks compensation for every day I'd spent inside! And all my own money back that I had on me when I got nicked. I chilled out in the Dam for a few days, and then went to Manchester where I caught up with Rab who was telling me about the Guvnors from Man City and how he'd been fighting in the town with them with the other Cowboys. I had a drink up in Collyhurst then headed back to Germany

I was now serious with Jana who kept telling me that the police in Germany solve many crimes by listening to people talk on phones, which was inadmissible in court but allowed them to get the picture. They'd sussed the amount of calls to Holland I'd been making from local phone boxes and thought I was in the drug biz. That August they burst into Jana's at seven in the morning. They found nothing, but towed in the Dutch car outside and found one leather coat and a few tops that had come via a stolen Visa card. I got three years.

The thing was, Jana and I had tried to get the okay to marry in Germany but because of my past and the marriage to Tum they not only said no way but now I was going to get a life ban from Germany. We planned instead to fly to Las Vegas and marry, then take all our documents to a lawyer and let him fight it out for us. But then I got nicked and it was all up the wall.

Oldenburg was an easy jail so I put in for an appeal,

which would keep me there till the next summer. United won the Double again and I got my Opal Fruit parcel in time for the run-in. German TV even showed the highlights of the Newcastle v the Reds game which really won us that league. Then it was the big England match against the Krauts in Euro 96 and that Wembley shootout, with the fucking Turks in the dorm all cheering for D-land. This was much worse than the Holland game; there was hate in the dorm. I'd gambled against Turkey all the way through the competition and had made a killing on them not even getting a goal.

So when Shearer got the first goal they all spat on the TV. I had to wipe it off in order to see. It was vital to me to keep cool, also in this dorm were two Germans who hated football but bit by bit just like all the German screws they were now screaming for the Fatherland to beat the English. I rate this as the worst moment in my life, never mind football. The full jail was down my neck all the rest of that summer.

The main Turks in all German jails are all in for smack. They believed it was good to fuck-up the kids in the West. They and the Chinks have been living side by side with opium since it came out of the earth. In the West, Holland had it first, then with the sixties and Flower Power London and San Francisco took over. By the late seventies it was on all council estates in England. The UK became the biggest drug market in Europe, and Manchester and Liverpool play a major role in this.

The Turks were all into Islam. There were murders in the room with me and my radio when United was on, as they all pray on a mat five times a day but no way would I ever turn it off. Most of the German cons who pass through the dorms are young, nothing, fucked-up kids and these Turks took great delight in bullying them till the point of cracking up.

Then it was up to the big appeal court, where I said I'd accept the three years, as I knew they were going to put more jail on my sentence if I carried on. This took only fifteen minutes but they still sent me a bill for wasting court time.

My old lady, Mark and James had a holiday in Oldenburg as it was Syl's birthday at the end of July. I got a small smoke from Mark and he said on the next visit he'd have a 'cigar' for going up my arse. I'd just got the great news that I was going to an open jail as well. Back on the wing I was back in another dorm, and as always I couldn't get along with the Turks and one of them grassed me up for having a smoke. I only had enough for the last joint which I was sharing with a Romanian guy when the screws burst in and caught me with the roach in my ashtray.

They took me outside and I had to sign a paper saying they'd searched and this stub was mine. As soon as they locked me up, another screw, not knowing what had just gone down, opened the door and said, 'Blaney, visit.' I bolted straight down and almost burst into the visiting room, as I knew any minute the scream would go up. James was straight on it and slipped me the cigar, which went not up my arse but straight down my throat – I'd be able to retrieve it later from my shit.

The same screws who had just nicked me were in within seconds and all came over to our table and stood round, almost touching us. It was very awkward and after a few minutes I gave Syl the wink and she said she felt ill and sacked the visit. I was strip-searched and they even asked me to bend over and the doctor had a wee poke up there – but the Denis was safe.

That same week I was shanghaied to the worst jail in North Germany, where the junkies had shooting galleries. It was full of bad seeds and I was put in this massive dorm which had fifteen cons in it. After a year you can get a double room, then another year on you get a single cell. It was full of Balkan bombs, a few Russkis and dreads, plenty of Turks and all the local Germans who were lifetime junkies. Every day was trouble big time. The food was the worst in all D-land, always that soya snide meat, so everyone needed to work to buy themselves better food. I went in the sewing shop doing all kinds on piecework.

All this time the Brit Embassy had a lawyer working for nothing challenging the German Government over them not allowing Jana and I to marry. He came to see me with the good news that he'd got them to change their minds, all to do with the harmonisation of laws across the European Union. So on September 22, amid the best sunshine of that year, we married. Mark came up with a cigar, Jana's best mate Emma arrived from Cork and I ordered a full Chink meal from a local gaff with non-alky wine. We even invited the screw to join us for a real slap-up job. Now I was married I was able to go before a parole board and also had the promise of a driving job to come out to in Oldenburg, so I was given early release in that November.

Walking out of jail, I was convinced my life on the road as a Cowboy was over.

Chapter Sixteen

The Demon Drink

THIS STORY SHOULD have had a happy ending. I enjoyed working on the building sites, doing the *Auf Wiedersehen, Pet* bit. I played football for a local team, played volleyball and ping-pong at the university midweek, and hardly ever went out on the town – just every other Saturday night to the local Irish pubs to throw the arrows. We acquired two cats and I even got Jana into *Coronation Street*, which Syl would video and send over every fortnight.

The only time Jana and I took a holiday would be for two or three days when United played in Europe. We loved it, as we could have a break and still see all my old friends, in places like Barca, Madrid and Milan, where all the shoplifters from Manchester ran riot in the fashion stores. We could get a suit, each worth several grand, off them for a bag of weed, or a binliner stuffed with silks and cashmere for a bag of coke. Jana said the Cowboys reminded her of the Ducky Boys in the film *The Wanderers*, as they were all little scallies who looked like death warmed up.

A game against Dortmund in the Champions League in 1997 was Jana's first. The weather was lovely and it was no surprise to bump into John McKee, Binzy, Jug and the Cavs, selling all kinds of merchandise. United played well but lost 1–0. As soon as we came out of the stadium, Jana spotted our Mark, James and Clint, so we finished off the day with a piss-up in the square. This would be the last time I'd ever see Clint. While selling tickets at the World Cup in France, he passed on a load to the lads, saying he'd had enough of it all. He went home, booked a holiday for his family and the next day when the kids went to wake him up they found him dead. The strange thing is, no-one who works as a ticket tout was shocked, as we all know how stressful life on the road actually is.

Our next break was when United played Feyenoord in Rotterdam. We stayed in Amsterdam the night before with around 1,000 other Reds. They were all over the red-light area, paying the hookers in fake £20 notes. The next day we met James and went to visit Mark, who by then was doing two years in an Amsterdam jail for a large amount of hash and weed. We got talking to a screw who loved English football. We gave him a United pin and hat and as time went on he got very close to Mark and in the end was sorting him out to watch *Match Of The Day* on Saturday nights with bottles of vodka that he would pass through the hatch in return for pieces of hash.

Back in the city, James met the thugs, who were going to ambush a few bars in Rotterdam. This later backfired, as throughout the game Reds were bombarded with bricks, bottles and coins from the upper tiers. Despite this, the whole section was in fine form and United won 3–1. Having lived in Rotterdam, I know that on their own turf they are one of the most feared firms in Europe, so for safety reasons Jana and I sat in the main stand – but I made the mistake of going to the bar, where my accent gave me away. I was lucky to escape with a busted eardrum.

My next trip with Jana was Bayern Munich, on our wedding anniversary. Mark was now out of jail, and with James we decided on a tour of all thirty-two Irish pubs in

the city. We'd made only one when Cockney Dougie said
all the lads were at the beer festival (the biggest in the
world) which had started that week. We got so pissed we
couldn't even attempt to find our hotel but the main Irish
pub let us all sleep under and on top of the pool tables.
The game itself is a blur. Being 2–1 with seconds left, we
decided to set off for the metro but as we turned to leave,
Munich got a scabby goal from a throw-in.

Despite the fact that I had settled down in Germany,
my drinking was becoming a serious problem – and with
United's success on the football field it was only going to
get worse. I was planning to go back to Manchester for
the end of that season because United were going for the
Treble, so I phoned Gags, who was sandblasting old
warehouses in the Castlefield area of Manchester for
conversion into yuppie apartments. He told me there was
enough work for as long as I needed it. I flew into
Birmingham and met Binzy and Jug at Villa Park because
they had tickets for the FA Cup semi-final replay against
Arsenal. In the last minute Arsenal got a penalty, so
we again decided to make our way to the exit when
Schmeichel pulled off a fantastic save and took the game
into extra time. Next came the Giggs goal that even
Maradona claimed was the best he'd ever seen.

Suffice to say the cracks were now starting between
Jana and me, mainly because of my drinking, and the
football that season would be the final straw. Roufy was
also a mess. I stayed at his place near Castlefield and had
no choice but to tell him how bad he looked. He looked
like he had cancer – yellow skin and bones sticking out,
no arse and pale as a ghost through drinking whisky all
day, then doing speed and coke almost every night. Gags
was paying me cash in hand on a daily basis, so after
work every day I'd get the shopping in and cook us a
good meal, but the weight was still dropping off him. I

saw his doctor and made him appointments, but he never kept them. He'd roadied for 808 State on their US tour the year before but when they came to play Bugged Out at Cream in Liverpool, he asked me to take the job, which wasn't the Roufy we all knew.

There was a feeling of things coming to an end, turning sour. Even the Hacienda, which was a symbol of all the Manchester scallies like us, was closing. The protest group Reclaim The Streets were planning to set up a sound system in the Hac for one final bash and we heard we could get in through the back doors but come Saturday night Roufy again wasn't interested at all. Henry and I got in around 11 P.M., Daft Charlie locked the doors and everyone stayed shut inside until 8 A.M. Sunday morning. The police attempted to break down the doors but with little success. Hundreds of punters also tried to get in for the last night of one of the most famous clubs in the world, with TV crews gathered outside to film the crazy scenes. The funny thing was, almost every kid inside was there for the first time, and H and I ended up giving them guided tours of the club. At closing time, they ripped up the dance floor and took the parts home as mementoes. For Roufy to miss this last night meant in itself he was losing the plot.

Soon after came the biggest test of all for United as we went for the Treble. First up was the last league game of the season against Spurs at Old Trafford. I got there early and was surprised by all the changes in ticket buying and selling that had taken place over the past two years. There were new laws giving undercover police the power to stop and search you, take your tickets and even take you into police custody and charge you. To stand any chance of making a few bob and getting yourself a ticket, you had to be working in a group with one person standing way off to one side whilst the others acted as runners, going to and fro and checking out the punters carefully. Now all this work can't be done if you're pissed, as I was by twelve bells, so I went to Plan B and hung around the main entrance, where the stewards check in the press and VIPs.

After twenty minutes or so I spotted a chance and ducked past them and up into the bar in the main stand, where I was rubbing shoulders with all the top jollies. Looking around, I realised how much football had changed. Some people call it Gold Trafford now but to me and many others it is Cold Trafford. All the money they have and they still won't provide a decent working-class social club. If Celtic can have one, why not us? That's why I agreed with the comments from Keano about the 'prawn sarnie brigade'. They never sing and get behind the Devils. Fact is, Man U have a better support at the big away games. A cheap section should be put aside for the local kids, who would create an atmosphere which would get the rest going, like it was up until the mid-nineties.

Once the players came out, the prawn sarnie lot headed to their private boxes, at which point I jumped down into the lower section and was over the moon to see Coco, who budged up and let me share his seat. As we were getting comfy, Ferdinand swiped a total miss-kick that flew past Schmeichel's napper. One-nil. That got everyone asking for a radio, as the Gunners were playing Villa at home and we could still fuck up. Then Beckham sent over a pinpoint pass to Yorke, who cracked a bullet into the top corner. Only two minutes into the second half and Cole lobbed a superb shot over Walker. Job done, next stop Wembley.

After the game we met up with Scotty Mick and Co. in Stevenson Square. These lads ran a travel firm and had laid on a spread. All the talk was of United at Wembley the next Saturday and the lads were after fellers like us who would act as stewards on the coaches, with the option of being a steward on a coach over to Barca in Spain for the European Final. There was no wage but there was a ticket waiting for the game and a decent piss-up, plus food.

Dicko phoned and told me to get to Wembley early because he had tickets to sell. I thought back to my son's twenty-first birthday on the day United beat Chelsea to win our first Double; I was locked up in a Swiss detention centre and resolved that if it could ever happen again, I'd love to be with my son. It did happen when we beat Liverpool but on that occasion I was banged up in a German jail. So there and then I knew I'd be off to Rhyl that Saturday to join Lee and watch the game on telly.

I got into the Prince of Wales pub for opening time and seconds later our Lee and Sparra came barging in with the Leg Iron Firm, an old school Rhyl mob with a massive rep in North Wales. We went over to the fairground to a pub called the Schooner, famous from the days of the great running battles between Mods and Rockers. The game against the Geordies was a walkover and more like a warm-up for the big Euro match that coming Wednesday. Eight minutes into the game and Roy Keane's right ankle went; it worked out for the best though because Teddy Sheringham took charge and scored a goal, then set up Scholes to win us the Double. Cue monster celebrations.

Back in Manchester on Sunday night I got a phone call from Mark and James asking me to get over to Holland, where they had hired a luxury coach with tickets. To this day I wonder why I turned them down, but having watched so many of the big games in the past with my mam, I knew it was only right I should watch it with her. Also, I didn't think it would be fair on Jana and was reaching that stage in my life (finally) where I'd come to realise there really were more important things to consider.

The day of the game, Gags and I worked a few hours then hit the pub to calm the nerves. It was amazing how quickly it all went by but luckily for me – my drinking was now getting out of control – Gags dropped me off back at Syl's in time for the game. After a good meal we were 1–0 down and Jana was on the phone, feeling as bad about it as we all were. We smoked a monster spliff and decided to sober up for the second half. Syl went into the garden and lit a candle under our nana's statue of the Virgin Mary. It all seemed in vain until Ferguson plays the greatest tactical move in United's history by bringing on the super subs, Teddy Sheringham and Ole Gunnar Solskjaer. Syl went into the kitchen and I shouted for her to stay there because it's weird but true that whenever she's with me United never seem to score from corners, which of course is bollocks but we only had three minutes left and this corner was our lifeline. Even Schmeichel went charging into the goalmouth and Becks only half cleared the ball out to Giggs who messed up his shot but Sheringham was there to poke the ball past the keeper and the Nou Camp went wild. But it wasn't over yet as Becks lines up to take another corner. Now I swear, with all the emotion running through us, we thought what happened next was a TV replay, as the ball went to the near post and Sheringham was there to flick it into the path of the baby-faced assassin, who buried it and Munich.

Whenever I think about the end of that game I think about George Best, who had left the stadium assuming United had lost and was probably on his way to sink a few! Little did I know that my life was about to go into a massive decline because of the demon drink too.

The next day I met Lee and the Rhyl Reds on the hottest day of the summer outside my grandad's old pub, the Dog and Partridge. There were thousands of fans from all over the UK and even a boatload of Dubliners who were all up for it, drinking and singing about who put the ball in the Munich net. We made our way down to the cricket ground and some of the lads with cameras scaled up the lampposts and trees. Minutes later came the police helicopters overhead and lines of dibble on horseback, both sides plus front and back. Even the dibble never stopped me and Becky – a Terrorhawk who was nine months pregnant – from breaking through the lines and getting in front of the bus, which had to stop for a second while we got down on our knees to give it a kiss. I got up and a black copper looked as if he was about to throttle me but I put out my fist in the style of a rapper and he started chuckling and gave me the same style fist back before telling me to fuck off lively.

We all walked down Deansgate, where the party really got underway. Gags started the ball rolling with jugs of sangria and declared there'd be no chance of us going back to work that week. In my case there would have been no chance of doing any work, because the party seemed to go on and on all over the place. I was partying with yuppie crowds, student crowds, gay crowds, you name it, and not once did I buy a drink. But it would all come falling down around my ears.

My birthday landed during Whit Week, so Lee and Syl came down to Billy Green's, the main pub where all the old Collyhurst lads meet. It was great to see Brian Hughes and have a chat about United and boxing. But Gags was not too happy – he pulled me aside and warned that the booze was getting the better of me. I tried half-heartedly to convince him I was sorting myself out. The rest of the afternoon was then spent talking about Whit Weeks of the past and mates we hadn't seen for years. The women and kids took over the stage and started singing, a tradition that will continue for many years to come. To finish off we went down to the Gay Village and met Dicko, Cotts, Mikey Williams and all the other City fans who'd just got back from Wembley after their amazing comeback the day before, when they beat Gillingham in the play-offs.

It all had to come to an end sometime. The next thing was Roufy getting busted with Es, weed and coke. The dibble reckoned he'd cop for three or four years; the poor fucker got nine. Money was raised for an appeal by an 808 State gig but the appeal was kicked out of court. One good thing to come out of it was that Roufy got his health back and works for the Samaritans as a listener, on twenty-four-hour standby for any prisoner feeling suicidal; they can go to his cell and talk through their problems.

I was in no state to move back to my mother's. My behaviour reminded her of Jimmy when he'd been off his head on booze. I thought about getting a couple of weeks' work with Gags and getting straight and back with Jana. I got a shock when I took my stuff out of the taxi and Gags told me he was not letting me stay – as he had promised only hours earlier – because his girlfriend wouldn't allow it. I felt even worse when I realised I had no choice but to move into the Salvation Army off Oxford Road.

I started drinking horrible strong cider, White Lightning (we called it Quite Frightening) and cheap wine on benches. Then came the DTs. You aren't able to walk through a crowd of people without feeling anxious, you get sweats that are hot and cold at the same time and panic attacks that convince you a heart attack is on its way, shits that run straight through you, spews that rip your stomach apart with blood, bile and heartburn, and then come the shakes that are so bad you're not even able to pick up a phone and you lie awake unable to sleep with just an empty feeling in your brain. A rumour went around Collyhurst that I was selling the *Big Issue* on Piccadilly.

I went to the doctors in this state and he recommended a top-of-the-range detox unit that had been opened by Princess Diana. Curly Watts from *Coronation Street* had apparently just come out of there – and it was in Collyhurst. It should have cost me a few grand but when I told them I'd just returned to the UK and my marriage had broken down, they said I wouldn't have to pay as long as I kept phoning in at certain times to show interest and commitment to the treatment.

The first three days were as bad as coming off drugs – or 'sleeping with the towels', as it was known (you needed the towels to soak up all your sweat). You had to stay in your room and were constantly monitored. After that we could go out for one hour during the day and a couple of hours after teatime and we were tested regularly for booze. Any sign of alcohol and you would be slung out. We had to attend meetings up to four times a day. One was in a room full of beanbags with dolphin music playing in the background. If you missed one you got a warning, two and you were booted out. The same if you were caught shagging or had anyone in your room. Almost every day people were thrown out. Some of them had paid the full three grand and had failed many times before. What really shocked me was how many young, good-looking, yuppie-type girls were in there and most of these were the ones least likely to last the three days. Another surprise was the amount of young, single-parent women who drink cheap plonk, stay at home and have their friends go to the shops for them.

I looked at it like being back in prison – keep your head down and get on with it and you'll get out when the time is right. When I got out I shot straight down to London and worked a Hyde Park concert with Dicko and Lincs –

and kept clean all weekend. But after all that, the demon drink got the better of me on the ferry to Holland to see Jana. The truth was, I was now a bad alcoholic. I had a bottle of gin and a good few pints and then worried about how I would look to Jana, who was picking me up. I must have broken her heart, and the problem became even worse when I turned into a secret drinker at our home. Jana was finding empty cans and bottles hidden in all sorts of stupid places.

Jana was pregnant but quite rightly told me I was not fit to look after myself, never mind a baby, so she had an abortion. Then her old feller told her he had cancer and he was taken into hospital. This was around Christmas and the Millennium New Year. I took on work cleaning up hotels and bars over the holiday period, anything that might occupy me and keep me off the booze.

On New Year's Day, the first thing I did was phone up my old man. We talked about how his favourite boxer, Sugar Ray, had beaten Ali (my favourite) to top spot as Boxer of the Century. Still, Ali did get voted Man of the Century. We also chatted about Nobby Stiles getting a OBE and our old mate Brian Hughes receiving an MBE for services to boxing. The last time I went up to his gym I'd just missed a visit by Iron Mike Tyson. The newspapers reported that Tyson said the gym was just like going back in time because it was so basic. Hanging up on the walls is a massive metal plaque featuring all the old bareknuckle fighters and it was said Tyson offered Brian £1 million for it but Brian said no chance.

That first day of the new century, Jana and I went for a meal and had a serious talk about our marriage and our future. Jana was willing to give it one more try but I immediately ruined that by going on a full bender the following day and ending up in hospital after fighting at a taxi rank. They let me crash out on a bed until Jana came and bailed me out. We both now faced up to the fact it was time to separate and once this was done we became better friends. But the day of parting was the saddest day of our lives. Jana drove us to Groningen in The Netherlands, our favourite town in the world. It held fantastic memories for us: we'd had our honeymoon there and used to meet up there for weekends. Many times we drove over the German border with my mother and Jana's parents for a day's shopping followed by a meal of fresh fish in the Old Square. When we finally said goodbye at the train station we both lost it and I was still in a state when I got on the plane in Amsterdam, so it's probably no surprise that I hit the gin.

* * *

Back in Manchester I knew I needed a job to stop me drifting into a life of crime, so at the Job Centre I asked about work on holiday camps. The first job that came up was as a chef at the Haven camp in Prestatyn, near Rhyl. Haven had taken over from Butlins and I was amazed at the poor standards throughout the camp. In the main bars they kept all the doors shut and it got so hot the drink sales were enormous and the prices were on a par with London. The dirty areas and general low standards were worse than Butlins all those years ago. The kitchen was terrible, with staff out of their heads on booze or drugs. The cooking utensils were so dirty I brought in my own. When it got really busy I even had to go out and serve food and drinks. I rented a caravan on the camp and cut right down on the drink. My son Lee lived a few miles down the road, so I also got to know my granddaughter, Natasha.

Whilst on a day off in Rhyl, the Job Centre told me about a post as a supervisor in the industrial cleaning business, and having a clean driving licence and good references got me straight in. I couldn't wait to start but first Haven gathered together the most senior staff they could muster to take me over to the bar while they gave me the bullet. It was a bit of a buzz because they honestly thought the job meant the world to me. The next day the cleaning job began and I loaded up a van with buffing, carpet cleaners and window cleaning stuff. I had to pick up all the lads, who were mainly dropouts or pissheads and on a minimal wage. It was hard to get them all going and I sussed out I needed to pick the best guy as my number two so I could give him all the cushy jobs as long as he told the others what's what.

The very first job was to clean the private boxes, offices and main reception at Old Trafford! It was a buzz to clean out Martin Edwards's office, more like an apartment really with all the mod cons. On the last day everybody was pinching little bits and pieces from the ground, as were the scaffolders, builders and roofers, as Old Trafford was getting its new tier. But tragedy struck when a local feller fell off the Stretford End roof through the safety net and was killed. We were kicked off the site and all the safety inspectors came in. The next job was at the swimming complex on Oxford Road, which was built for the Commonwealth Games. We worked in trunks and were even allowed to use the jacuzzis.

As ever, things soon started going downhill. I found myself getting up at three in the morning, picking up lads in Chester and Stoke and driving down to Reading for a job. I would put them to work and then go to find us some cheap accommodation. I was told anything over £20 and we had to pay ourselves. On our way back up north we were told not to stop in Birmingham but to carry on to Carlisle, which pissed us all right off but was just the start of a non-stop trek around the country on various jobs for the next few weeks. We were earning hardly a carrot and by the time we got home we were skint, so some of the lads walked away and eventually I followed.

A job was going at a local builders, dropping tools and parts at sites all over North Wales, and the pay was decent with good hours and a few perks thrown in, so I moved to Rhyl itself. It was rundown and tacky and had problems with drugs, violent crime and poor health, but it was my kind of town because the people were down to earth. Jana came over to stay and we got on really well. We know we'll be best friends for life and it's better not to rock the boat by trying to get back together.

Indeed, things could not have been going better for me by Christmas. The company hired out a room for all the workers to enjoy free booze and a buffet, with curry and a disco to round things off. I don't remember much about that Christmas and New Year at all but I had the shock of my life when on New Year's Day the police came round and charged me with sexual assault.

This was alleged to have happened at three in the morning at the curry house. I couldn't even remember being there, though I could recall we talked about going for a curry beforehand. Everybody at work seemed to find it one big joke; to me it was anything but. I knew that if found guilty I would go to prison and be put on the sex offenders' register. So with this hanging over my head, my drinking got worse again. I started turning up late for work, stinking of booze, and missing days with stupid excuses because I had to make seven court appearances before the trial. It came as no surprise when I finally lost the best job I'd ever had.

Life on the dole was something I'd never had to deal with and soon the debts mounted up. Trying to survive on £50 per week meant I had to shop late at night in the

big stores for out-of-date food and damaged tinned stuff.
I ate pancakes to fill me up and drank the cheapest cider
I could find as there was no chance of going to the pub. If
I was lucky I could stretch to £5 for a block of hash and a
pouch of tobacco. The temptation to get back into crime
was at its peak but I remained determined to stay on the
straight and narrow for Jana and my mother's sake.

In May United won the League but more than the
celebrations I enjoyed seeing Fat Neck as the twelfth man,
gatecrashing the team line-up in Munich in full strip. He
was like a vision stood there with his chest pumped out
and that Ancoats grin all over his face. Next thing you
know he's on morning TV, quiz and chat shows and was
even the subject of a documentary, *Britain's Biggest
Hoaxer*.

My trial was supposed to take a full day but it was a
farce and was thrown out before lunch. The woman who
made the complaint had also been on a works night out
on the piss, and when all her mates pulled fellers she
apparently started coming on to me in the curry house.
They even got the staff in to testify to this. When I
showed no interest, she got pissed off and what made it
worse was the fact her husband was a copper so she had
made up this story to take the heat off her situation. Her
mistake was not complaining until ten days later. I think
women who do things like that should be made to stand
in the dock themselves and see how they cope with the
stress of it all.

Soon after this, my neighbour, Fenton, won a big
payout from a car crash in which his wife and her friend
had died and he had been left with a steel plate in his
skull. He invited me and a few friends over to the
bungalow he had just bought and all was going well until
a gatecrasher arrived and caused a bit of bother at the
doorway. In the melee that followed a woman fell into

some bushes and scratched her face. The police got involved and before I knew it I was back at the same court. Again we got a not guilty within an hour and we were in the pub having a few by dinnertime. Yet I could not seem to avoid trouble.

In the New Year I was invited to a house in Rhyl to watch the Man Utd–Fulham game. One of the lads there was a real dodgy dude who claimed he was a member of the Gooch gang from Moss Side, but he could only throw up one name that I knew, so I was sure he was talking bollocks. Turns out I was right and he was a snide bastard, robbing people's houses and bullying folk. He left but later returned, smacked and coked out of his mind. He was told to fuck off but instead pulled out a butterfly knife and went to plunge me. I got a good grip of him and we got him out of the house but he was full of gear and was trying to throw me all over the place. Luckily a local hard nut steamed in to help me and the lad ended up in a heap on the pavement. Soon dibble were everywhere and there was even a helicopter overhead shouting down through a megaphone for us all to freeze.

It was so cold in my cell I remember having to put my mattress on the floor near the air vents that had a trickle of heat coming through. I drove the police mad for hours, banging away demanding more blankets. Eventually we got bail and I spent the New Year celebrations asleep in the corner of a sweaty back street pub. It turns out the feller we assaulted was wanted by police all over North Wales and by various gangsters, so it was no surprise he cut himself a deal to get a short jail sentence. Good for us too, because the charges were dropped.

Only weeks later, I was at a funeral and went into a Rhyl wine bar after with a lad who, unbeknown to me, was not liked in there because of his drug dealing. So when I left the bar I was followed by the bouncers until I was out of range of the CCTV cameras, then was jumped from behind. I woke up in Irish Kitty's with an ambulance outside. My face was busted up badly and there was a lot of blood loss.

* * *

The World Cup in 2002 started on my forty-sixth birthday. My biggest problem was the early morning kick-offs, as by half-time I'd be losing it, but the comp itself was the best since Mexico 1970. My big comedown came after we beat the Argies. I got on my bike and two minutes later was flat out in the main road: I'd gone bang into the side of a bus. I saw a helicopter hovering above me, then passed out. When I came around they had plastered up my broken wrist and arm. They told me at midnight that I was okay to go home but all my bits of money had fallen from my pockets after the crash, so I asked the ambulance fellers for a lift back to Rhyl, as it was a good few miles, I had cracked ribs and the buses had stopped running. They really did not want me near them, so I thought, fuck it, I'll have to insult them, get the police to arrest me and take me back to the dibble shop in Rhyl.

When the police turned up I was still giving it out so they slung me into the back of the van, drove me round and round the block, then up to some dirt track and dumped me outside an old castle. The dibble were having a ball, calling me an English twat and saying, 'Enjoy your walk home.' It took me six hours to walk back.

The Commonwealth Games put the buzz back in Manchester and gave me the opportunity to get away from Rhyl. It was a shame the media at first dismissed the event by conjuring up every available northern cliché they could think of including flat caps, crumbling venues and shitty weather. Despite this the Games were a massive success. Over a billion people in more than seventy countries tuned in to see the opening ceremony. It got better and better as we won more and more medals and hometown girl Paula Radcliffe broke the Commonwealth and world records.

We knew the great weather couldn't last and when it broke it absolutely pissed down. I felt sorry for the athletes in the walking race that day. We were under cover near Old Trafford and were all talking about City's new ground at Eastlands and what a top venue it was. Some of us were off to watch the boxing later that evening over in Wythenshawe, which was sold out because the British team were outstanding. Dicko asked me if we should split the work up with him doing the Velodrome and me the G-MEX because the judo had just started.

Suddenly this deep thought entered my head. I started thinking about United in the Champions League final and if they made it would I still be there to see it – the chances were I'd be in hospital or prison. It was a sad truth about the way my life was but there you go, and I launched myself into a drinking bender with a death wish.

After a few days I crawled up the ramp at Piccadilly Station to catch a train back to Wales. My family and friends had had enough and were giving me the elbow. At first I was hurt but in time I realised it was my own fault. Munchen had got nine years for robbing some tourists and at that time I wished I was with him. At the entrance to Piccadilly I saw two godsends in the shape of two Leeds carrying bags full of Strongbow. We got off the train in Chester but soon the local redneck Teddy Boys had run us out of town.

Once back in Rhyl I was letting in all kinds of pissheads so long as there was a drink in it for me. Within a few weeks I was crashing out on the kitchen floor and in the bath, leaving the gas on, lit fags left lying around. Things were getting robbed, with everybody accusing each other, and I gave up buying phones after they kept getting nicked; I used the phone box. Then it was cash, credit cards, clothes and eventually, yes, even the spoons went as the dreaded smackheads moved in. The place went from bad to worse when they descended and ambulances were calling daily to tend to people with ghost-white faces and purple lips.

Eventually it would be my time for the ambulance. I'd not eaten for days and was taking handfuls of pills without a clue as to what they were. I was spewing up buckets of bile and blood, which tore my stomach apart, and my sugar level was all over the place. The craving for liquid was unreal and they put a drip in my arm which slowly started to work with the painkillers and sleeping pills. I wanted to ask for a priest as I felt 100 per cent I was not going to pull through; my breathing was full of panic. Just before I took the nod I phoned Jana to ask her to make sure my ashes were scattered not over the Stretford End but over the railway bridge that leads from the Stretford End to my grandparents' home on Railway Road. I had so many happy thoughts of walking over the bridge with Grandad and all the trains and the smog and the dark rain as we headed for the Stretford End with him always telling me United's history. Finally I dropped into a kind of coma.

* * *

A few days later I started to come round, and eventually got a full meal down without being sick. I also got a call from CAIS, an organisation that helps people in North Wales on drink or drugs to get straight, and they soon had me admitted to Hafen Wen in Wrexham. I was there six weeks. I was able to visit the town library during the day and I'd even go to a pub during the evening if there was a football game on and drink orange. The staff at the centre were fantastic but had to test me on my return with breathalysers. Then Jana came and picked me up and we had a few days together.

I knew that the Christmas and New Year coming up would be the biggest test for me. I just had to beat the booze, as the fact is I can't take it anymore; I get ill after a few pints or finish up barred from the pub or nicked. Knowing it was going to be a white-knuckle ride to get through the festive season, I got myself a decent bag of weed and sank into the soaps on TV. I took three sleeping pills to get through New Year's Eve and thank fuck when 2003 rang in. On New Year's Day I went with Lee to the rugby club to watch the Man U game. We got the winner in the last minute and I felt fantastic, as I'd had only a pint of orange juice. I knew that feeling would not be with me for always so I thought I'd savour it while I could.

One thing I feel especially bad about is that I upset every close friend I had, and even worse all my family. There were times when they would cross the road to avoid me staggering along, times when I'd call and they'd shoot out the back way to the neighbours or shops. Invites to go for meals, family functions or birthdays dried up. Also out the window was my sex life. I could not for the life of me pull women, like I'd been able to do all my life, be it in a bus stop, library, shopping, any kind of normal way. I was only ever able to pull while out of my brains on booze in the shite happy-hour theme pubs, and I'd wake up with girls younger than my son or women as old as my mam. Most times they'd tell me I was a bag of shite but worst for my head to take was when they would be saying how good it was, yet I could never remember a fucking thing. I'd be left shaking bad once they left and in desperate need of a strong drink. Losing the plot in this way does give your system a jolt as it leaves you not only sexually frustrated but very bitter with life. My temper became wicked; in shops I was a nightmare, getting barred from many, and who can blame the shopkeepers or public? I was a walking pain in the arse.

If I'd had the chance to have lived a nine-to-five, Postman Pat life, I would gladly swop. But that's like saying if shit was rice pudding you'd never go hungry.

Afterword

Have I had a life of Reilly? I find it hard to say: my life has always been up and down. Maybe I'm the typical Gemini. Even with this book, I could write another book alone about the amount of writing night and day, only to fuck up and cancel all the work by pressing a wrong button; no wonder youngsters at university throw themselves off roofs after losing all their work. I lost a year's worth and threw in the towel a few times. In the end I had to cut off from the world in the library for six weeks and get stuck in.

Now I'm nearing my fifties I look back and see how everything has changed. For example, the atmosphere has gone at Old Trafford. My God, you can see people leaving the ground with ten minutes still to play. The lads can't get all in one section together and have a sing-song, half of them are barred anyway for singing whilst pissed or standing up too much, and the fucking fellers who come and deal with you are fucking rubber necks from the sticks. Worst of all, there's no part of the ground for local young kids to get in cheap on the day. Nowadays all the lads look forward more to the away games in Europe. The modern game in England has no room for Cowboys. I'm not saying this is a bad thing, just the way it seems to be.

My next big test is trying to avoid thinking about life as a series of tests.

I went to another cup final against Liverpool at the Millennium Stadium. Coming back from that game with the Manchester lads and being able to stay sober and go into a pub and chat with decent company was a breakthrough. I had to keep myself occupied by playing pool and the fruit machines, but did it. Don't get me wrong, being alcoholic is a fucker of a thing to have hanging over me, but we all have our demons to fight.

Living in Wales, I started to watch Wrexham – which is a hotbed of Man U fans – and also saw their deadly rivals Chester have a top season coming back up into the big time. I ended up staying local and supporting the Lilywhites, Rhyl, who had the best season in their history, winning the Welsh league and two cups. They even got into Europe for the first time ever. I enjoy the chillout part of football, be it local or big time. Trouble I know how to avoid but it's still a fact that it will always pop up now and again no matter what my age is.

As for the grafters, any left these days are all old school; really there's no more young ones coming through, the odd one now and then via family. Today all the kids think they're fucking gangsters. They've all got major attitudes, with their hoods and mountain bikes and shooters, stuck on their poxy little patches of turf on sink housing estates. Imagine sticking a firm of them slap in Piccadilly on a Sunday night, no dosh, no phones, no tickets, then give them the script: Get grafting all the way to Barca for the Wednesday night, might have to split into two or three teams, the odd chance you may have an offmans or on top, then solo it'll be. The main meet, seven bells sharpish in the bar inside the ground, wedged and clobbered up. Could they do it? Not a chance; they'd be in Shit Strasse. The current gangs are ninety per cent involved in heavy drugs and weapons and my kind wouldn't last two minutes these days – but they wouldn't have lasted two minutes in our day. In a way I feel sorry for them as their world is so small, the pace of life is so fast and the drugs are all shite. Maybe the best thing is going straight after all.

Strangely I don't feel any remorse for all the things we stole. My only regret is for the times we occasionally stole women's purses, and even then if they had photos and personal stuff in we'd often leave them somewhere they could be found. Otherwise, when I look back I think of how much we blew, and the stuff that slipped through our fingers. Like the clear Russian diamond ring our Mark liberated from the cutting department of a top diamond gaff in Antwerp; it was worth £20,000 and had photos and papers confirming its value – and I lost the fucker. Or the time I lost the only gold chain with coins that I ever bought, and with it a diamond ring that was our only bit of profit from a shit week of graft around the Flatlands; that was down to being pissed and asleep on a ferry when it had been cleared of all passengers and even customs had gone home. I left the tom in the cabin and sussed it when I got to London. And then there was the massive wad I left on top of a telly in the Holiday Inn in Brussels. We twigged at the airport and rushed back but the Turkish women cleaners must have already had it away. Easy come, easy go, they say – well it goes a lot easier than it comes, believe me.

As for the lads, Gagzy now runs his own cleaning company, as does Eric. Roufy runs a pub kitchen, while Chike died suddenly; no-one really knew what it was down to but some said his hedonistic lifestyle. George cleans the market that took over from Smithfield, Steve Wilson lives out on the Lancashire coast, OB retired to the hills growing his weed, Munchen's doing nine years, Maca's into fraud and our Mark and Renno will be grafters for life. Of the ladies, Bev runs a music business in Rotterdam, Tum runs a Thai restaurant in Manchester and Jana and I are going through a divorce but are still the best of friends.

As for where my life's up to, I'm happy to still have some health, as every day I get up the thought of the demon drink is there. It's a twat but a fact that I have to live with. I look at the George Bests of this world and shit myself. Yet to stay off the booze is such a battle. My biggest joy is turning up clean and sober at family dinners or friends. Talking helps me, but it's hard to find people who have time to small-talk. I'd love to get involved in acting, just any old project to keep active, but Rhyl where I live has fuck-all, only back street pubs and campsites full of *Hi-de-His*. It looks for cert I will move soon. I'm looking forward even if in the back of my head I know any good times won't last long.

So get the most out of life while the going's good.